THE ILLUMINATED BOOK OF PSALMS

THE ILLUMINATED
BOOK OF PSALMS

The Illustrated Text

of All 150 Prayers

and Hymns

BLACK DOG
& LEVENTHAL
PUBLISHERS
NEW YORK

Cover image: King David from the Egbert Psalter, 12th century; courtesy of Getty Images.

Image credits:
Pages 2, 6, 9, 20, 25, 48, 57, 72, 84, 87, 95, 106, 118, 126, 142, 162, 166, 171, 184, 191, 195, 196, 201, 226, 245, 249: © British Library Board / Robana / Art Resource, NY
Pages 17, 237: The Pierpont Morgan Library / Art Resource, NY
Pages 31, 38, 136: British Library / The Art Archive at Art Resource, NY
Pages 52, 78, 101, 147, 154, 176, 223: Dover
Pages 68: © BnF, Dist. RMN-Grand Palais / Art Resource, NY
Page 92: Getty Images
Page 133: Hessisches Landesmuseum, Darmstadt, Germany
Page 217: Gianni Dagli Orti / The Art Archive at Art Resource, NY
Page 220: Finsiel/Alinari / Art Resource, NY
Page 231: V&A Images, London / Art Resource, NY

Black Dog & Leventhal Publishers
Hachette Book Group
1290 Avenue of the Americas
New York, NY 10104
www.blackdogandleventhal.com

Printed in Malaysia

Cover and interior design by Liz Driesbach

IM

First Edition: September 2015
10 9 8 7 6 5 4 3 2 1

Black Dog & Leventhal Publishers is an imprint of Hachette Books, a division of Hachette Book Group.

The Black Dog & Leventhal Publishers name and logo are trademarks of Hachette Book Group, Inc.

Library of Congress Cataloging-in-Publication Data available upon request.

CONTENTS

BOOK I

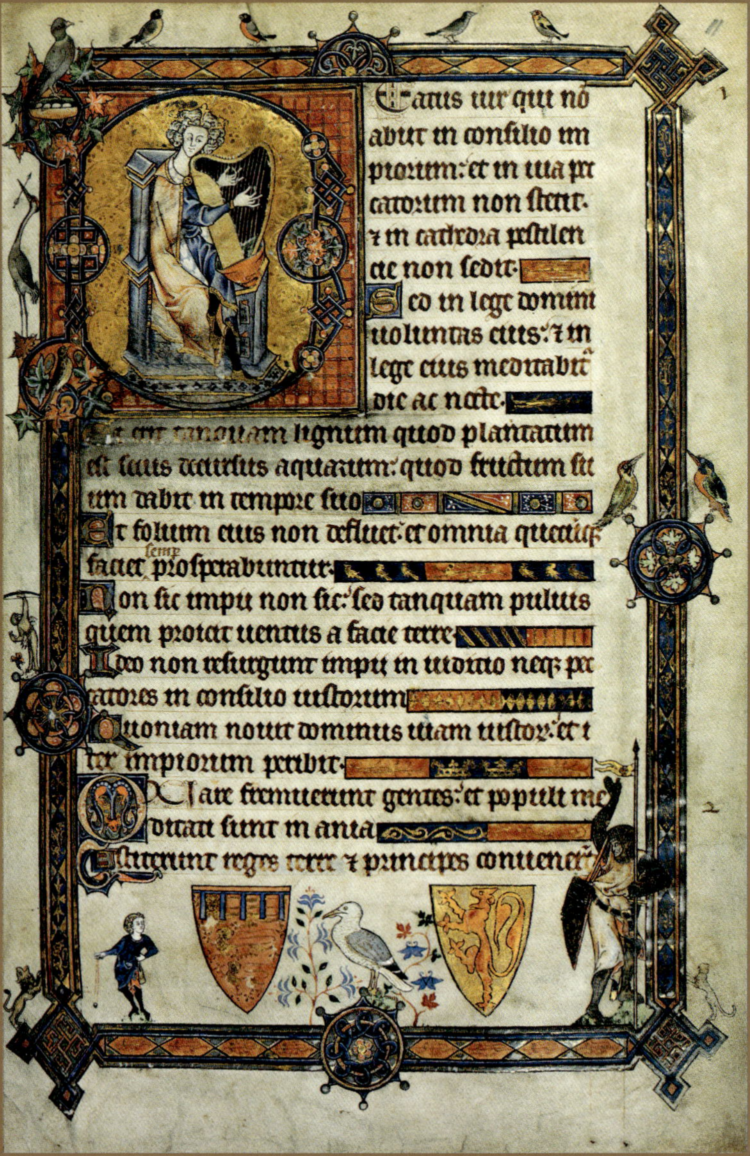

Alfonso Psalter, England, Psalm 1, ca. 1316

PSALM 1

Blessed is the man that walketh not in the counsel
of the ungodly, nor standeth in the way of sinners,
nor sitteth in the seat of the scornful.
2 But his delight is in the law of the LORD; and in his law
doth he meditate day and night.
3 And he shall be like a tree planted by the rivers of water,
that bringeth forth his fruit in his season; his leaf also shall
not wither; and whatsoever he doeth shall prosper.
4 The ungodly are not so: but are like the chaff which the
wind driveth away.
5 Therefore the ungodly shall not stand in the judgment,
nor sinners in the congregation of the righteous.
6 For the LORD knoweth the way of the righteous: but the
way of the ungodly shall perish.

PSALM 2

Why do the heathen rage, and the people imagine
a vain thing?
2 The kings of the earth set themselves, and the rulers
take counsel together, against the LORD, and against his
anointed, saying,
3 Let us break their bands asunder, and cast away their cords
from us.
4 He that sitteth in the heavens shall laugh: the LORD shall
have them in derision.
5 Then shall he speak unto them in his wrath, and vex them
in his sore displeasure.

6 Yet have I set my king upon my holy hill of Zion.
7 I will declare the decree: the LORD hath said unto me,
Thou art my Son; this day have I begotten thee.
8 Ask of me, and I shall give thee the heathen for thine
inheritance, and the uttermost parts of the earth for thy
possession.
9 Thou shalt break them with a rod of iron; thou shalt dash
them in pieces like a potter's vessel.
10 Be wise now therefore, O ye kings: be instructed, ye
judges of the earth.
11 Serve the LORD with fear, and rejoice
with trembling.
12 Kiss the Son, lest he be angry, and ye
perish from the way, when his wrath
is kindled but a little. Blessed are all
they that put their trust in him.

PSALM 3

A Psalm of David, when he fled from Absalom his son.

LORD, how are they increased that trouble me!
many are they that rise up against me.
2 Many there be which say of my soul, There is no help for
him in God. Selah.
3 But thou, O LORD, art a shield for me; my glory, and the
lifter up of mine head.
4 I cried unto the LORD with my voice, and he heard me
out of his holy hill. Selah.

5I laid me down and slept; I awaked; for the LORD
sustained me.
6I will not be afraid of ten thousands of people, that have
set themselves against me round about.
7Arise, O LORD; save me, O my God: for thou hast
smitten all mine enemies upon the cheek bone; thou hast
broken the teeth of the ungodly.
8Salvation belongeth unto the LORD: thy blessing is upon
thy people. Selah.

PSALM 4

To the chief Musician on Neginoth,
A Psalm of David.

Hear me when I call, O God of my righteousness: thou
hast enlarged me when I was in distress; have mercy
upon me, and hear my prayer.
2O ye sons of men, how long will ye turn my glory into
shame? how long will ye love vanity, and seek after leasing?
Selah.
3But know that the LORD hath set apart him that is godly
for himself: the LORD will hear when I call unto him.
4Stand in awe, and sin not: commune with your own heart
upon your bed, and be still. Selah.
5Offer the sacrifices of righteousness, and put your trust in
the LORD.

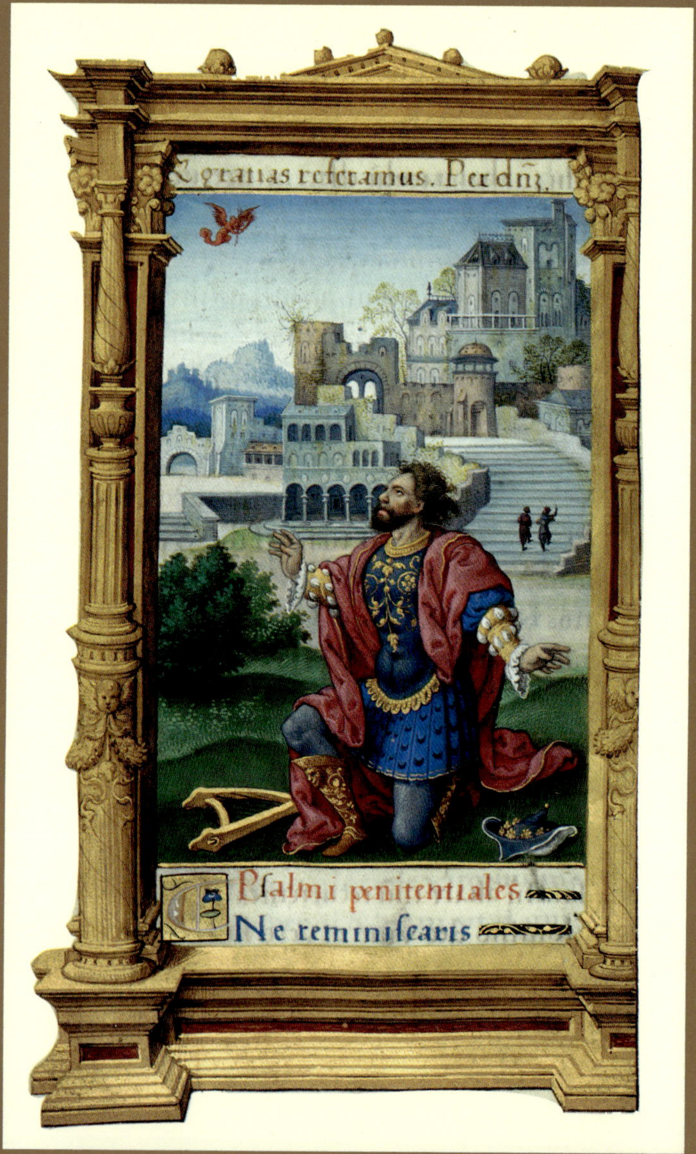

Book of Hours, France, Psalm 6, 16th century

6There be many that say, Who will shew us any good?
LORD, lift thou up the light of thy countenance upon us.
7Thou hast put gladness in my heart, more than in the time
that their corn and their wine increased.
8I will both lay me down in peace, and sleep: for thou,
LORD, only makest me dwell in safety.

PSALM 5

To the chief Musician upon Nehiloth,
A Psalm of David.

Give ear to my words, O LORD, consider my
meditation.
2Hearken unto the voice of my cry, my King, and my God:
for unto thee will I pray.
3My voice shalt thou hear in the morning, O LORD; in the
morning will I direct my prayer unto thee, and will look up.
4For thou art not a God that hath pleasure in wickedness:
neither shall evil dwell with thee.
5The foolish shall not stand in thy sight: thou hatest all
workers of iniquity.
6Thou shalt destroy them that speak leasing: the LORD
will abhor the bloody and deceitful man.
7But as for me, I will come into thy house in the multitude
of thy mercy: and in thy fear will I worship toward thy holy
temple.
8Lead me, O LORD, in thy righteousness because of mine
enemies; make thy way straight before my face.
9For there is no faithfulness in their mouth; their inward

part is very wickedness; their throat is an open
sepulchre; they flatter with their tongue.
10 Destroy thou them, O God; let them
fall by their own counsels; cast them out in
the multitude of their transgressions;
for they have rebelled against thee.
11 But let all those that put their trust in thee rejoice: let
them ever shout for joy, because thou defendest them: let
them also that love thy name be joyful in thee.
12 For thou, LORD, wilt bless the righteous; with favour wilt
thou compass him as with a shield.

PSALM 6

*To the chief Musician on Neginoth upon
Sheminith, A Psalm of David.*

O LORD, rebuke me not in thine anger, neither
chasten me in thy hot displeasure.
2 Have mercy upon me, O LORD; for I am weak: O LORD,
heal me; for my bones are vexed.
3 My soul is also sore vexed: but thou, O LORD, how long?
4 Return, O LORD, deliver my soul: oh save me for thy
mercies' sake.
5 For in death there is no remembrance of thee: in the
grave who shall give thee thanks?
6 I am weary with my groaning; all the night make I
my bed to swim; I water my couch with my tears.
7 Mine eye is consumed because of grief; it waxeth old
because of all mine enemies.

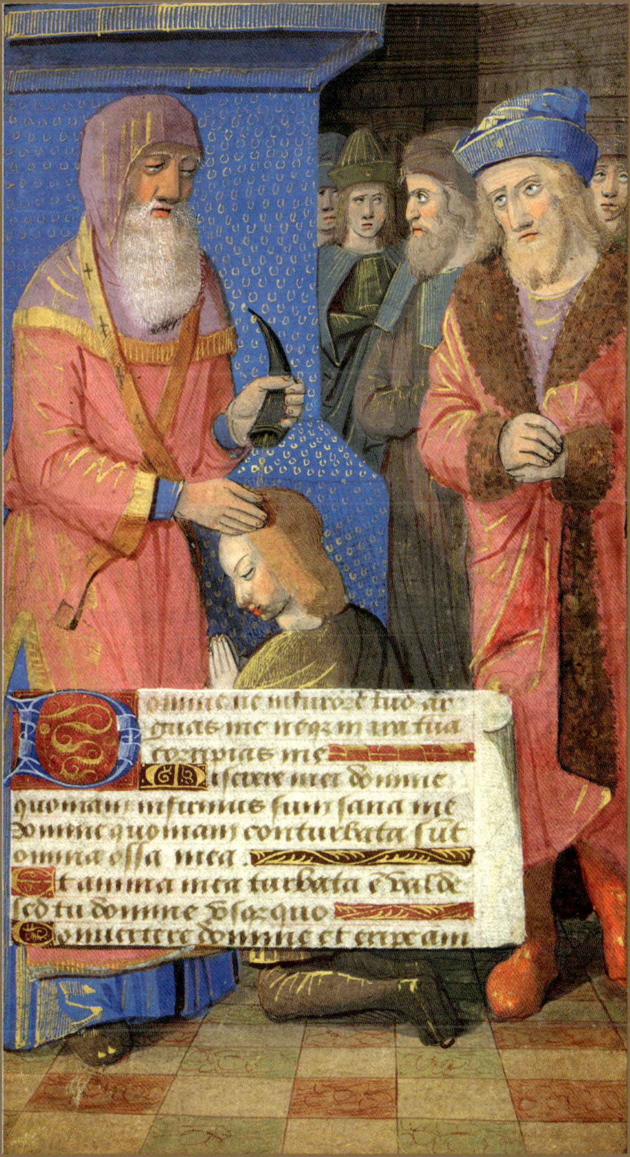

Book of Hours, France, Psalm 6, 15th century

8Depart from me, all ye workers of iniquity; for the LORD
hath heard the voice of my weeping.
9The LORD hath heard my supplication; the LORD will
receive my prayer.
10Let all mine enemies be ashamed and sore vexed: let them
return and be ashamed suddenly.

PSALM 7

Shiggaion of David, which he sang unto the LORD, concerning the words of Cush the Benjamite.

O LORD my God, in thee do I put my trust: save me
from all them that persecute me, and deliver me:
2Lest he tear my soul like a lion, rending it in pieces, while
there is none to deliver.
3O LORD my God, if I have done this; if there be iniquity
in my hands;
4If I have rewarded evil unto him that was at peace with
me; (yea, I have delivered him that without cause is mine
enemy:)
5Let the enemy persecute my soul, and take it; yea, let him
tread down my life upon the earth, and lay mine honour in
the dust. Selah.
6Arise, O LORD, in thine anger, lift up thyself because of
the rage of mine enemies: and awake for me to the judgment
that thou hast commanded.
7So shall the congregation of the people compass thee
about: for their sakes therefore return thou on high.
8The LORD shall judge the people: judge me, O LORD,

according to my righteousness, and
according to mine integrity that is in me.
9 Oh let the wickedness of the wicked
come to an end; but establish the just: for
the righteous God trieth the hearts and reins.
10 My defence is of God, which saveth the upright in heart.
11 God judgeth the righteous, and God is angry with the
wicked every day.
12 If he turn not, he will whet his sword; he hath bent his
bow, and made it ready.
13 He hath also prepared for him the instruments of death;
he ordaineth his arrows against the persecutors.
14 Behold, he travaileth with iniquity, and hath conceived
mischief, and brought forth falsehood.
15 He made a pit, and digged it, and is fallen into the ditch
which he made.
16 His mischief shall return upon his own head, and his
violent dealing shall come down upon his own pate.
17 I will praise the LORD according to his righteousness:
and will sing praise to the name of the LORD most high.

PSALM 8

To the chief Musician upon Gittith,
A Psalm of David.

O LORD our LORD, how excellent is thy name in all the
earth! who hast set thy glory above the heavens.
2 Out of the mouth of babes and sucklings hast thou
ordained strength because of thine enemies, that thou

mightest still the enemy and the avenger.
3When I consider thy heavens, the work of thy fingers, the
moon and the stars, which thou hast ordained;
4What is man, that thou art mindful of him? and the son of
man, that thou visitest him?
5For thou hast made him a little lower than the angels, and
hast crowned him with glory and honour.
6Thou madest him to have dominion over the works of thy
hands; thou hast put all things under his feet:
7All sheep and oxen, yea, and the beasts of the field;
8The fowl of the air, and the fish of the sea, and whatsoever
passeth through the paths of the seas.
9O LORD our LORD, how excellent is thy name in all the
earth!

PSALM 9

To the chief Musician upon Muthlabben,
A Psalm of David.

I will praise thee, O LORD, with my whole heart;
I will shew forth all thy marvellous works.
2I will be glad and rejoice in thee: I will sing praise to thy
name, O thou most High.
3When mine enemies are turned back, they shall fall and
perish at thy presence.
4For thou hast maintained my right and my cause; thou
satest in the throne judging right.
5Thou hast rebuked the heathen, thou hast destroyed the
wicked, thou hast put out their name for ever and ever.
6O thou enemy, destructions are come to a perpetual end:

and thou hast destroyed cities; their memorial is perished
with them.
7 But the LORD shall endure for ever: he hath prepared his
throne for judgment.
8 And he shall judge the world in righteousness, he shall
minister judgment to the people in uprightness.
9 The LORD also will be a refuge for the oppressed, a
refuge in times of trouble.
10 And they that know thy name will put their trust in thee:
for thou, LORD, hast not forsaken them that seek thee.
11 Sing praises to the LORD, which dwelleth in Zion:
declare among the people his doings.
12 When he maketh inquisition for blood, he remembereth
them: he forgetteth not the cry of the humble.
13 Have mercy upon me, O LORD; consider my trouble
which I suffer of them that hate me, thou that liftest me up
from the gates of death:
14 That I may shew forth all thy praise in the gates of the
daughter of Zion: I will rejoice in thy salvation.
15 The heathen are sunk down in the pit that they made: in
the net which they hid is their own foot taken.
16 The LORD is known by the judgment which he
executeth: the wicked is snared in the work of his own hands.
Higgaion. Selah.
17 The wicked shall be turned into hell, and all the nations
that forget God.
18 For the needy shall not alway be forgotten: the
expectation of the poor shall not perish for ever.
19 Arise, O LORD; let not man prevail: let the heathen be
judged in thy sight.
20 Put them in fear, O LORD: that the nations may know
themselves to be but men. Selah.

PSALM 10

Why standest thou afar off, O LORD? why hidest
thou thyself in times of trouble?
2 The wicked in his pride doth persecute the poor: let them
be taken in the devices that they have imagined.
3 For the wicked boasteth of his heart's desire, and blesseth
the covetous, whom the LORD abhorreth.
4 The wicked, through the pride of his countenance, will not
seek after God: God is not in all his thoughts.
5 His ways are always grievous; thy judgments are far above
out of his sight: as for all his enemies, he puffeth at them.
6 He hath said in his heart, I shall not be moved: for I shall
never be in adversity.
7 His mouth is full of cursing and deceit and fraud: under
his tongue is mischief and vanity.
8 He sitteth in the lurking places of the villages: in the secret
places doth he murder the innocent: his eyes are privily set
against the poor.
9 He lieth in wait secretly as a lion in his den: he lieth in wait
to catch the poor: he doth catch the poor, when he draweth
him into his net.
10 He croucheth, and humbleth himself, that the poor may
fall by his strong ones.
11 He hath said in his heart, God hath forgotten: he hideth
his face; he will never see it.

12 Arise, O LORD; O God, lift up thine hand: forget not
the humble.
13 Wherefore doth the wicked contemn God? he hath said in
his heart, Thou wilt not require it.
14 Thou hast seen it; for thou beholdest mischief and spite,
to requite it with thy hand: the poor committeth himself
unto thee; thou art the helper of the fatherless.
15 Break thou the arm of the wicked and the evil man: seek
out his wickedness till thou find none.
16 The LORD is King for ever and ever: the heathen are
perished out of his land.
17 LORD, thou hast heard the desire of the humble: thou
wilt prepare their heart, thou wilt cause thine ear to hear:
18 To judge the fatherless and the oppressed, that the man of
the earth may no more oppress.

PSALM 11

To the chief Musician, A Psalm of David.

In the LORD put I my trust: How say ye to my soul,
Flee as a bird to your mountain?
2 For, lo, the wicked bend their bow, they make ready their
arrow upon the string, that they may privily shoot at the
upright in heart.
3 If the foundations be destroyed, what can the righteous do?
4 The LORD is in his holy temple, the LORD'S throne is in
heaven: his eyes behold, his eyelids try, the children of men.
5 The LORD trieth the righteous: but the wicked and him
that loveth violence his soul hateth.

6 Upon the wicked he shall rain snares, fire and brimstone, and an horrible tempest: this shall be the portion of their cup.
7 For the righteous LORD loveth righteousness; his countenance doth behold the upright.

PSALM 12

To the chief Musician upon Sheminith, A Psalm of David.

Help, LORD; for the godly man ceaseth; for the faithful fail from among the children of men.
2 They speak vanity every one with his neighbour: with flattering lips and with a double heart do they speak.
3 The LORD shall cut off all flattering lips, and the tongue that speaketh proud things:
4 Who have said, With our tongue will we prevail; our lips are our own: who is lord over us?
5 For the oppression of the poor, for the sighing of the needy, now will I arise, saith the LORD; I will set him in safety from him that puffeth at him.
6 The words of the LORD are pure words: as silver tried in a furnace of earth, purified seven times.
7 Thou shalt keep them, O LORD, thou shalt preserve them from this generation for ever.
8 The wicked walk on every side, when the vilest men are exalted.

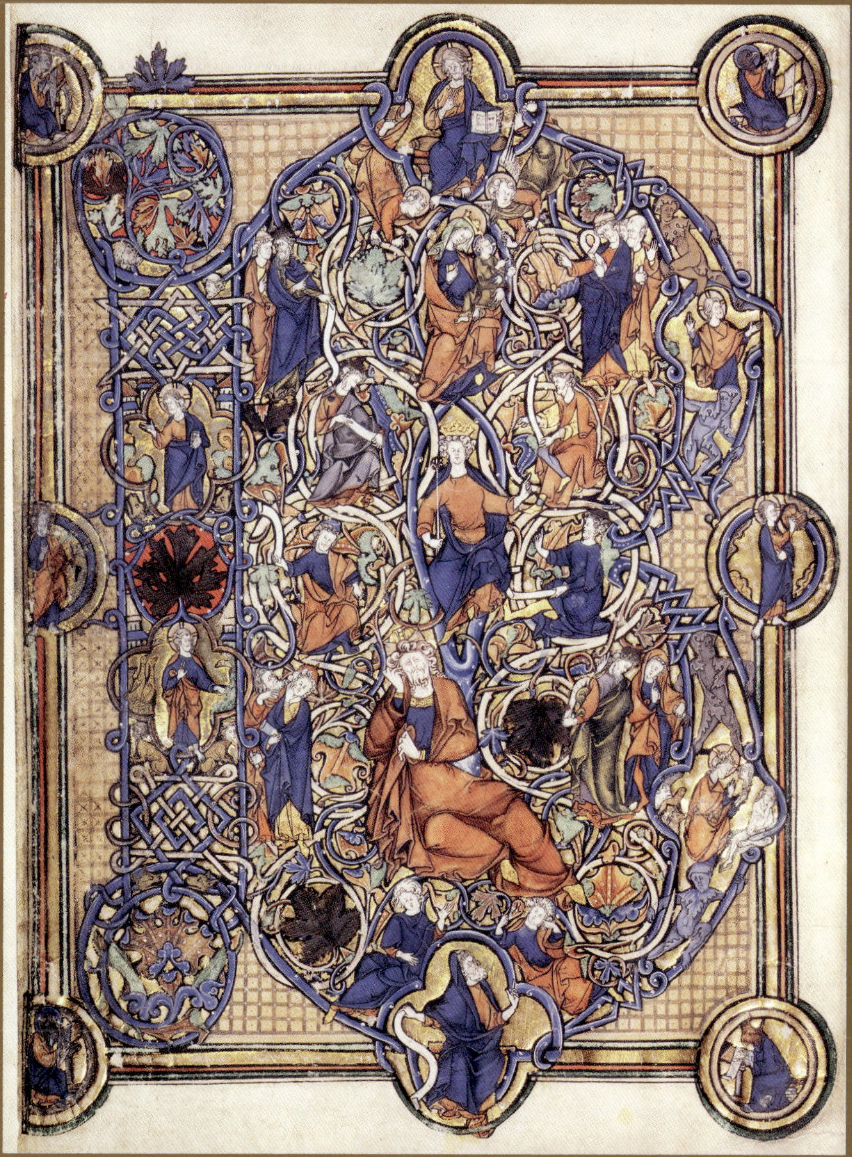

Windmill Psalter, England, ca. 1270–1280

PSALM 13

To the chief Musician, A Psalm of David.

How long wilt thou forget me, O LORD? for ever?
how long wilt thou hide thy face from me?
2 How long shall I take counsel in my soul, having sorrow in my
heart daily? how long shall mine enemy be exalted over me?
3 Consider and hear me, O LORD my God: lighten mine
eyes, lest I sleep the sleep of death;
4 Lest mine enemy say, I have prevailed against him; and
those that trouble me rejoice when I am moved.
5 But I have trusted in thy mercy; my heart shall rejoice in
thy salvation.
6 I will sing unto the LORD, because he hath dealt
bountifully with me.

PSALM 14

To the chief Musician, A Psalm of David.

The fool hath said in his heart, There is no God.
They are corrupt, they have done abominable works,
there is none that doeth good.
2 The LORD looked down from heaven upon the children
of men, to see if there were any that did understand, and
seek God.
3 They are all gone aside, they are all together become filthy:
there is none that doeth good, no, not one.
4 Have all the workers of iniquity no knowledge? who eat up

my people as they eat bread, and call not upon the LORD.
5There were they in great fear: for God is in the generation
of the righteous.
6Ye have shamed the counsel of the poor, because the
LORD is his refuge.
7Oh that the salvation of Israel were come out of Zion!
when the LORD bringeth back the captivity of his people,
Jacob shall rejoice, and Israel shall be glad.

PSALM 15

A Psalm of David.

LORD, who shall abide in thy tabernacle? who shall
dwell in thy holy hill?
2He that walketh uprightly, and worketh righteousness, and
speaketh the truth in his heart.
3He that backbiteth not with his tongue, nor doeth evil to his
neighbour, nor taketh up a reproach against his neighbour.
4In whose eyes a vile person is contemned; but he
honoureth them that fear the LORD. He that sweareth to
his own hurt, and changeth not.
5He that putteth not out his money to usury, nor taketh
reward against the innocent. He that doeth these things shall
never be moved.

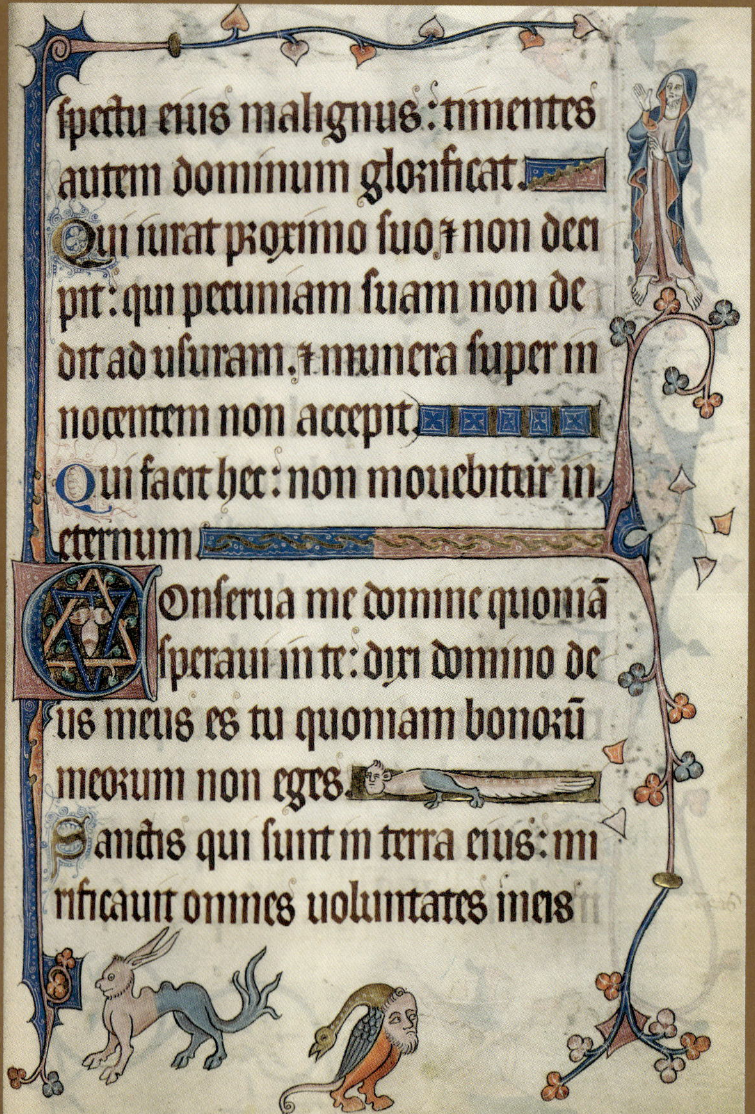
spectu eius malignus: timentes
autem dominum glorificat.
Qui iurat proximo suo & non deci
pit: qui pecuniam suam non de
dit ad usuram. & munera super in
nocentem non accepit.
Qui facit hec: non mouebitur in
eternum
Conserua me domine quoniã
speraui in te: dixi domino de
us meus es tu quoniam bonorũ
meorum non eges.
Sanctis qui sunt in terra eius: mi
rificauit omnes uoluntates meas

Luttrell Psalter, England, Psalm 15, ca. 1325–1335

PSALM 16

Michtam of David.

Preserve me, O God: for in thee do I put my trust.
2 O my soul, thou hast said unto the LORD, Thou
art my LORD: my goodness extendeth not to thee;
3 But to the saints that are in the earth, and to the excellent,
in whom is all my delight.
4 Their sorrows shall be multiplied that hasten after another
god: their drink offerings of blood will I not offer, nor take
up their names into my lips.
5 The LORD is the portion of mine inheritance and of my
cup: thou maintainest my lot.
6 The lines are fallen unto me in pleasant places; yea, I have
a goodly heritage.
7 I will bless the LORD, who hath given me counsel: my
reins also instruct me in the night seasons.
8 I have set the LORD always before me: because he is at
my right hand, I shall not be moved.
9 Therefore my heart is glad, and my glory rejoiceth: my
flesh also shall rest in hope.
10 For thou wilt not leave my soul in hell; neither wilt thou
suffer thine Holy One to see corruption.
11 Thou wilt shew me the path of life: in thy presence is
fulness of joy; at thy right hand there are pleasures for
evermore.

PSALM 17

A Prayer of David.

Hear the right, O LORD, attend unto my cry, give ear
unto my prayer, that goeth not out of feigned lips.
2 Let my sentence come forth from thy presence; let thine
eyes behold the things that are equal.
3 Thou hast proved mine heart; thou hast visited me in
the night; thou hast tried me, and shalt find nothing; I am
purposed that my mouth shall not transgress.
4 Concerning the words of men, by the word of thy lips I
have kept me from the paths of the destroyer.
5 Hold up my goings in thy paths, that my footsteps slip not.
6 I have called upon thee, for thou wilt hear me, O God:
incline thine ear unto me, and hear my speech.
7 Shew thy marvellous lovingkindness, O thou that savest by
thy right hand them which put their trust in thee from those
that rise up against them.
8 Keep me as the apple of the eye, hide me under the
shadow of thy wings,
9 From the wicked that oppress me, from my deadly
enemies, who compass me about.
10 They are inclosed in their own fat: with their mouth they
speak proudly.
11 They have now compassed us in our steps: they have set
their eyes bowing down to the earth;
12 Like as a lion that is greedy of his prey, and as it were a
young lion lurking in secret places.
13 Arise, O LORD, disappoint him, cast him down: deliver
my soul from the wicked, which is thy sword:
14 From men which are thy hand, O LORD, from men of

the world, which have their portion in this life, and whose
belly thou fillest with thy hid treasure: they are full of
children, and leave the rest of their substance to their babes.
15 As for me, I will behold thy face in righteousness: I shall
be satisfied, when I awake, with thy likeness.

PSALM 18

To the chief Musician, A Psalm of David, the servant of the LORD, who spake unto the LORD the words of this song in the day that the LORD delivered him from the hand of all his enemies, and from the hand of Saul: And he said,

I will love thee, O LORD, my strength.
2 The LORD is my rock, and my fortress, and my
deliverer; my God, my strength, in whom I will trust; my
buckler, and the horn of my salvation, and my high tower.
3 I will call upon the LORD, who is worthy to be praised: so
shall I be saved from mine enemies.
4 The sorrows of death compassed me, and the floods of
ungodly men made me afraid.
5 The sorrows of hell compassed me about: the snares of
death prevented me.
6 In my distress I called upon the LORD, and cried unto my
God: he heard my voice out of his temple, and my cry came
before him, even into his ears.
7 Then the earth shook and trembled; the foundations also
of the hills moved and were shaken, because he was wroth.
8 There went up a smoke out of his nostrils, and fire out of
his mouth devoured: coals were kindled by it.

[9]He bowed the heavens also, and came down: and darkness
was under his feet.
[10]And he rode upon a cherub, and did fly: yea, he did fly
upon the wings of the wind.
[11]He made darkness his secret place; his pavilion round
about him were dark waters and thick clouds of the skies.
[12]At the brightness that was before him his thick clouds
passed, hail stones and coals of fire.
[13]The LORD also thundered in the heavens, and the
Highest gave his voice; hail stones and coals of fire.
[14]Yea, he sent out his arrows, and scattered them; and he
shot out lightnings, and discomfited them.
[15]Then the channels of waters were seen, and the
foundations of the world were discovered at thy rebuke, O
LORD, at the blast of the breath of thy nostrils.
[16]He sent from above, he took me, he drew me out of many
waters.
[17]He delivered me from my strong enemy, and from them
which hated me: for they were too strong for me.
[18]They prevented me in the day of my calamity: but the
LORD was my stay.
[19]He brought me forth also into a large place; he delivered
me, because he delighted in me.
[20]The LORD rewarded me according to my righteousness;
according to the cleanness of my hands hath he recompensed
me.
[21]For I have kept the ways of the LORD, and have not
wickedly departed from my God.
[22]For all his judgments were before me, and I did not put
away his statutes from me.
[23]I was also upright before him, and I kept myself from
mine iniquity.

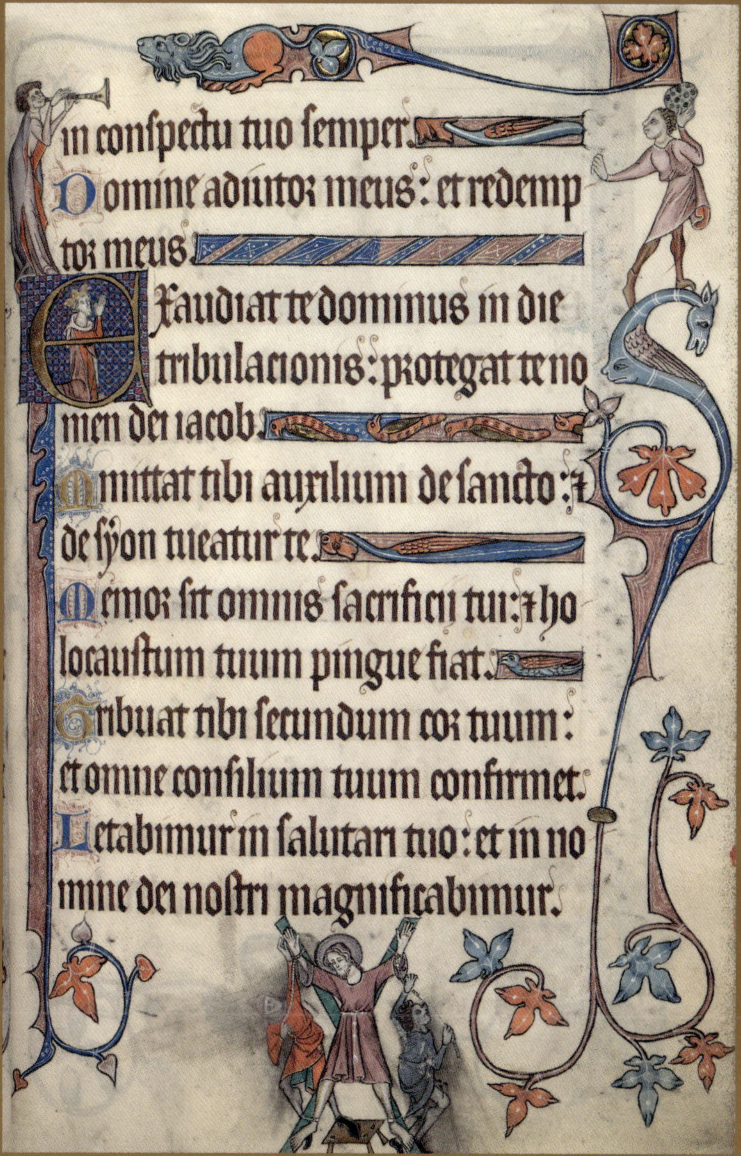
in conspectu tuo semper.
Domine adiutor meus: et redemp
tor meus.
Exaudiat te dominus in die
tribulacionis: protegat te no
men dei iacob.
Mittat tibi auxilium de sancto: et
de syon tueatur te.
Memor sit omnis sacrificij tui: et ho
locaustum tuum pingue fiat.
Tribuat tibi secundum cor tuum:
et omne consilium tuum confirmet.
Letabimur in salutari tuo: et in no
mine dei nostri magnificabimur.

Luttrell Psalter, England, Psalm 19, ca. 1325–1335

24Therefore hath the LORD recompensed me according to
my righteousness, according to the cleanness of my hands in
his eyesight.
25With the merciful thou wilt shew thyself merciful; with an
upright man thou wilt shew thyself upright;
26With the pure thou wilt shew thyself pure; and with the
froward thou wilt shew thyself froward.
27For thou wilt save the afflicted people; but wilt bring
down high looks.
28For thou wilt light my candle: the LORD my God will
enlighten my darkness.
29For by thee I have run through a troop; and by my God
have I leaped over a wall.
30As for God, his way is perfect: the word of the LORD is
tried: he is a buckler to all those that trust in him.
31For who is God save the LORD? or who is a rock save our
God?
32It is God that girdeth me with strength, and maketh my
way perfect.
33He maketh my feet like hinds' feet, and setteth me upon
my high places.
34He teacheth my hands to war, so that a bow of steel is
broken by mine arms.
35Thou hast also given me the shield of thy salvation: and
thy right hand hath holden me up, and thy gentleness hath
made me great.
36Thou hast enlarged my steps under me, that my feet did
not slip.
37I have pursued mine enemies, and overtaken them:
neither did I turn again till they were consumed.
38I have wounded them that they were not able to rise: they
are fallen under my feet.

39 For thou hast girded me with strength unto the battle:
thou hast subdued under me those that rose up against me.
40 Thou hast also given me the necks of mine enemies; that
I might destroy them that hate me.
41 They cried, but there was none to save them: even unto
the LORD, but he answered them not.
42 Then did I beat them small as the dust before the wind: I
did cast them out as the dirt in the streets.
43 Thou hast delivered me from the strivings of the people;
and thou hast made me the head of the heathen: a people
whom I have not known shall serve me.
44 As soon as they hear of me, they shall obey me: the
strangers shall submit themselves unto me.
45 The strangers shall fade away, and be afraid out of their
close places.
46 The LORD liveth; and blessed be my rock; and let the
God of my salvation be exalted.
47 It is God that avengeth me, and subdueth the people
under me.
48 He delivereth me from mine enemies: yea, thou liftest me
up above those that rise up against me: thou hast delivered
me from the violent man.
49 Therefore will I give thanks unto thee, O LORD, among
the heathen, and sing praises unto thy name.
50 Great deliverance giveth he to his king; and sheweth mercy
to his anointed, to David, and to his seed for evermore.

PSALM 19

To the chief Musician, A Psalm of David.

The heavens declare the glory of God; and the
firmament sheweth his handywork.
2 Day unto day uttereth speech, and night unto night
sheweth knowledge.
3 There is no speech nor language, where their voice is not
heard.
4 Their line is gone out through all the earth, and their
words to the end of the world. In them hath he set a
tabernacle for the sun,
5 Which is as a bridegroom coming out of his chamber, and
rejoiceth as a strong man to run a race.
6 His going forth is from the end of the heaven, and his
circuit unto the ends of it: and there is nothing hid from the
heat thereof.
7 The law of the LORD is perfect, converting the soul: the
testimony of the LORD is sure, making wise the simple.
8 The statutes of the LORD are right, rejoicing the heart: the
commandment of the LORD is pure, enlightening the eyes.
9 The fear of the LORD is clean, enduring for ever: the
judgments of the LORD are true and righteous altogether.
10 More to be desired are they than gold, yea, than much fine
gold: sweeter also than honey and the honeycomb.
11 Moreover by them is thy servant warned: and in keeping
of them there is great reward.
12 Who can understand his errors?
cleanse thou me from secret faults.
13 Keep back thy servant also from
presumptuous sins; let them not have

dominion over me: then shall I be upright,
and I shall be innocent from the great
transgression.
14Let the words of my mouth, and the
meditation of my heart, be acceptable in thy
sight, O LORD, my strength, and my redeemer.

PSALM 20

To the chief Musician, A Psalm of David.

The LORD hear thee in the day of trouble; the name
of the God of Jacob defend thee;
2Send thee help from the sanctuary, and strengthen thee out
of Zion;
3Remember all thy offerings, and accept thy burnt sacrifice;
Selah.
4Grant thee according to thine own heart, and fulfil all thy
counsel.
5We will rejoice in thy salvation, and in the name of our
God we will set up our banners: the LORD fulfil all thy
petitions.
6Now know I that the LORD saveth his anointed; he will
hear him from his holy heaven with the saving strength of his
right hand.
7Some trust in chariots, and some in horses: but we will
remember the name of the LORD our God.
8They are brought down and fallen: but we are risen, and
stand upright.
9Save, LORD: let the king hear us when we call.

PSALM 21

To the chief Musician, A Psalm of David.

The king shall joy in thy strength, O LORD; and in
thy salvation how greatly shall he rejoice!
2 Thou hast given him his heart's desire, and hast not
withholden the request of his lips. Selah.
3 For thou preventest him with the blessings of goodness:
thou settest a crown of pure gold on his head.
4 He asked life of thee, and thou gavest it him, even length
of days for ever and ever.
5 His glory is great in thy salvation: honour and majesty hast
thou laid upon him.
6 For thou hast made him most blessed for ever: thou hast
made him exceeding glad with thy countenance.
7 For the king trusteth in the LORD, and through the mercy
of the most High he shall not be moved.
8 Thine hand shall find out all thine enemies: thy right hand
shall find out those that hate thee.
9 Thou shalt make them as a fiery oven in the time of thine
anger: the LORD shall swallow them up in his wrath, and
the fire shall devour them.
10 Their fruit shalt thou destroy from the earth, and their
seed from among the children of men.
11 For they intended evil against thee: they imagined a
mischievous device, which they are not able to perform.
12 Therefore shalt thou make them turn their back, when
thou shalt make ready thine arrows upon thy strings against
the face of them.
13 Be thou exalted, LORD, in thine own strength: so will we
sing and praise thy power.

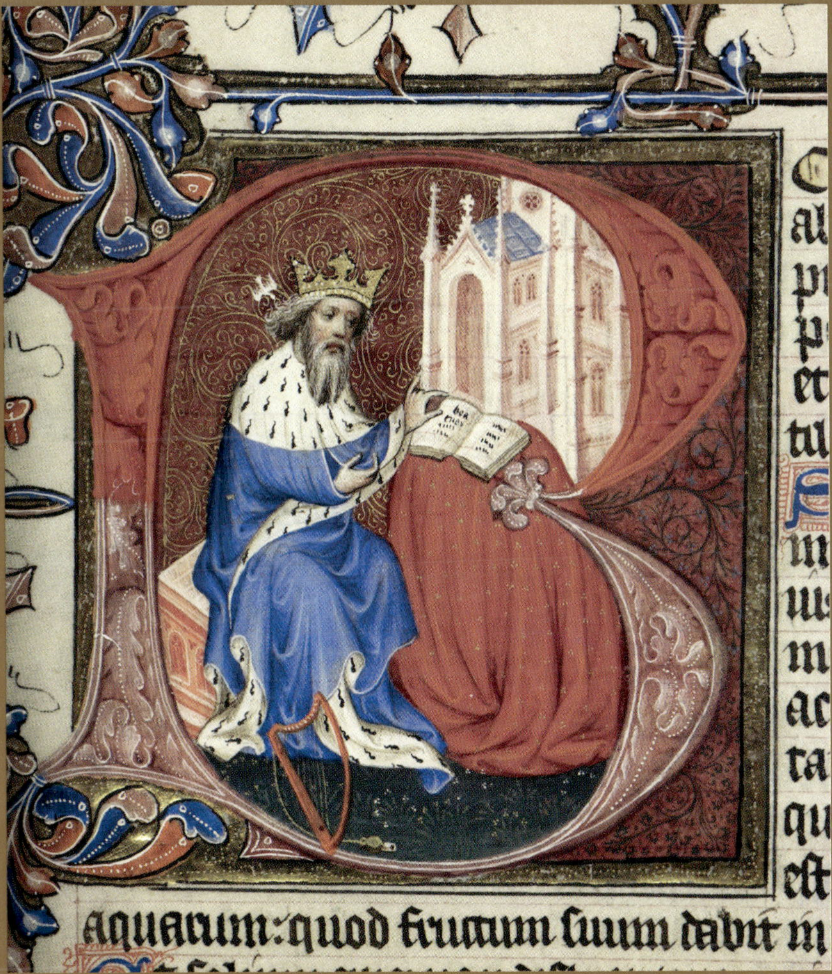

The Great Bible (St. Jerome version), England, 1405–1415

PSALM 22

To the chief Musician upon Aijeleth Shahar,
A Psalm of David.

My God, my God, why hast thou forsaken me? why
art thou so far from helping me, and from the
words of my roaring?
2 O my God, I cry in the daytime, but thou hearest not; and
in the night season, and am not silent.
3 But thou art holy, O thou that inhabitest the praises of Israel.
4 Our fathers trusted in thee: they trusted, and thou didst
deliver them.
5 They cried unto thee, and were delivered: they trusted in
thee, and were not confounded.
6 But I am a worm, and no man; a reproach of men, and
despised of the people.
7 All they that see me laugh me to scorn: they shoot out the
lip, they shake the head saying,
8 He trusted on the LORD that he would deliver him: let
him deliver him, seeing he delighted in him.
9 But thou art he that took me out of the womb: thou didst
make me hope when I was upon my mother's breasts.
10 I was cast upon thee from the womb: thou art my God
from my mother's belly.

11 Be not far from me; for trouble is near; for there is none
to help.
12 Many bulls have compassed me: strong bulls of Bashan
have beset me round.
13 They gaped upon me with their mouths, as a ravening and
a roaring lion.
14 I am poured out like water, and all my bones are out of joint:
my heart is like wax; it is melted in the midst of my bowels.
15 My strength is dried up like a potsherd; and my tongue
cleaveth to my jaws; and thou hast brought me into the dust
of death.
16 For dogs have compassed me: the assembly of the wicked
have inclosed me: they pierced my hands and my feet.
17 I may tell all my bones: they look and stare upon me.
18 They part my garments among them, and cast lots upon
my vesture.
19 But be not thou far from me, O LORD: O my strength,
haste thee to help me.
20 Deliver my soul from the sword; my darling from the
power of the dog.
21 Save me from the lion's mouth: for thou hast heard me
from the horns of the unicorns.
22 I will declare thy name unto my brethren: in the midst of
the congregation will I praise thee.
23 Ye that fear the LORD, praise him; all ye the seed of
Jacob, glorify him; and fear him, all ye the seed of Israel.
24 For he hath not despised nor abhorred the affliction of
the afflicted; neither hath he hid his face from him; but when
he cried unto him, he heard.
25 My praise shall be of thee in the great congregation: I will
pay my vows before them that fear him.
26 The meek shall eat and be satisfied: they shall praise the

LORD that seek him: your heart shall live for ever.
27 All the ends of the world shall remember and turn unto
the LORD: and all the kindreds of the nations shall worship
before thee.
28 For the kingdom is the LORD'S: and he is the governor
among the nations.
29 All they that be fat upon earth shall eat and worship: all
they that go down to the dust shall bow before him: and
none can keep alive his own soul.
30 A seed shall serve him; it shall be accounted to the LORD
for a generation.
31 They shall come, and shall declare his righteousness unto
a people that shall be born, that he hath done this.

PSALM 23

A Psalm of David.

The LORD is my shepherd; I shall not want.
2 He maketh me to lie down in green pastures: he
leadeth me beside the still waters.
3 He restoreth my soul: he leadeth me in the paths of
righteousness for his name's sake.
4 Yea, though I walk through the valley of the shadow of
death, I will fear no evil: for thou art with me; thy rod and
thy staff they comfort me.
5 Thou preparest a table before me in the presence of mine
enemies: thou anointest my head with oil; my cup runneth over.
6 Surely goodness and mercy shall follow me all the days of
my life: and I will dwell in the house of the LORD for ever.

PSALM 24

A Psalm of David.

The earth is the LORD'S, and the fulness thereof; the
world, and they that dwell therein.
2 For he hath founded it upon the seas, and established it
upon the floods.
3 Who shall ascend into the hill of the LORD? or who shall
stand in his holy place?
4 He that hath clean hands, and a pure heart; who hath not
lifted up his soul unto vanity, nor sworn deceitfully.
5 He shall receive the blessing from the LORD, and
righteousness from the God of his salvation.
6 This is the generation of them that seek him, that seek thy
face, O Jacob. Selah.
7 Lift up your heads, O ye gates; and be ye lift up, ye
everlasting doors; and the King of glory shall come in.
8 Who is this King of glory? The LORD strong and mighty,
the LORD mighty in battle.
9 Lift up your heads, O ye gates; even lift them up, ye
everlasting doors; and the King of glory shall come in.
10 Who is this King of glory? The LORD of hosts, he is the
King of glory. Selah.

PSALM 25

A Psalm of David.

Unto thee, O LORD, do I lift up my soul.
2 O my God, I trust in thee: let me not be ashamed,
let not mine enemies triumph over me.
3 Yea, let none that wait on thee be ashamed: let them be
ashamed which transgress without cause.
4 Shew me thy ways, O LORD; teach me thy paths.
5 Lead me in thy truth, and teach me: for thou art the God
of my salvation; on thee do I wait all the day.
6 Remember, O LORD, thy tender mercies and thy
lovingkindnesses; for they have been ever of old.
7 Remember not the sins of my youth, nor my
transgressions: according to thy mercy remember thou me
for thy goodness' sake, O LORD.
8 Good and upright is the LORD: therefore will he teach
sinners in the way.
9 The meek will he guide in judgment: and the meek will he
teach his way.
10 All the paths of the LORD are mercy and truth unto such
as keep his covenant and his testimonies.
11 For thy name's sake, O LORD, pardon mine iniquity; for
it is great.
12 What man is he that feareth the LORD? him shall he
teach in the way that he shall choose.
13 His soul shall dwell at ease; and his seed shall inherit the earth.
14 The secret of the LORD is with them that fear him; and
he will shew them his covenant.
15 Mine eyes are ever toward the LORD; for he shall pluck
my feet out of the net.

[16]Turn thee unto me, and have mercy upon me; for I am
desolate and afflicted.
[17]The troubles of my heart are enlarged: O bring thou me
out of my distresses.
[18]Look upon mine affliction and my pain; and forgive all my
sins.
[19]Consider mine enemies; for they are many; and they hate
me with cruel hatred.
[20]O keep my soul, and deliver me: let me not be ashamed;
for I put my trust in thee.
[21]Let integrity and uprightness preserve me; for I wait on thee.
[22]Redeem Israel, O God, out of all his troubles.

PSALM 26

A Psalm of David.

Judge me, O LORD; for I have walked in mine
integrity: I have trusted also in the LORD; therefore
I shall not slide.
[2]Examine me, O LORD, and prove me; try my reins and
my heart.
[3]For thy lovingkindness is before mine eyes: and I have
walked in thy truth.
[4]I have not sat with vain persons, neither will I go in with
dissemblers.
[5]I have hated the congregation of evildoers; and will not sit
with the wicked.
[6]I will wash mine hands in innocency: so will I compass
thine altar, O LORD:

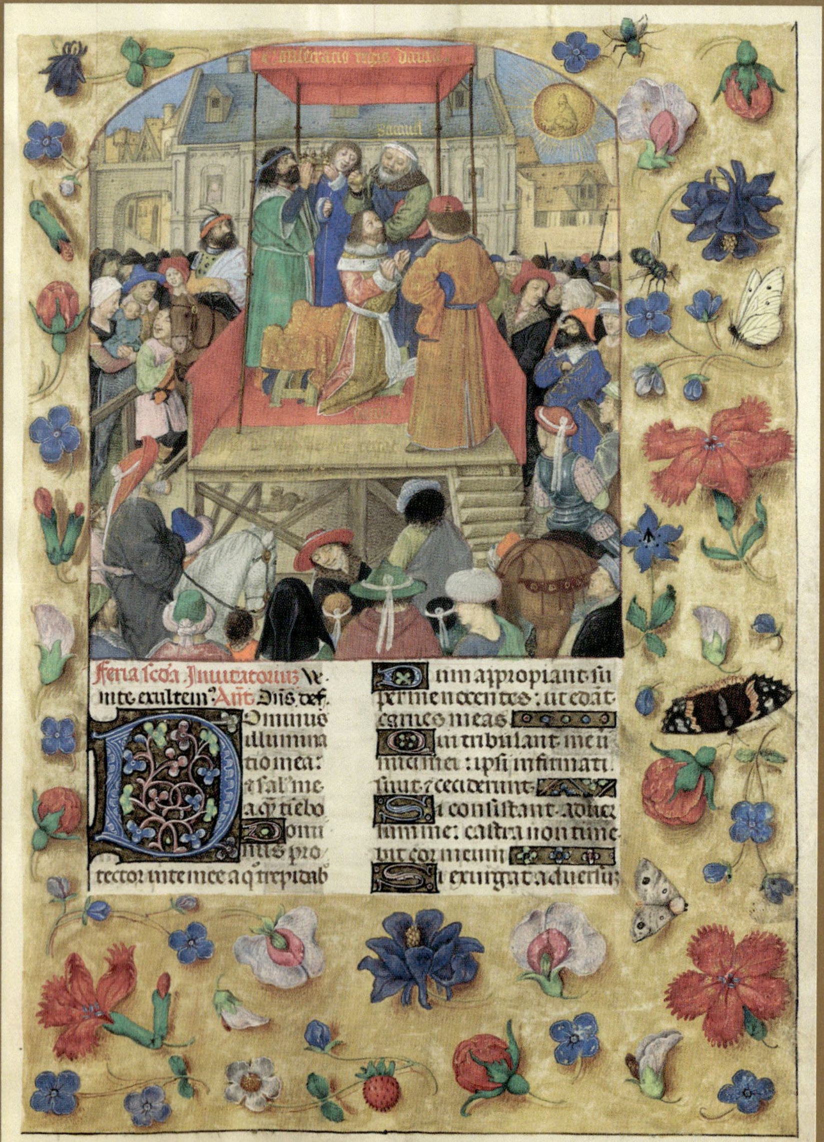

Isabella Breviary, South Netherlands, Psalm 26, ca. 1490–1497

7That I may publish with the voice of thanksgiving, and tell
of all thy wondrous works.
8LORD, I have loved the habitation of thy house,
and the place where thine honour dwelleth.
9Gather not my soul with sinners, nor
my life with bloody men:
10In whose hands is mischief, and
their right hand is full of bribes.
11But as for me, I will walk in mine
integrity: redeem me, and be merciful unto me.
12My foot standeth in an even place: in the congregations
will I bless the LORD.

PSALM 27

A Psalm of David.

The LORD is my light and my salvation; whom shall
I fear? the LORD is the strength of my life; of
whom shall I be afraid?
2When the wicked, even mine enemies and my foes, came
upon me to eat up my flesh, they stumbled and fell.
3Though an host should encamp against me, my heart shall
not fear: though war should rise against me, in this will I be
confident.
4One thing have I desired of the LORD, that will I seek
after; that I may dwell in the house of the LORD all the days
of my life, to behold the beauty of the LORD, and to enquire
in his temple.

5For in the time of trouble he shall hide me in his pavilion:
in the secret of his tabernacle shall he hide me; he shall set
me up upon a rock.
6And now shall mine head be lifted up above mine enemies
round about me: therefore will I offer in his tabernacle
sacrifices of joy; I will sing, yea, I will sing praises unto the
LORD.
7Hear, O LORD, when I cry with my voice: have mercy also
upon me, and answer me.
8When thou saidst, Seek ye my face; my heart said unto
thee, Thy face, LORD, will I seek.
9Hide not thy face far from me; put not thy servant away in
anger: thou hast been my help; leave me not, neither forsake
me, O God of my salvation.
10When my father and my mother forsake me, then the
LORD will take me up.
11Teach me thy way, O LORD, and lead me in a plain path,
because of mine enemies.
12Deliver me not over unto the will of mine enemies: for
false witnesses are risen up against me, and such as breathe
out cruelty.
13I had fainted, unless I had believed to see the goodness of
the LORD in the land of the living.
14Wait on the LORD: be of good courage, and he shall
strengthen thine heart: wait, I say, on the LORD.

PSALM 28

A Psalm of David.

Unto thee will I cry, O LORD my rock; be not silent
to me: lest, if thou be silent to me, I become like
them that go down into the pit.
2 Hear the voice of my supplications, when I cry unto thee,
when I lift up my hands toward thy holy oracle.
3 Draw me not away with the wicked, and with the workers
of iniquity, which speak peace to their neighbours, but
mischief is in their hearts.
4 Give them according to their deeds, and according to the
wickedness of their endeavours: give them after the work of
their hands; render to them their desert.
5 Because they regard not the works of the LORD, nor the
operation of his hands, he shall destroy them, and not build
them up.
6 Blessed be the LORD, because he hath heard the voice of
my supplications.
7 The LORD is my strength and my shield; my heart trusted
in him, and I am helped: therefore my heart greatly rejoiceth;
and with my song will I praise him.
8 The LORD is their strength, and he is the saving strength
of his anointed.
9 Save thy people, and bless thine inheritance: feed them
also, and lift them up for ever.

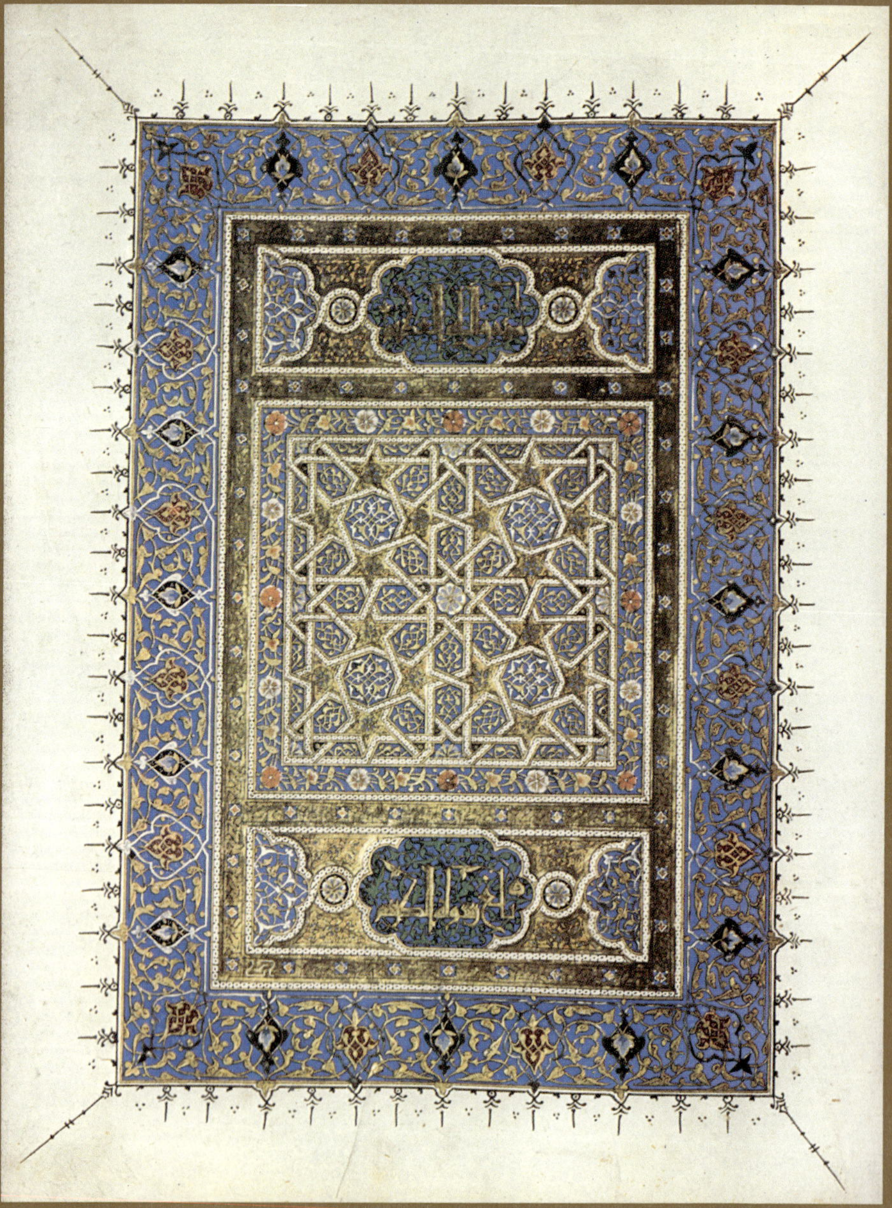

PSALM 29

A Psalm of David.

Give unto the LORD, O ye mighty, give unto the
LORD glory and strength.
2 Give unto the LORD the glory due unto his name;
worship the LORD in the beauty of holiness.
3 The voice of the LORD is upon the waters: the God of
glory thundereth: the LORD is upon many waters.
4 The voice of the LORD is powerful; the voice of the
LORD is full of majesty.
5 The voice of the LORD breaketh the cedars; yea, the
LORD breaketh the cedars of Lebanon.
6 He maketh them also to skip like a calf; Lebanon and
Sirion like a young unicorn.
7 The voice of the LORD divideth the flames of fire.
8 The voice of the LORD shaketh the wilderness; the
LORD shaketh the wilderness of Kadesh.
9 The voice of the LORD maketh the hinds to calve, and
discovereth the forests: and in his temple doth every one
speak of his glory.
10 The LORD sitteth upon the flood; yea, the LORD sitteth
King for ever.
11 The LORD will give strength unto his people; the LORD
will bless his people with peace.

PSALM 30

A Psalm and Song at the dedication
of the house of David.

I will extol thee, O LORD; for thou hast lifted me up,
and hast not made my foes to rejoice over me.
2 O LORD my God, I cried unto thee, and thou hast healed me.
3 O LORD, thou hast brought up my soul from the grave:
thou hast kept me alive, that I should not go down to the pit.
4 Sing unto the LORD, O ye saints of his, and give thanks at
the remembrance of his holiness.
5 For his anger endureth but a moment; in his favour is life:
weeping may endure for a night, but joy cometh in the morning.
6 And in my prosperity I said, I shall never be moved.
7 LORD, by thy favour thou hast made my mountain to
stand strong: thou didst hide thy face, and I was troubled.
8 I cried to thee, O LORD; and unto the LORD I made
supplication.
9 What profit is there in my blood, when I go down to the
pit? Shall the dust praise thee? shall it declare thy truth?
10 Hear, O LORD, and have mercy upon me: LORD, be
thou my helper.
11 Thou hast turned for me my mourning into dancing: thou
hast put off my sackcloth, and girded me with gladness;
12 To the end that my glory may sing praise to thee, and
not be silent. O LORD my God, I will give thanks unto thee
for ever.

PSALM 31

To the chief Musician, A Psalm of David.

In thee, O LORD, do I put my trust; let me never be
ashamed: deliver me in thy righteousness.
2 Bow down thine ear to me; deliver me speedily: be thou
my strong rock, for an house of defence to save me.
3 For thou art my rock and my fortress; therefore for thy
name's sake lead me, and guide me.
4 Pull me out of the net that they have laid privily for me:
for thou art my strength.
5 Into thine hand I commit my spirit: thou hast redeemed
me, O LORD God of truth.
6 I have hated them that regard lying vanities: but I trust in
the LORD.
7 I will be glad and rejoice in thy mercy: for thou hast
considered my trouble; thou hast known my soul in
adversities;
8 And hast not shut me up into the hand of the enemy: thou
hast set my feet in a large room.
9 Have mercy upon me, O LORD, for I am in trouble: mine
eye is consumed with grief, yea, my soul and my belly.
10 For my life is spent with grief, and my years with sighing:
my strength faileth because of mine iniquity, and my bones
are consumed.
11 I was a reproach among all mine enemies, but especially
among my neighbours, and a fear to mine acquaintance: they
that did see me without fled from me.
12 I am forgotten as a dead man out of mind: I am like a
broken vessel.
13 For I have heard the slander of many: fear was on every

side: while they took counsel together against me, they
devised to take away my life.
14 But I trusted in thee, O LORD: I said, Thou art my God.
15 My times are in thy hand: deliver me from the hand of
mine enemies, and from them that persecute me.
16 Make thy face to shine upon thy servant: save me for thy
mercies' sake.
17 Let me not be ashamed, O LORD; for I have called upon
thee: let the wicked be ashamed, and let them be silent in
the grave.
18 Let the lying lips be put to silence; which speak grievous
things proudly and contemptuously against the righteous.
19 Oh how great is thy goodness, which thou hast laid up for
them that fear thee; which thou hast wrought for them that
trust in thee before the sons of men!
20 Thou shalt hide them in the secret of thy presence from
the pride of man: thou shalt keep them secretly in a pavilion
from the strife of tongues.
21 Blessed be the LORD: for he hath shewed me his
marvellous kindness in a strong city.
22 For I said in my haste, I am cut off from before thine eyes:
nevertheless thou heardest the voice of my
supplications when I cried unto thee.
23 O love the LORD, all ye his saints: for the
LORD preserveth the faithful, and plentifully
rewardeth the proud doer.
24 Be of good courage, and he shall strengthen
your heart, all ye that hope in the LORD.

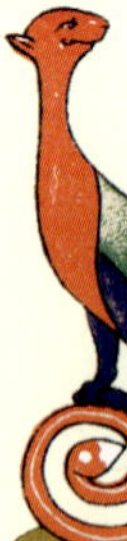

PSALM 32

A Psalm of David, Maschil.

Blessed is he whose transgression is forgiven, whose
sin is covered.
2 Blessed is the man unto whom the LORD imputeth not
iniquity, and in whose spirit there is no guile.
3 When I kept silence, my bones waxed old through my
roaring all the day long.
4 For day and night thy hand was heavy upon me: my
moisture is turned into the drought of summer. Selah.
5 I acknowledged my sin unto thee, and mine iniquity have
I not hid. I said, I will confess my transgressions unto the
LORD; and thou forgavest the iniquity of my sin. Selah.
6 For this shall every one that is godly pray unto thee in a
time when thou mayest be found: surely in the floods of great
waters they shall not come nigh unto him.
7 Thou art my hiding place; thou shalt preserve me
from trouble; thou shalt compass me about with songs of
deliverance. Selah.
8 I will instruct thee and teach thee in the way which thou
shalt go: I will guide thee with mine eye.
9 Be ye not as the horse, or as the mule, which have no
understanding: whose mouth must be held in with bit and
bridle, lest they come near unto thee.
10 Many sorrows shall be to the wicked: but he that trusteth
in the LORD, mercy shall compass him about.
11 Be glad in the LORD, and rejoice, ye righteous: and shout
for joy, all ye that are upright in heart.

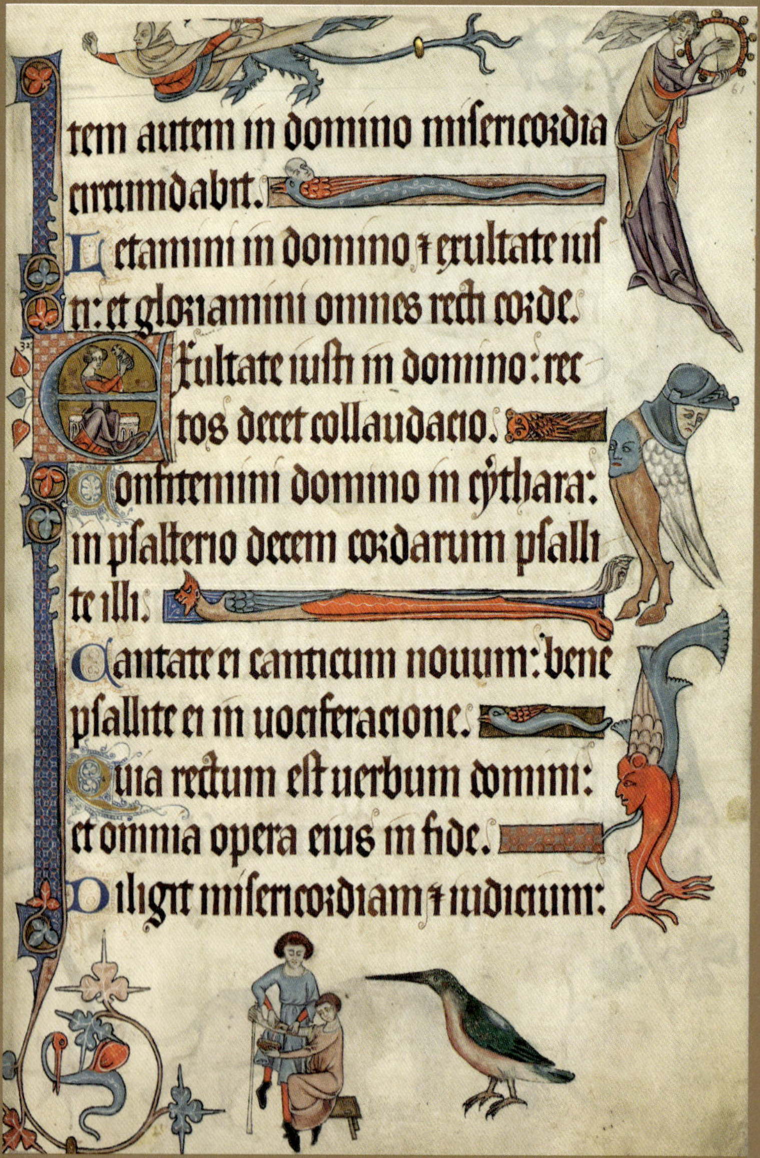

61

tem autem in domino misericordia
circumdabit.
Letamini in domino et exultate iusti: et gloriamini omnes recti corde.
32 Exultate iusti in domino: rec
tos decet collaudacio.
Confitemini domino in cythara:
in psalterio decem cordarum psalli
te illi.
Cantate ei canticum nouum: bene
psallite ei in uociferacione.
Quia rectum est uerbum domini:
et omnia opera eius in fide.
Diligit misericordiam et iudicium:

Luttrell Psalter, England, Psalm 32, ca. 1325–1335

PSALM 33

Rejoice in the LORD, O ye righteous: for praise is
comely for the upright.
2 Praise the LORD with harp: sing unto him with the
psaltery and an instrument of ten strings.
3 Sing unto him a new song; play skilfully with a loud noise.
4 For the word of the LORD is right; and all his works are
done in truth.
5 He loveth righteousness and judgment: the earth is full of
the goodness of the LORD.
6 By the word of the LORD were the heavens made; and all
the host of them by the breath of his mouth.
7 He gathereth the waters of the sea together as an heap: he
layeth up the depth in storehouses.
8 Let all the earth fear the LORD: let all the inhabitants of
the world stand in awe of him.
9 For he spake, and it was done; he commanded, and it stood
fast.
10 The LORD bringeth the counsel of the heathen to
nought: he maketh the devices of the people of none effect.
11 The counsel of the LORD standeth for ever, the thoughts
of his heart to all generations.
12 Blessed is the nation whose God is the LORD: and the
people whom he hath chosen for his own inheritance.
13 The LORD looketh from heaven; he beholdeth all the
sons of men.
14 From the place of his habitation he looketh upon all the
inhabitants of the earth.
15 He fashioneth their hearts alike; he considereth all their
works.
16 There is no king saved by the multitude of an host: a

mighty man is not delivered by much strength.
17 An horse is a vain thing for safety: neither shall he deliver
any by his great strength.
18 Behold, the eye of the LORD is upon them that fear him,
upon them that hope in his mercy;
19 To deliver their soul from death, and to keep them alive in
famine.
20 Our soul waiteth for the LORD: he is our help and our
shield.
21 For our heart shall rejoice in him, because we have trusted
in his holy name.
22 Let thy mercy, O LORD, be upon us, according as we
hope in thee.

PSALM 34

A Psalm of David, when he changed his behaviour before Abimelech; who drove him away, and he departed.

I will bless the LORD at all times: his praise shall
continually be in my mouth.
2 My soul shall make her boast in the LORD: the humble
shall hear thereof, and be glad.
3 O magnify the LORD with me, and let us exalt his name
together.
4 I sought the LORD, and he heard me, and delivered me
from all my fears.
5 They looked unto him, and were lightened: and their faces
were not ashamed.
6 This poor man cried, and the LORD heard him, and saved
him out of all his troubles.

7 The angel of the LORD encampeth round about them
that fear him, and delivereth them.
8 O taste and see that the LORD is good: blessed is the man
that trusteth in him.
9 O fear the LORD, ye his saints: for there is no want to
them that fear him.
10 The young lions do lack, and suffer hunger: but they that
seek the LORD shall not want any good thing.
11 Come, ye children, hearken unto me: I will teach you the
fear of the LORD.
12 What man is he that desireth life, and loveth many days,
that he may see good?
13 Keep thy tongue from evil, and thy lips from speaking guile.
14 Depart from evil, and do good; seek peace, and pursue it.
15 The eyes of the LORD are upon the righteous, and his
ears are open unto their cry.
16 The face of the LORD is against them that do evil, to cut
off the remembrance of them from the earth.
17 The righteous cry, and the LORD heareth, and delivereth
them out of all their troubles.
18 The LORD is nigh unto them that are of a broken heart;
and saveth such as be of a contrite spirit.
19 Many are the afflictions of the righteous: but the LORD
delivereth him out of them all.
20 He keepeth all his bones: not one of them is broken.
21 Evil shall slay the wicked: and they that hate
the righteous shall be desolate.
22 The LORD redeemeth the soul of
his servants: and none of them that
trust in him shall be desolate.

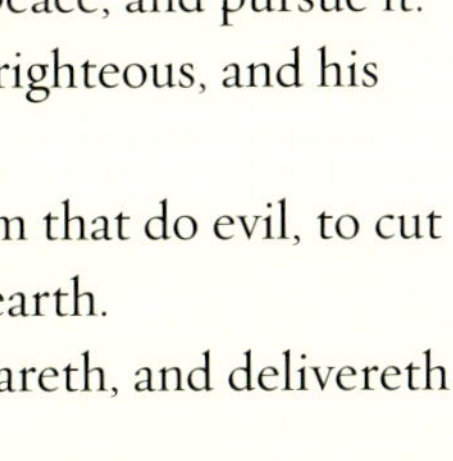

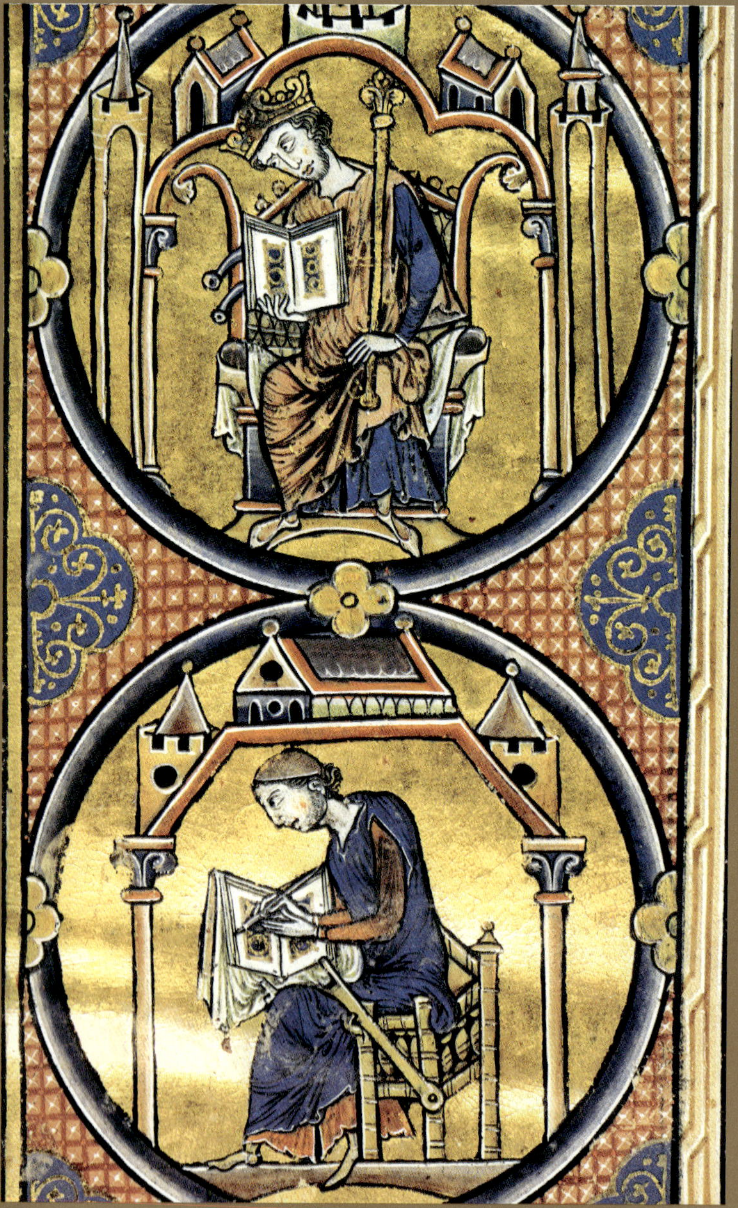

PSALM 35

A Psalm of David.

Plead my cause, O LORD, with them that strive with
me: fight against them that fight against me.
2 Take hold of shield and buckler, and stand up for mine help.
3 Draw out also the spear, and stop the way against them
that persecute me: say unto my soul, I am thy salvation.
4 Let them be confounded and put to shame that seek after
my soul: let them be turned back and brought to confusion
that devise my hurt.
5 Let them be as chaff before the wind: and let the angel of
the LORD chase them.
6 Let their way be dark and slippery: and let the angel of the
LORD persecute them.
7 For without cause have they hid for me their net in a pit,
which without cause they have digged for my soul.
8 Let destruction come upon him at unawares; and let his
net that he hath hid catch himself: into that very destruction
let him fall.
9 And my soul shall be joyful in the LORD: it shall rejoice
in his salvation.
10 All my bones shall say, LORD, who is like unto thee,
which deliverest the poor from him that is too strong for
him, yea, the poor and the needy from him that spoileth him?
11 False witnesses did rise up; they laid to my charge things
that I knew not.
12 They rewarded me evil for good to the spoiling of my soul.
13 But as for me, when they were sick, my clothing was
sackcloth: I humbled my soul with fasting; and my prayer
returned into mine own bosom.

14 I behaved myself as though he had been my friend or
brother: I bowed down heavily, as one that mourneth for his
mother.
15 But in mine adversity they rejoiced, and gathered
themselves together: yea, the abjects gathered themselves
together against me, and I knew it not; they did tear me, and
ceased not:
16 With hypocritical mockers in feasts, they gnashed upon
me with their teeth.
17 LORD, how long wilt thou look on? rescue my soul from
their destructions, my darling from the lions.
18 I will give thee thanks in the great congregation: I will
praise thee among much people.
19 Let not them that are mine enemies wrongfully rejoice
over me: neither let them wink with the eye that hate me
without a cause.
20 For they speak not peace: but they devise deceitful
matters against them that are quiet in the land.
21 Yea, they opened their mouth wide against me, and said,
Aha, aha, our eye hath seen it.
22 This thou hast seen, O LORD: keep not silence: O LORD,
be not far from me.
23 Stir up thyself, and awake to my judgment, even unto my
cause, my God and my LORD.
24 Judge me, O LORD my God, according to thy
righteousness; and let them not rejoice over me.

25 Let them not say in their hearts, Ah, so would we have it:
let them not say, We have swallowed him up.
26 Let them be ashamed and brought to confusion together
that rejoice at mine hurt: let them be clothed with shame and
dishonour that magnify themselves against me.
27 Let them shout for joy, and be glad, that favour my
righteous cause: yea, let them say continually, Let the LORD be
magnified, which hath pleasure in the prosperity of his servant.
28 And my tongue shall speak of thy righteousness and of thy
praise all the day long.

PSALM 36

To the chief Musician, A Psalm of David,
the servant of the LORD.

The transgression of the wicked saith within my
heart, that there is no fear of God before his eyes.
2 For he flattereth himself in his own eyes, until his iniquity
be found to be hateful.
3 The words of his mouth are iniquity and deceit: he hath
left off to be wise, and to do good.
4 He deviseth mischief upon his bed; he setteth himself in a
way that is not good; he abhorreth not evil.
5 Thy mercy, O LORD, is in the heavens; and thy
faithfulness reacheth unto the clouds.
6 Thy righteousness is like the great mountains; thy
judgments are a great deep: O LORD, thou preservest man
and beast.
7 How excellent is thy lovingkindness, O God! therefore the
children of men put their trust under the shadow of thy wings.

8 They shall be abundantly satisfied with the fatness of thy
house; and thou shalt make them drink of the river of thy
pleasures.
9 For with thee is the fountain of life: in thy light shall we
see light.
10 O continue thy lovingkindness unto them that know thee;
and thy righteousness to the upright in heart.
11 Let not the foot of pride come against me, and let not the
hand of the wicked remove me.
12 There are the workers of iniquity fallen: they are cast down,
and shall not be able to rise.

PSALM 37

A Psalm of David.

Fret not thyself because of evildoers, neither be thou
envious against the workers of iniquity.
2 For they shall soon be cut down like the grass, and wither
as the green herb.
3 Trust in the LORD, and do good; so shalt thou dwell in
the land, and verily thou shalt be fed.
4 Delight thyself also in the LORD; and he shall give thee
the desires of thine heart.
5 Commit thy way unto the LORD; trust also in him; and he
shall bring it to pass.
6 And he shall bring forth thy righteousness as the light, and
thy judgment as the noonday.
7 Rest in the LORD, and wait patiently for him: fret not
thyself because of him who prospereth in his way, because of
the man who bringeth wicked devices to pass.

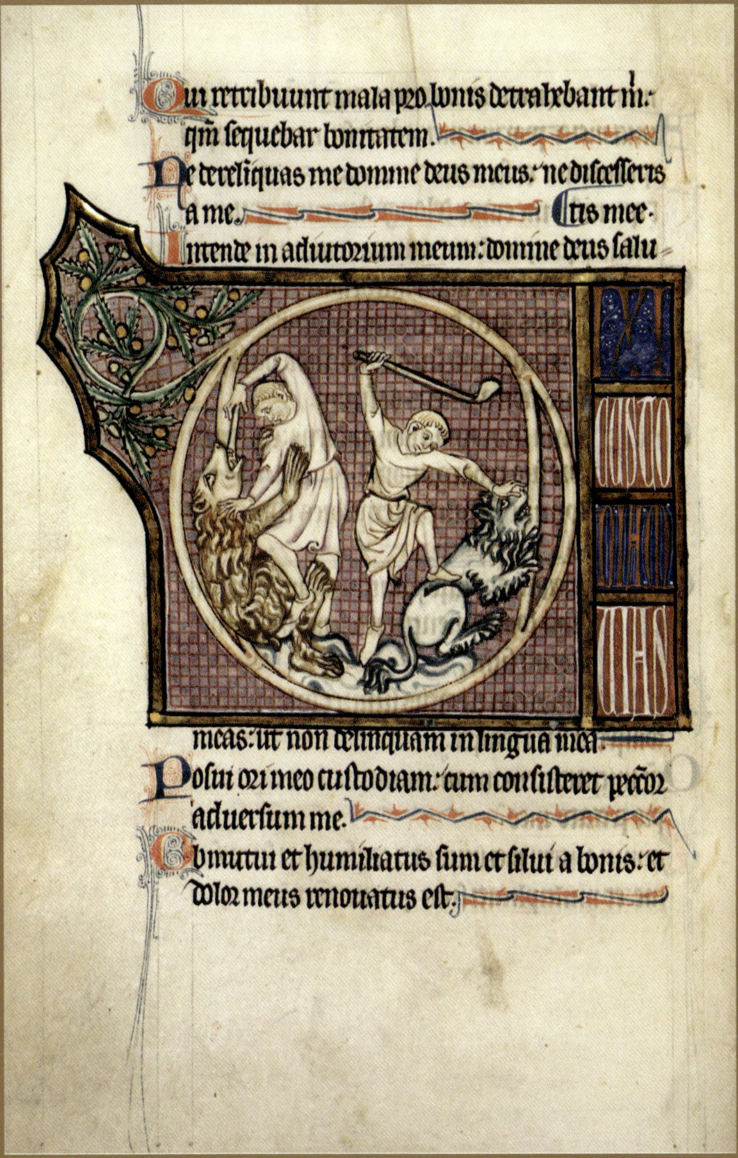

Lire Abbey Psalter, Psalm 37-38, France, late 13th-early 14th century

8 Cease from anger, and forsake wrath: fret not thyself in
any wise to do evil.
9 For evildoers shall be cut off: but those that wait upon the
LORD, they shall inherit the earth.
10 For yet a little while, and the wicked shall not be: yea,
thou shalt diligently consider his place, and it shall not be.
11 But the meek shall inherit the earth; and shall delight
themselves in the abundance of peace.
12 The wicked plotteth against the just, and gnasheth upon
him with his teeth.
13 The LORD shall laugh at him: for he seeth that his day is
coming.
14 The wicked have drawn out the sword, and have bent
their bow, to cast down the poor and needy, and to slay such
as be of upright conversation.
15 Their sword shall enter into their own heart, and their
bows shall be broken.
16 A little that a righteous man hath is better than the riches
of many wicked.
17 For the arms of the wicked shall be broken: but the
LORD upholdeth the righteous.
18 The LORD knoweth the days of the upright: and their
inheritance shall be for ever.
19 They shall not be ashamed in the evil time: and in the
days of famine they shall be satisfied.
20 But the wicked shall perish, and the enemies of the
LORD shall be as the fat of lambs: they shall consume; into
smoke shall they consume away.
21 The wicked borroweth, and payeth not again: but the
righteous sheweth mercy, and giveth.
22 For such as be blessed of him shall inherit the earth; and
they that be cursed of him shall be cut off.

23 The steps of a good man are ordered by the LORD: and
he delighteth in his way.
24 Though he fall, he shall not be utterly cast down: for the
LORD upholdeth him with his hand.
25 I have been young, and now am old; yet have I not seen
the righteous forsaken, nor his seed begging bread.
26 He is ever merciful, and lendeth; and his seed is blessed.
27 Depart from evil, and do good; and dwell for evermore.
28 For the LORD loveth judgment, and forsaketh not his
saints; they are preserved for ever: but the seed of the wicked
shall be cut off.
29 The righteous shall inherit the land, and dwell therein for ever.
30 The mouth of the righteous speaketh wisdom, and his
tongue talketh of judgment.
31 The law of his God is in his heart; none of his steps shall
slide.
32 The wicked watcheth the righteous, and seeketh to slay him.
33 The LORD will not leave him in his hand, nor condemn
him when he is judged.
34 Wait on the LORD, and keep his way, and he shall exalt
thee to inherit the land: when the wicked are cut off, thou
shalt see it.

35 I have seen the wicked in great power, and
spreading himself like a green bay tree.

36 Yet he passed away, and, lo, he was not:
yea, I sought him, but he could not be found.

37 Mark the perfect man, and behold the
upright: for the end of that man is peace.

38 But the transgressors shall be destroyed together: the end
of the wicked shall be cut off.

39 But the salvation of the righteous is of the LORD: he is
their strength in the time of trouble.

40 And the LORD shall help them and deliver them: he shall
deliver them from the wicked, and save them, because they
trust in him.

PSALM 38

A Psalm of David, to bring to remembrance.

O LORD, rebuke me not in thy wrath: neither chasten
me in thy hot displeasure.

2 For thine arrows stick fast in me, and thy hand presseth
me sore.

3 There is no soundness in my flesh because of thine anger;
neither is there any rest in my bones because of my sin.

4 For mine iniquities are gone over mine head: as an heavy
burden they are too heavy for me.

5 My wounds stink and are corrupt because of my foolishness.

6 I am troubled; I am bowed down greatly; I go mourning
all the day long.

7 For my loins are filled with a loathsome disease: and there
is no soundness in my flesh.

8 I am feeble and sore broken: I have roared by reason of
the disquietness of my heart.
9 LORD, all my desire is before thee; and my groaning is not
hid from thee.
10 My heart panteth, my strength faileth me: as for the light
of mine eyes, it also is gone from me.
11 My lovers and my friends stand aloof from my sore; and
my kinsmen stand afar off.
12 They also that seek after my life lay snares for me: and
they that seek my hurt speak mischievous things, and imagine
deceits all the day long.
13 But I, as a deaf man, heard not; and I was as a dumb man
that openeth not his mouth.
14 Thus I was as a man that heareth not, and in whose
mouth are no reproofs.
15 For in thee, O LORD, do I hope: thou wilt hear, O LORD
my God.
16 For I said, Hear me, lest otherwise they should rejoice
over me: when my foot slippeth, they magnify themselves
against me.
17 For I am ready to halt, and my sorrow is continually
before me.
18 For I will declare mine iniquity; I will be sorry for my sin.
19 But mine enemies are lively, and they are strong: and they
that hate me wrongfully are multiplied.
20 They also that render evil for good are mine adversaries;
because I follow the thing that good is.
21 Forsake me not, O LORD: O my God, be not far from me.
22 Make haste to help me, O LORD my salvation.

PSALM 39

To the chief Musician, even to Jeduthun,
A Psalm of David.

I said, I will take heed to my ways, that I sin not with
my tongue: I will keep my mouth with a bridle, while
the wicked is before me.
2 I was dumb with silence, I held my peace, even from good;
and my sorrow was stirred.
3 My heart was hot within me, while I was musing the fire
burned: then spake I with my tongue,
4 LORD, make me to know mine end, and the measure of
my days, what it is; that I may know how frail I am.
5 Behold, thou hast made my days as an handbreadth; and
mine age is as nothing before thee: verily every man at his
best state is altogether vanity. Selah.
6 Surely every man walketh in a vain shew: surely they are
disquieted in vain: he heapeth up riches, and knoweth not
who shall gather them.
7 And now, LORD, what wait I for? my hope is in thee.
8 Deliver me from all my transgressions: make me not the
reproach of the foolish.
9 I was dumb, I opened not my mouth; because thou didst it.
10 Remove thy stroke away from me: I am consumed by the
blow of thine hand.

11When thou with rebukes dost correct man for iniquity,
thou makest his beauty to consume away like a moth: surely
every man is vanity. Selah.
12Hear my prayer, O LORD, and give ear unto my cry;
hold not thy peace at my tears: for I am a stranger with
thee, and a sojourner, as all my fathers were.
13O spare me, that I may recover strength, before I go
hence, and be no more.

PSALM 40

To the chief Musician,
A Psalm of David.

I waited patiently for the LORD; and he inclined
me, and heard my cry.
2He brought me up also out of an horrible pit, out of the
miry clay, and set my feet upon a rock, and established my
goings.
3And he hath put a new song in my mouth, even praise
unto our God: many shall see it, and fear, and shall trust in
the LORD.
4Blessed is that man that maketh the LORD his trust,
and respecteth not the proud, nor such as turn aside to lies.
5Many, O LORD my God, are thy wonderful works
which thou hast done, and thy thoughts which are to us-
ward: they cannot be reckoned up in order unto thee: if I
would declare and speak of them, they are more than can
be numbered.
6Sacrifice and offering thou didst not desire; mine ears

hast thou opened: burnt offering and sin offering hast thou
not required.
7Then said I, Lo, I come: in the volume of the book it is
written of me,
8I delight to do thy will, O my God: yea, thy law is within
my heart.
9I have preached righteousness in the great congregation:
lo, I have not refrained my lips, O LORD, thou knowest.
10I have not hid thy righteousness within my heart; I
have declared thy faithfulness and thy salvation: I have not
concealed thy lovingkindness and thy truth from the great
congregation.
11Withhold not thou thy tender mercies from me, O LORD:
let thy lovingkindness and thy truth continually preserve me.
12For innumerable evils have compassed me about: mine
iniquities have taken hold upon me, so that I am not able to
look up; they are more than the hairs of mine head: therefore
my heart faileth me.
13Be pleased, O LORD, to deliver me: O LORD, make
haste to help me.
14Let them be ashamed and confounded together that seek
after my soul to destroy it; let them be driven backward and
put to shame that wish me evil.
15Let them be desolate for a reward of their shame that say
unto me, Aha, aha.
16Let all those that seek thee rejoice and be glad in thee:
let such as love thy salvation say continually, The LORD be
magnified.
17But I am poor and needy; yet the LORD thinketh upon
me: thou art my help and my deliverer; make no tarrying, O
my God.

PSALM 41

To the chief Musician,
A Psalm of David.

Blessed is he that considereth the poor: the LORD
will deliver him in time of trouble.
2 The LORD will preserve him, and keep him alive; and he
shall be blessed upon the earth: and thou wilt not deliver him
unto the will of his enemies.
3 The LORD will strengthen him upon the bed of
languishing: thou wilt make all his bed in his sickness.
4 I said, LORD, be merciful unto me: heal my soul; for I
have sinned against thee.
5 Mine enemies speak evil of me, When shall he die, and his
name perish?
6 And if he come to see me, he speaketh vanity: his heart
gathereth iniquity to itself; when he goeth abroad, he telleth it.
7 All that hate me whisper together against me: against me
do they devise my hurt.

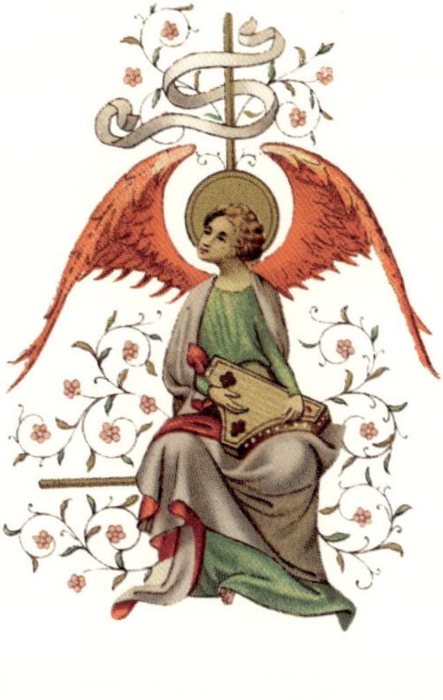

8 An evil disease, say they, cleaveth fast unto him: and now
that he lieth he shall rise up no more.
9 Yea, mine own familiar friend, in whom I trusted, which
did eat of my bread, hath lifted up his heel against me.
10 But thou, O LORD, be merciful unto me, and raise me
up, that I may requite them.
11 By this I know that thou favourest me, because mine
enemy doth not triumph over me.
12 And as for me, thou upholdest me in mine integrity, and
settest me before thy face for ever.
13 Blessed be the LORD God of Israel from everlasting, and
to everlasting. Amen, and Amen.

BOOK II

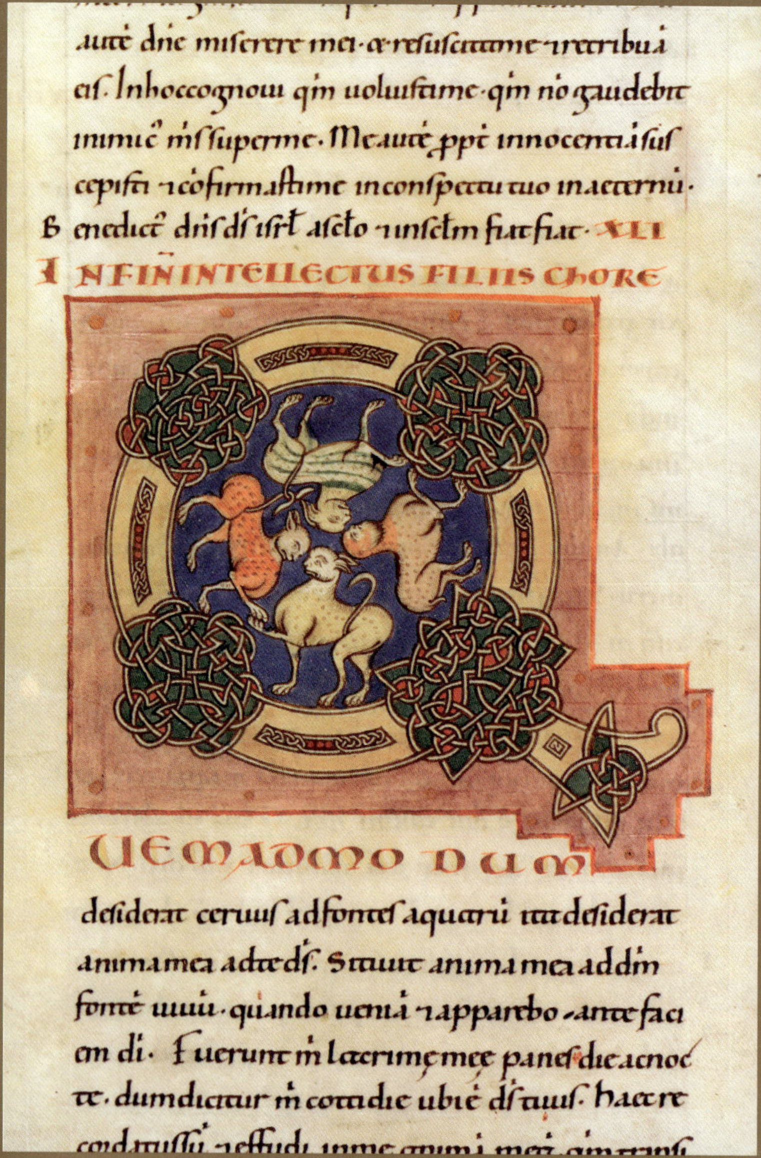

Second Bible of Saint-Martial de Limoges, Psalm 41, ca. 1100

PSALM 42

To the chief Musician, Maschil,
for the sons of Korah.

As the hart panteth after the water brooks, so panteth
my soul after thee, O God.
2 My soul thirsteth for God, for the living God: when shall I
come and appear before God?
3 My tears have been my meat day and night, while they
continually say unto me, Where is thy God?
4 When I remember these things, I pour out my soul in
me: for I had gone with the multitude, I went with them to
the house of God, with the voice of joy and praise, with a
multitude that kept holyday.
5 Why art thou cast down, O my soul? and why art thou
disquieted in me? hope thou in God: for I shall yet praise
him for the help of his countenance.
6 O my God, my soul is cast down within me: therefore
will I remember thee from the land of Jordan, and of the
Hermonites, from the hill Mizar.
7 Deep calleth unto deep at the noise of thy waterspouts: all
thy waves and thy billows are gone
over me.
8 Yet the LORD will command his
lovingkindness in the daytime, and in
the night his song shall be with me,
and my prayer unto the God of my life.
9 I will say unto God my rock, Why
hast thou forgotten me? why go I
mourning because of the oppression
of the enemy?

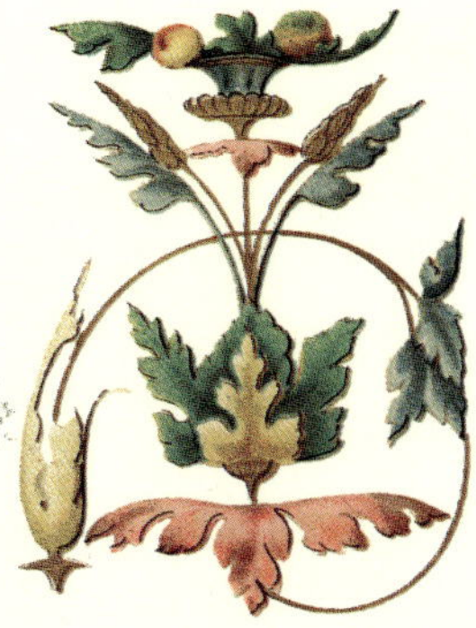

10 As with a sword in my bones, mine enemies reproach me;
while they say daily unto me, Where is thy God?
11 Why art thou cast down, O my soul? and why art thou
disquieted within me? hope thou in God: for I shall yet praise
him, who is the health of my countenance, and my God.

PSALM 43

Judge me, O God, and plead my cause against an
ungodly nation: O deliver me from the deceitful
and unjust man.
2 For thou art the God of my strength: why dost thou cast
me off? why go I mourning because of the oppression of the
enemy?
3 O send out thy light and thy truth: let them lead me; let
them bring me unto thy holy hill, and to thy tabernacles.
4 Then will I go unto the altar of God, unto God my
exceeding joy: yea, upon the harp will I praise thee, O God
my God.
5 Why art thou cast down, O my soul? and why art thou
disquieted within me? hope in God: for I shall yet praise him,
who is the health of my countenance, and my God.

PSALM 44

*To the chief Musician for the
sons of Korah, Maschil.*

We have heard with our ears, O God, our fathers have
told us, what work thou didst in their days, in the
times of old.
2 How thou didst drive out the heathen with thy hand, and
plantedst them; how thou didst afflict the people, and cast
them out.
3 For they got not the land in possession by their own sword,
neither did their own arm save them: but thy right hand, and
thine arm, and the light of thy countenance, because thou
hadst a favour unto them.
4 Thou art my King, O God: command deliverances for Jacob.
5 Through thee will we push down our enemies: through thy
name will we tread them under that rise up against us.
6 For I will not trust in my bow, neither shall my sword
save me.
7 But thou hast saved us from our enemies, and hast put
them to shame that hated us.
8 In God we boast all the day long, and praise thy name for
ever. Selah.
9 But thou hast cast off, and put us to shame; and goest not
forth with our armies.
10 Thou makest us to turn back from the enemy: and they
which hate us spoil for themselves.
11 Thou hast given us like sheep appointed for meat; and
hast scattered us among the heathen.
12 Thou sellest thy people for nought, and dost not increase
thy wealth by their price.

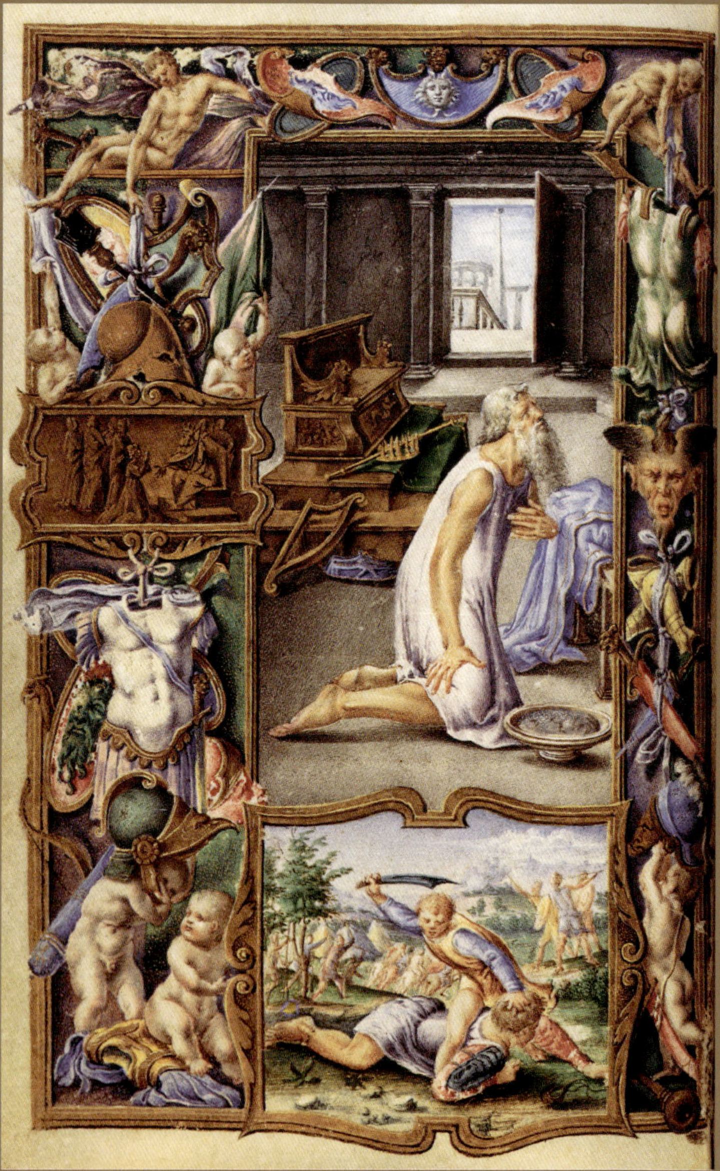

Stuart de Rothesay Hours, Italy, ca. 1511

13Thou makest us a reproach to our neighbours, a scorn and
a derision to them that are round about us.
14Thou makest us a byword among the heathen, a shaking
of the head among the people.
15My confusion is continually before me, and the shame of
my face hath covered me,
16For the voice of him that reproacheth and blasphemeth;
by reason of the enemy and avenger.
17All this is come upon us; yet have we not forgotten thee,
neither have we dealt falsely in thy covenant.
18Our heart is not turned back, neither have our steps
declined from thy way;
19Though thou hast sore broken us in the place of dragons,
and covered us with the shadow of death.
20If we have forgotten the name of our God, or stretched
out our hands to a strange god;
21Shall not God search this out? for he knoweth the secrets
of the heart.
22Yea, for thy sake are we killed all the day long; we are
counted as sheep for the slaughter.
23Awake, why sleepest thou, O LORD? arise, cast us not off
for ever.
24Wherefore hidest thou thy face, and forgettest our
affliction and our oppression?
25For our soul is bowed down to the dust: our belly cleaveth
unto the earth.
26Arise for our help, and redeem us for thy mercies' sake.

PSALM 45

To the chief Musician upon Shoshannim, for the sons of Korah, Maschil, A Song of loves.

My heart is inditing a good matter: I speak of the things which I have made touching the king: my tongue is the pen of a ready writer.

2 Thou art fairer than the children of men: grace is poured into thy lips: therefore God hath blessed thee for ever.

3 Gird thy sword upon thy thigh, O most mighty, with thy glory and thy majesty.

4 And in thy majesty ride prosperously because of truth and meekness and righteousness; and thy right hand shall teach thee terrible things.

5 Thine arrows are sharp in the heart of the king's enemies; whereby the people fall under thee.

6 Thy throne, O God, is for ever and ever: the sceptre of thy kingdom is a right sceptre.

7 Thou lovest righteousness, and hatest wickedness: therefore God, thy God, hath anointed thee with the oil of gladness above thy fellows.

8 All thy garments smell of myrrh, and aloes, and cassia, out of the ivory palaces, whereby they have made thee glad.

9 Kings' daughters were among thy honourable women: upon thy right hand did stand the queen in gold of Ophir.

10 Hearken, O daughter, and consider, and incline thine ear; forget also thine own people, and thy father's house;

11 So shall the king greatly desire thy beauty: for he is thy LORD; and worship thou him.

12 And the daughter of Tyre shall be there with a gift; even the rich among the people shall intreat thy favour.

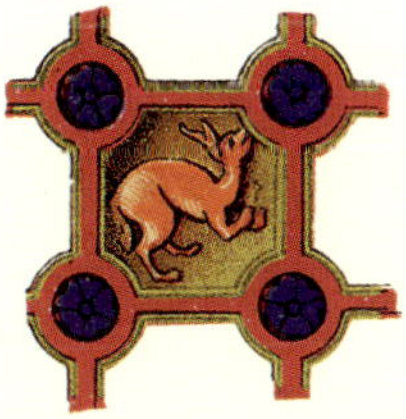

13 The king's daughter is all glorious
within: her clothing is of wrought gold.
14 She shall be brought unto the king
in raiment of needlework: the virgins
her companions that follow her shall
be brought unto thee.
15 With gladness and rejoicing shall they be brought:
they shall enter into the king's palace.
16 Instead of thy fathers shall be thy children, whom thou
mayest make princes in all the earth.
17 I will make thy name to be remembered in all generations:
therefore shall the people praise thee for ever and ever.

PSALM 46

To the chief Musician for the sons of Korah,
A Song upon Alamoth.

God is our refuge and strength, a very present help in
trouble.
2 Therefore will not we fear, though the earth be removed,
and though the mountains be carried into the midst of the sea;
3 Though the waters thereof roar and be troubled, though
the mountains shake with the swelling thereof. Selah.
4 There is a river, the streams whereof shall make glad the city
of God, the holy place of the tabernacles of the most High.
5 God is in the midst of her; she shall not be moved: God
shall help her, and that right early.
6 The heathen raged, the kingdoms were moved: he uttered
his voice, the earth melted.

7 The LORD of hosts is with us; the God of Jacob is our
refuge. Selah.
8 Come, behold the works of the LORD, what desolations
he hath made in the earth.
9 He maketh wars to cease unto the end of the earth;
he breaketh the bow, and cutteth the spear in sunder; he
burneth the chariot in the fire.
10 Be still, and know that I am God: I will be exalted among
the heathen, I will be exalted in the earth.
11 The LORD of hosts is with us; the God of Jacob is our
refuge. Selah.

PSALM 47

To the chief Musician,
A Psalm for the sons of Korah.

O clap your hands, all ye people; shout unto God with
the voice of triumph.
2 For the LORD most high is terrible; he is a great King
over all the earth.
3 He shall subdue the people under us, and the nations
under our feet.
4 He shall choose our inheritance for us, the excellency of
Jacob whom he loved. Selah.
5 God is gone up with a shout, the LORD
with the sound of a trumpet.
6 Sing praises to God, sing praises: sing
praises unto our King, sing praises.
7 For God is the King of all the earth:
sing ye praises with understanding.

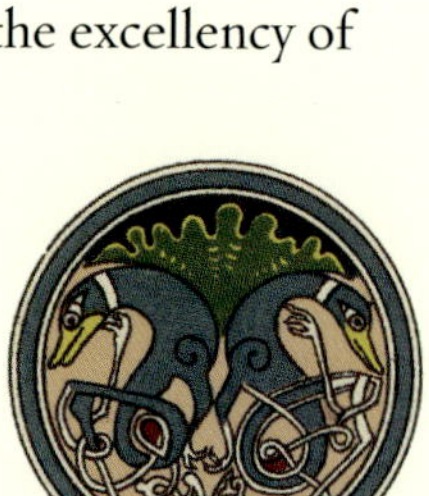

8God reigneth over the heathen: God sitteth upon the
throne of his holiness.
9The princes of the people are gathered together, even the
people of the God of Abraham: for the shields of the earth
belong unto God: he is greatly exalted.

PSALM 48

A Song and Psalm for the sons of Korah.

Great is the LORD, and greatly to be praised in the city
of our God, in the mountain of his holiness.
2Beautiful for situation, the joy of the whole earth, is mount
Zion, on the sides of the north, the city of the great King.
3God is known in her palaces for a refuge.
4For, lo, the kings were assembled, they passed by together.
5They saw it, and so they marvelled; they were troubled,
and hasted away.
6Fear took hold upon them there, and pain, as of a woman
in travail.
7Thou breakest the ships of Tarshish with an east wind.
8As we have heard, so have we seen in the city of the
LORD of hosts, in the city of our God: God will establish it
for ever. Selah.
9We have thought of thy lovingkindness, O God, in the
midst of thy temple.
10According to thy name, O God, so is thy praise unto the
ends of the earth: thy right hand is full of righteousness.
11Let mount Zion rejoice, let the daughters of Judah be glad,
because of thy judgments.

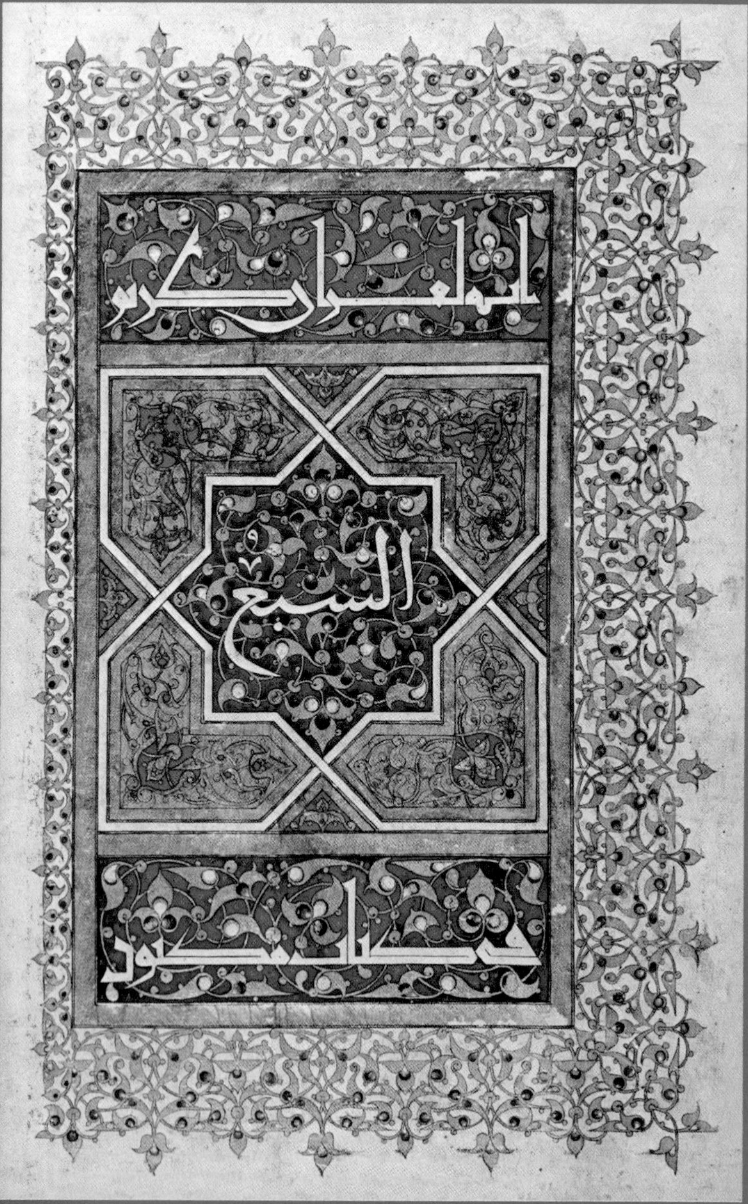
انه لقران كريم
السبع
في كتاب مكنون

12Walk about Zion, and go round about her: tell the towers
thereof.
13Mark ye well her bulwarks, consider her palaces; that ye
may tell it to the generation following.
14For this God is our God for ever and ever: he will be our
guide even unto death.

PSALM 49

To the chief Musician,
A Psalm for the sons of Korah.

Hear this, all ye people; give ear, all ye inhabitants of
the world:
2Both low and high, rich and poor, together.
3My mouth shall speak of wisdom; and the meditation of
my heart shall be of understanding.
4I will incline mine ear to a parable: I will open my dark
saying upon the harp.
5Wherefore should I fear in the days of evil, when the
iniquity of my heels shall compass me about?
6They that trust in their wealth, and boast themselves in
the multitude of their riches;
7None of them can by any means redeem his brother, nor
give to God a ransom for him:
8(For the redemption of their soul is precious, and it
ceaseth for ever:)
9That he should still live for ever, and not see corruption.
10For he seeth that wise men die, likewise the fool and the
brutish person perish, and leave their wealth to others.

11 Their inward thought is, that their houses shall continue
for ever, and their dwelling places to all generations; they call
their lands after their own names.
12 Nevertheless man being in honour abideth not: he is like
the beasts that perish.
13 This their way is their folly: yet their posterity approve
their sayings. Selah.
14 Like sheep they are laid in the grave; death shall feed on
them; and the upright shall have dominion over them in the
morning; and their beauty shall consume in the grave from
their dwelling.
15 But God will redeem my soul from the power of the grave:
for he shall receive me. Selah.
16 Be not thou afraid when one is made rich, when the glory
of his house is increased;
17 For when he dieth he shall carry nothing away: his glory
shall not descend after him.
18 Though while he lived he blessed his soul: and men will
praise thee, when thou doest well to thyself.
19 He shall go to the generation of his fathers; they shall
never see light.
20 Man that is in honour, and understandeth not, is like the
beasts that perish.

PSALM 50

A Psalm of Asaph.

The mighty God, even the LORD, hath spoken, and
called the earth from the rising of the sun unto the
going down thereof.
2 Out of Zion, the perfection of beauty, God hath shined.
3 Our God shall come, and shall not keep silence: a fire shall
devour before him, and it shall be very tempestuous round
about him.
4 He shall call to the heavens from above, and to the earth,
that he may judge his people.
5 Gather my saints together unto me; those that have made a
covenant with me by sacrifice.
6 And the heavens shall declare his righteousness: for God is
[illegible]
[illegible] speak; O Israel, and I will
[illegible] God.
[illegible] thy burnt
offer[illegible]
9 I will take [illegible]
thy folds.
10 For every beast of the forest is [illegible]
thousand hills.
11 I know all the fowls of the mountains: and the wild beasts
of the field are mine.
12 If I were hungry, I would not tell thee: for the world is
mine, and the fulness thereof.
13 Will I eat the flesh of bulls, or drink the blood of goats?
14 Offer unto God thanksgiving; and pay thy vows unto the
most High:

15 And call upon me in the day of trouble: I will deliver thee,
and thou shalt glorify me.
16 But unto the wicked God saith, What hast thou to do to
declare my statutes, or that thou shouldest take my covenant
in thy mouth?
17 Seeing thou hatest instruction, and castest my words
behind thee.
18 When thou sawest a thief, then thou consentedst with
him, and hast been partaker with adulterers.
19 Thou givest thy mouth to evil, and thy tongue frameth deceit.
20 Thou sittest and speakest against thy brother; thou
slanderest thine own mother's son.
21 These things hast thou done, and I kept silence; thou
thoughtest that I was altogether such an one as thyself: but I
will reprove thee, and set them in order before thine eyes.
22 Now consider this, ye that forget God, lest I tear you in
pieces, and there be none to deliver.
23 Whoso offereth praise glorifieth me: and to him that
ordereth his conversation aright will I shew the salvation of
God.

PSALM 51

To the chief Musician, A Psalm of David,
when Nathan the prophet came unto him,
after he had gone in to Bathsheba.

Have mercy upon me, O God, according to thy lovingkindness: according unto the multitude of thy tender mercies blot out my transgressions.

2 Wash me throughly from mine iniquity,
and cleanse me from my sin.
3 For I acknowledge my transgressions:
and my sin is ever before me.
4 Against thee, thee only, have I sinned, and
done this evil in thy sight: that thou mightest be
justified when thou speakest, and be clear when thou judgest.
5 Behold, I was shapen in iniquity; and in sin did my mother
conceive me.
6 Behold, thou desirest truth in the inward parts: and in the
hidden part thou shalt make me to know wisdom.
7 Purge me with hyssop, and I shall be clean: wash me, and I
shall be whiter than snow.
8 Make me to hear joy and gladness; that the bones which
thou hast broken may rejoice.
9 Hide thy face from my sins, and blot out all mine
iniquities.
10 Create in me a clean heart, O God; and renew a right
spirit within me.
11 Cast me not away from thy presence; and take not thy
holy spirit from me.
12 Restore unto me the joy of thy salvation; and uphold me
with thy free spirit.
13 Then will I teach transgressors thy ways; and sinners shall
be converted unto thee.
14 Deliver me from bloodguiltiness, O God, thou God
of my salvation: and my tongue shall sing aloud of thy
righteousness.
15 O LORD, open thou my lips; and my mouth shall shew
forth thy praise.
16 For thou desirest not sacrifice; else would I give it: thou
delightest not in burnt offering.

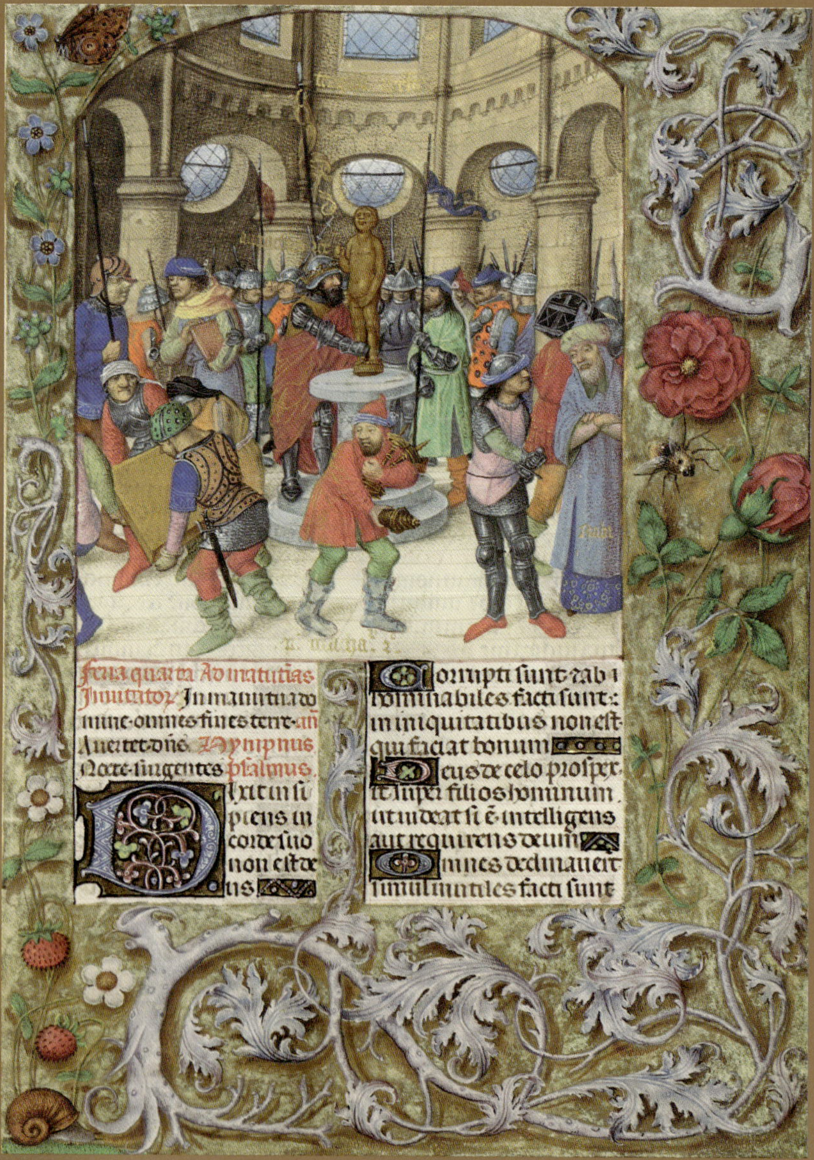

Isabella Breviary, South Netherlands, Psalm 52, ca. 1490–1497

17 The sacrifices of God are a broken spirit: a broken and a
contrite heart, O God, thou wilt not despise.
18 Do good in thy good pleasure unto Zion: build thou the
walls of Jerusalem.
19 Then shalt thou be pleased with the sacrifices of
righteousness, with burnt offering and whole burnt offering:
then shall they offer bullocks upon thine altar.

PSALM 52

To the chief Musician, Maschil, A Psalm of David, when Doeg the Edomite came and told Saul, and said unto him, David is come to the house of Ahimelech.

Why boastest thou thyself in mischief, O mighty man?
the goodness of God endureth continually.
2 Thy tongue deviseth mischiefs; like a sharp rasor, working
deceitfully.
3 Thou lovest evil more than good; and lying rather than to
speak righteousness. Selah.
4 Thou lovest all devouring words, O thou deceitful tongue.
5 God shall likewise destroy thee for ever, he shall take thee
away, and pluck thee out of thy dwelling place, and root thee
out of the land of the living. Selah.
6 The righteous also shall see, and fear, and shall laugh at him:
7 Lo, this is the man that made not God his strength; but

trusted in the abundance of his riches, and strengthened
himself in his wickedness.
8 But I am like a green olive tree in the house of God: I trust
in the mercy of God for ever and ever.
9 I will praise thee for ever, because thou hast done it: and I
will wait on thy name; for it is good before thy saints.

PSALM 53

To the chief Musician upon Mahalath,
Maschil, A Psalm of David.

The fool hath said in his heart, There is no God.
Corrupt are they, and have done abominable
iniquity: there is none that doeth good.
2 God looked down from heaven upon the children of men,
to see if there were any that did understand, that did seek
God.
3 Every one of them is gone back: they are altogether
become filthy; there is none that doeth good, no, not one.
4 Have the workers of iniquity no knowledge? who eat up
my people as they eat bread: they have not called upon God.
5 There were they in great fear, where no fear was: for God
hath scattered the bones of him that encampeth against thee:
thou hast put them to shame, because God hath despised
them.
6 Oh that the salvation of Israel were come out of Zion!
When God bringeth back the captivity of his people, Jacob
shall rejoice, and Israel shall be glad.

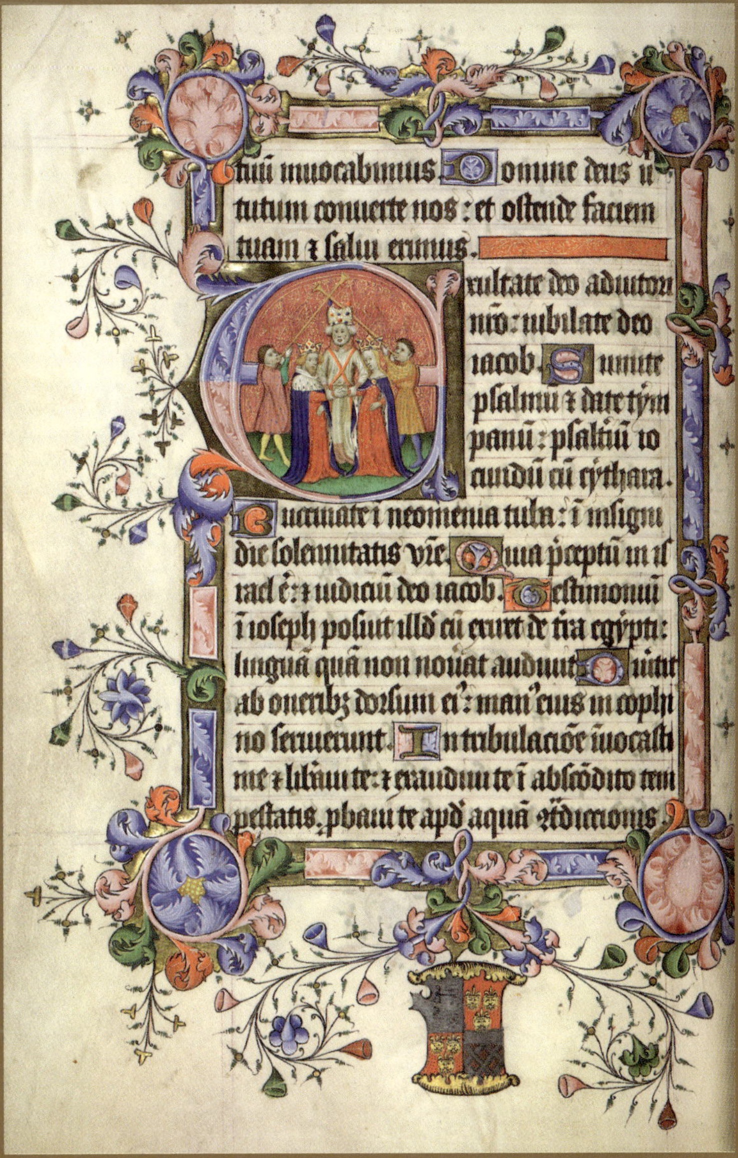

tuũ inuocabimus. Domine deus u
tutum conuerte nos: et ostende faciem
tuam ⁊ salui erimus.
Exultate deo adiutori
nr̃o: iubilate deo
iacob. Sumite
psalmũ ⁊ date tym
panũ: psaltiũ io
cundũ cũ cythara.
Buccinate i neomenia tuba: i insigni
die solemnitatis vr̃e. Quia pceptũ in is
rael ẽ: ⁊ iudiciũ deo iacob. Testimoniũ
i ioseph posuit illđ cũ exiret de tra egypti:
linguã quã non nouat audiuit. Diuertit
ab oneribz dorsum ei': man' eius in cophi
no seruierunt. In tribulacõe inuocasti
me ⁊ liberaui te: ⁊ exaudiui te i abscõdito tem
pestatis. pbaui te apđ aquã cõdiccionis.

Bedford Hours and Psalter, Psalm 53, 15th century

PSALM 54

To the chief Musician on Neginoth, Maschil,
A Psalm of David, when the Ziphims came and said to Saul,
Doth not David hide himself with us?

Save me, O God, by thy name, and judge me by thy
strength.
2 Hear my prayer, O God; give ear to the words of my mouth.
3 For strangers are risen up against me, and oppressors seek
after my soul: they have not set God before them. Selah.
4 Behold, God is mine helper: the LORD is with them that
uphold my soul.
5 He shall reward evil unto mine enemies: cut them off in
thy truth.
6 I will freely sacrifice unto thee: I will praise thy name, O
LORD; for it is good.
7 For he hath delivered me out of all trouble: and mine eye
hath seen his desire upon mine enemies.

PSALM 55

To the chief Musician on Neginoth, Maschil,
A Psalm of David.

Give ear to my prayer, O God; and hide not thyself
from my supplication.
2 Attend unto me, and hear me: I mourn in my complaint,
and make a noise;
3 Because of the voice of the enemy, because of the

oppression of the wicked: for they cast iniquity
upon me, and in wrath they hate me.

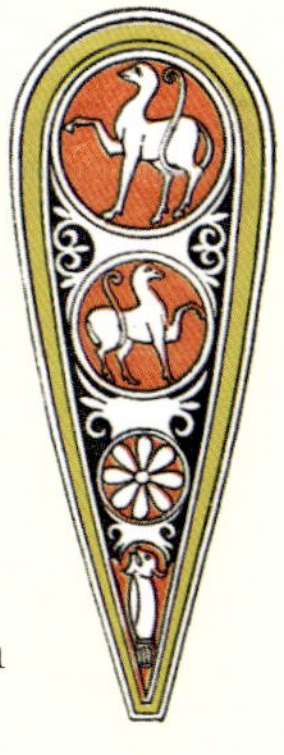

4 My heart is sore pained within me: and the
terrors of death are fallen upon me.
5 Fearfulness and trembling are come upon
me, and horror hath overwhelmed me.
6 And I said, Oh that I had wings like a dove!
for then would I fly away, and be at rest.
7 Lo, then would I wander far off, and remain in
the wilderness. Selah.
8 I would hasten my escape from the windy storm and tempest.
9 Destroy, O LORD, and divide their tongues: for I have
seen violence and strife in the city.
10 Day and night they go about it upon the walls thereof:
mischief also and sorrow are in the midst of it.
11 Wickedness is in the midst thereof: deceit and guile
depart not from her streets.
12 For it was not an enemy that reproached me; then I
could have borne it: neither was it he that hated me that did
magnify himself against me; then I would have hid myself
from him:
13 But it was thou, a man mine equal, my guide, and mine
acquaintance.
14 We took sweet counsel together, and walked unto the
house of God in company.
15 Let death seize upon them, and let them go down quick
into hell: for wickedness is in their dwellings, and among them.
16 As for me, I will call upon God; and the LORD shall save me.
17 Evening, and morning, and at noon, will I pray, and cry
aloud: and he shall hear my voice.
18 He hath delivered my soul in peace from the battle that
was against me: for there were many with me.

19God shall hear, and afflict them, even he that abideth of
old. Selah. Because they have no changes, therefore they fear
not God.
20He hath put forth his hands against such as be at peace
with him: he hath broken his covenant.
21The words of his mouth were smoother than butter, but
war was in his heart: his words were softer than oil, yet were
they drawn swords.
22Cast thy burden upon the LORD, and he shall sustain
thee: he shall never suffer the righteous to be moved.
23But thou, O God, shalt bring them down into the pit of
destruction: bloody and deceitful men shall not live out half
their days; but I will trust in thee.

PSALM 56

*To the chief Musician upon
Jonathelemrechokim, Michtam of David,
when the Philistines took him in Gath.*

Be merciful unto me, O God: for man would swallow
me up; he fighting daily oppresseth me.
2Mine enemies would daily swallow me up: for they be
many that fight against me, O thou most High.
3What time I am afraid, I will trust in thee.
4In God I will praise his word, in God I have put my trust;
I will not fear what flesh can do unto me.
5Every day they wrest my words: all their thoughts are
against me for evil.
6They gather themselves together, they hide themselves, they

mark my steps, when they wait for my soul.
7Shall they escape by iniquity? in thine
anger cast down the people, O God.
8Thou tellest my wanderings: put thou my
tears into thy bottle: are they not in thy book?
9When I cry unto thee, then shall mine enemies turn back:
this I know; for God is for me.
10In God will I praise his word: in the LORD will I praise
his word.
11In God have I put my trust: I will not be afraid what man
can do unto me.
12Thy vows are upon me, O God: I will render praises unto thee.
13For thou hast delivered my soul from death: wilt not thou
deliver my feet from falling, that I may walk before God in
the light of the living?

PSALM 57

To the chief Musician, Altaschith, Michtam of David, when he fled from Saul in the cave.

Be merciful unto me, O God, be merciful unto me:
for my soul trusteth in thee: yea, in the shadow of
thy wings will I make my refuge, until these calamities be
overpast.
2I will cry unto God most high; unto God that performeth
all things for me.
3He shall send from heaven, and save from the reproach of
him that would swallow me up. Selah. God shall send forth
his mercy and his truth.

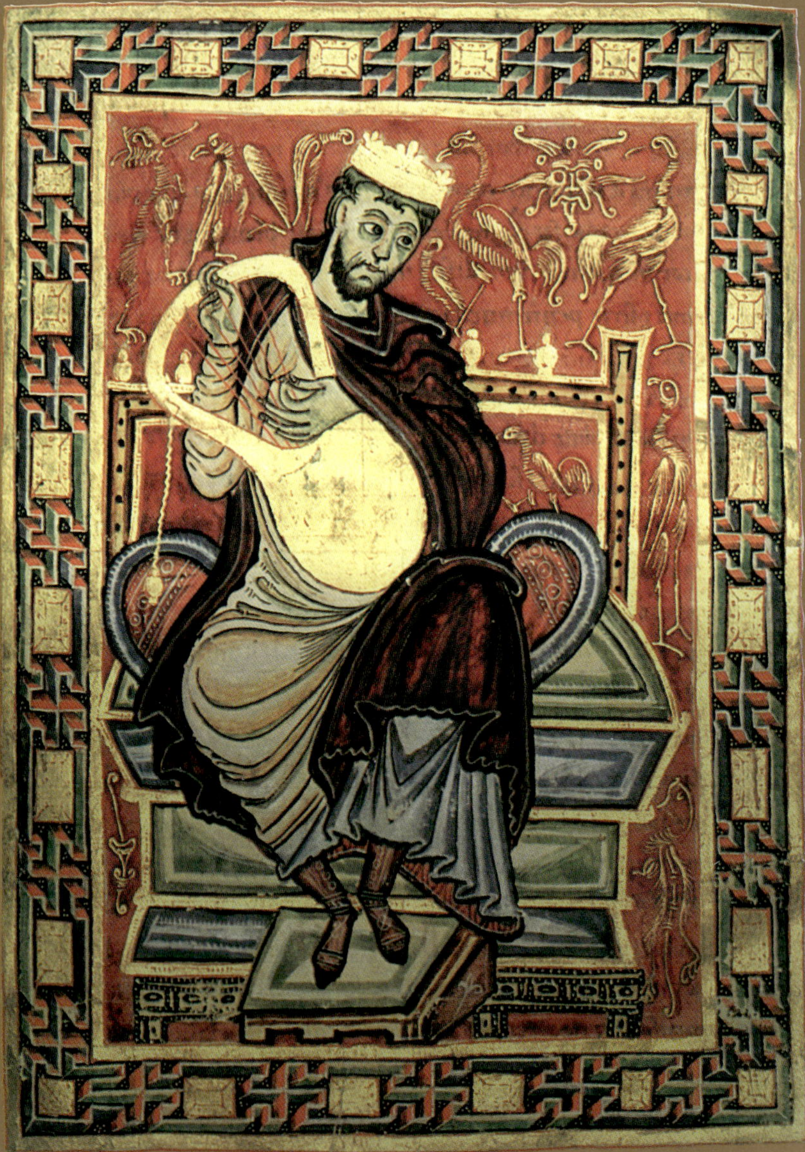

Egbert Psalter, Italy, 12th century

4My soul is among lions: and I lie even among them that
are set on fire, even the sons of men, whose teeth are spears
and arrows, and their tongue a sharp sword.
5Be thou exalted, O God, above the heavens; let thy glory
be above all the earth.
6They have prepared a net for my steps; my soul is bowed
down: they have digged a pit before me, into the midst
whereof they are fallen themselves. Selah.
7My heart is fixed, O God, my heart is fixed: I will sing and
give praise.
8Awake up, my glory; awake, psaltery and harp: I myself will
awake early.
9I will praise thee, O LORD, among the people: I will sing
unto thee among the nations.
10For thy mercy is great unto the heavens, and thy truth
unto the clouds.
11Be thou exalted, O God, above the heavens: let thy glory
be above all the earth.

PSALM 58

*To the chief Musician, Altaschith,
Michtam of David.*

Do ye indeed speak righteousness, O congregation?
do ye judge uprightly, O ye sons of men?
2Yea, in heart ye work wickedness; ye weigh the violence of
your hands in the earth.
3The wicked are estranged from the womb: they go astray
as soon as they be born, speaking lies.

[4]Their poison is like the poison of a serpent: they are like
the deaf adder that stoppeth her ear;
[5]Which will not hearken to the voice of charmers, charming
never so wisely.
[6]Break their teeth, O God, in their mouth: break out the
great teeth of the young lions, O LORD.
[7]Let them melt away as waters which run continually: when
he bendeth his bow to shoot his arrows, let them be as cut in
pieces.
[8]As a snail which melteth, let every one of them pass away:
like the untimely birth of a woman, that they may not see the
sun.
[9]Before your pots can feel the thorns, he shall take them
away as with a whirlwind, both living, and in his wrath.
[10]The righteous shall rejoice when he seeth the vengeance:
he shall wash his feet in the blood of the wicked.
[11]So that a man shall say, Verily there is a reward for the
righteous: verily he is a God that judgeth in the earth.

PSALM 59

To the chief Musician, Altaschith, Michtam of David;
when Saul sent, and they watched the house to kill him.

Deliver me from mine enemies, O my God: defend
me from them that rise up against me.
[2]Deliver me from the workers of iniquity, and save me from
bloody men.
[3]For, lo, they lie in wait for my soul: the mighty are gathered
against me; not for my transgression, nor for my sin, O LORD.

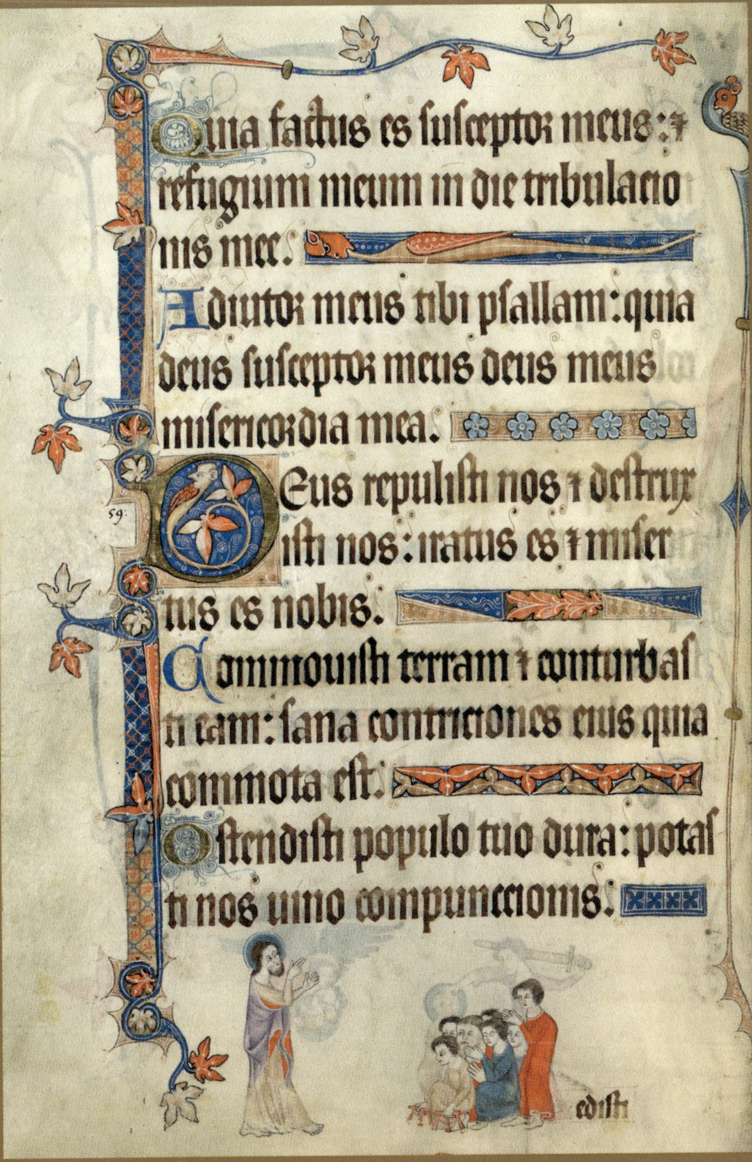
Quia factus es susceptor meus: et
refugium meum in die tribulatio
nis mee.
Adiutor meus tibi psallam: quia
deus susceptor meus deus meus
misericordia mea.
59. Deus repulisti nos et destrux
isti nos: iratus es et miser
tus es nobis.
Commouisti terram et conturbas
ti eam: sana contriciones eius quia
commota est.
Ostendisti populo tuo dura: potas
ti nos uino compunccionis.
edisti

Luttrell Psalter, England, Psalm 59, ca. 1325–1335

4 They run and prepare themselves without my fault: awake
to help me, and behold.
5 Thou therefore, O LORD God of hosts, the God of Israel,
awake to visit all the heathen: be not merciful to any wicked
transgressors. Selah.
6 They return at evening: they make a noise like a dog, and
go round about the city.
7 Behold, they belch out with their mouth: swords are in
their lips: for who, say they, doth hear?
8 But thou, O LORD, shalt laugh at them; thou shalt have
all the heathen in derision.
9 Because of his strength will I wait upon thee: for God is
my defence.
10 The God of my mercy shall prevent me: God shall let me
see my desire upon mine enemies.
11 Slay them not, lest my people forget: scatter them by thy
power; and bring them down, O LORD our shield.
12 For the sin of their mouth and the words of their lips let
them even be taken in their pride: and for cursing and lying
which they speak.
13 Consume them in wrath, consume them, that they may
not be: and let them know that God ruleth in Jacob unto the
ends of the earth. Selah.
14 And at evening let them return; and let them make a noise
like a dog, and go round about the city.
15 Let them wander up and down for meat, and grudge if
they be not satisfied.
16 But I will sing of thy power; yea, I will sing aloud of thy
mercy in the morning: for thou hast been my defence and
refuge in the day of my trouble.
17 Unto thee, O my strength, will I sing: for God is my
defence, and the God of my mercy.

PSALM 60

*To the chief Musician upon Shushan-eduth,
Michtam of David, to teach; when he strove with Aram-naharaim
and with Aram-zobah, when Joab returned, and smote of Edom
in the valley of salt twelve thousand.*

O God, thou hast cast us off, thou hast scattered us,
thou hast been displeased; O turn thyself to us again.
2 Thou hast made the earth to tremble; thou hast broken it:
heal the breaches thereof; for it shaketh.
3 Thou hast shewed thy people hard things: thou hast made
us to drink the wine of astonishment.
4 Thou hast given a banner to them that fear thee, that it
may be displayed because of the truth. Selah.
5 That thy beloved may be delivered; save with thy right
hand, and hear me.
6 God hath spoken in his holiness; I will rejoice, I will divide
Shechem, and mete out the valley of Succoth.
7 Gilead is mine, and Manasseh is mine; Ephraim also is the
strength of mine head; Judah is my lawgiver;
8 Moab is my washpot; over Edom will I cast out my shoe:
Philistia, triumph thou because of me.
9 Who will bring me into the strong city? who will lead me
into Edom?
10 Wilt not thou, O God, which hadst cast us off? and thou,
O God, which didst not go out with our armies?
11 Give us help from trouble: for vain is the help of man.
12 Through God we shall do valiantly: for he it is that shall
tread down our enemies.

PSALM 61

To the chief Musician upon Neginah,
A Psalm of David.

Hear my cry, O God; attend unto my prayer.
[2]From the end of the earth will I cry unto thee,
when my heart is overwhelmed: lead me to the rock that is
higher than I.
[3]For thou hast been a shelter for me, and a strong tower
from the enemy.
[4]I will abide in thy tabernacle for ever: I will trust in the
covert of thy wings. Selah.
[5]For thou, O God, hast heard my vows: thou hast given me
the heritage of those that fear thy name.
[6]Thou wilt prolong the king's life: and his years as many
generations.
[7]He shall abide before God for ever: O prepare mercy and
truth, which may preserve him.
[8]So will I sing praise unto thy name for ever, that I may
daily perform my vows.

PSALM 62

To the chief Musician, to Jeduthun,
A Psalm of David.

Truly my soul waiteth upon God: from him cometh
my salvation.
2 He only is my rock and my salvation; he is my defence; I
shall not be greatly moved.
3 How long will ye imagine mischief against a man? ye
shall be slain all of you: as a bowing wall shall ye be, and as a
tottering fence.
4 They only consult to cast him down from his excellency:
they delight in lies: they bless with their mouth, but they
curse inwardly. Selah.
5 My soul, wait thou only upon God; for my expectation is
from him.
6 He only is my rock and my salvation: he is my defence; I
shall not be moved.
7 In God is my salvation and my glory: the rock of my
strength, and my refuge, is in God.
8 Trust in him at all times; ye people, pour out your heart
before him: God is a refuge for us. Selah.
9 Surely men of low degree are vanity, and men of high
degree are a lie: to be laid in the balance, they are altogether
lighter than vanity.
10 Trust not in oppression, and become not vain in robbery:
if riches increase, set not your heart upon them.
11 God hath spoken once; twice have I heard this; that power
belongeth unto God.
12 Also unto thee, O LORD, belongeth mercy: for thou
renderest to every man according to his work.

PSALM 63

A Psalm of David,
when he was in the wilderness of Judah.

O God, thou art my God; early will I seek thee: my
soul thirsteth for thee, my flesh longeth for thee in a
dry and thirsty land, where no water is;
2 To see thy power and thy glory, so as I have seen thee in
the sanctuary.
3 Because thy lovingkindness is better than life, my lips shall
praise thee.
4 Thus will I bless thee while I live: I will lift up my hands
in thy name.
5 My soul shall be satisfied as with marrow and fatness; and
my mouth shall praise thee with joyful lips:
6 When I remember thee upon my bed, and meditate on
thee in the night watches.
7 Because thou hast been my help, therefore in the shadow
of thy wings will I rejoice.
8 My soul followeth hard after thee: thy right hand
upholdeth me.
9 But those that seek my soul, to destroy it, shall go into the
lower parts of the earth.
10 They shall fall by the sword: they shall be a portion for foxes.
11 But the king shall rejoice in God; every one that sweareth
by him shall glory: but the mouth of them that speak lies
shall be stopped.

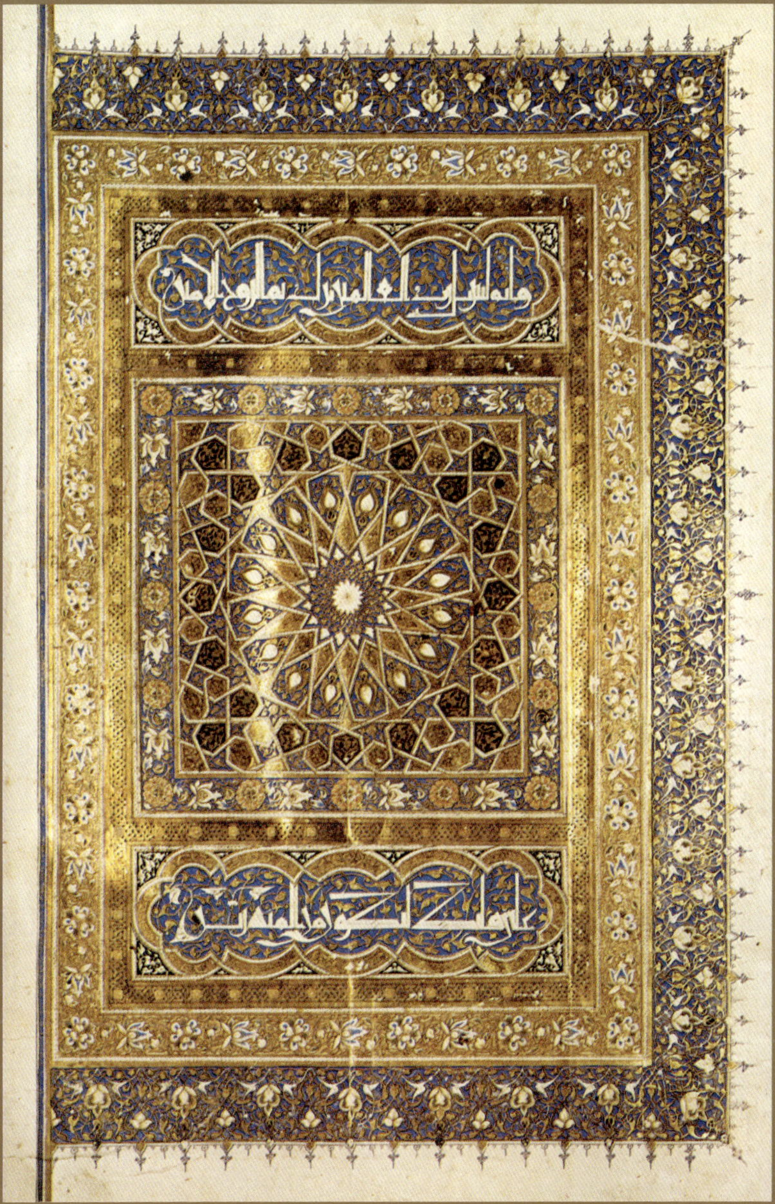

PSALM 64

To the chief Musician,
A Psalm of David.

Hear my voice, O God, in my prayer: preserve my life
from fear of the enemy.
2 Hide me from the secret counsel of the wicked; from the
insurrection of the workers of iniquity:
3 Who whet their tongue like a sword, and bend their bows
to shoot their arrows, even bitter words:
4 That they may shoot in secret at the perfect: suddenly do
they shoot at him, and fear not.
5 They encourage themselves in an evil matter: they
commune of laying snares privily; they say, Who shall see them?
6 They search out iniquities; they accomplish a diligent
search: both the inward thought of every one of them, and
the heart, is deep.
7 But God shall shoot at them with an arrow; suddenly shall
they be wounded.
8 So they shall make their own tongue to fall upon
themselves: all that see them shall flee away.
9 And all men shall fear, and shall declare the work of God;
for they shall wisely consider of his doing.
10 The righteous shall be glad in the LORD, and shall trust
in him; and all the upright in heart shall glory.

PSALM 65

To the chief Musician,
A Psalm and Song of David.

Praise waiteth for thee, O God, in Sion: and unto thee
shall the vow be performed.
2O thou that hearest prayer, unto thee shall all flesh come.
3Iniquities prevail against me: as for our transgressions,
thou shalt purge them away.
4Blessed is the man whom thou choosest, and causest to
approach unto thee, that he may dwell in thy courts: we shall
be satisfied with the goodness of thy house, even of thy holy
temple.
5By terrible things in righteousness wilt thou answer us, O
God of our salvation; who art the confidence of all the ends
of the earth, and of them that are afar off upon the sea:
6Which by his strength setteth fast the mountains; being
girded with power:
7Which stilleth the noise of the seas, the noise of their
waves, and the tumult of the people.
8They also that dwell in the uttermost parts are afraid at
thy tokens: thou makest the outgoings of the morning and
evening to rejoice.
9Thou visitest the earth, and waterest it: thou greatly
enrichest it with the river of God, which is full of water: thou
preparest them corn, when thou hast so provided for it.
10Thou waterest the ridges thereof abundantly: thou settlest
the furrows thereof: thou makest it soft with
showers: thou blessest the springing thereof.
11Thou crownest the year with thy
goodness; and thy paths drop fatness.

[12]They drop upon the pastures of the wilderness: and the
little hills rejoice on every side.
[13]The pastures are clothed with flocks; the valleys also are
covered over with corn; they shout for joy, they also sing.

PSALM 66

To the chief Musician,
A Song or Psalm.

Make a joyful noise unto God, all ye lands:
[2]Sing forth the honour of his name: make his praise
glorious.
[3]Say unto God, How terrible art thou in thy works! through
the greatness of thy power shall thine enemies submit
themselves unto thee.
[4]All the earth shall worship thee, and shall sing unto thee;
they shall sing to thy name. Selah.
[5]Come and see the works of God: he is terrible in his doing
toward the children of men.
[6]He turned the sea into dry land: they went through the
flood on foot: there did we rejoice in him.
[7]He ruleth by his power for ever; his eyes behold the
nations: let not the rebellious exalt themselves. Selah.
[8]O bless our God, ye people, and make the
voice of his praise to be heard:
[9]Which holdeth our soul in life, and
suffereth not our feet to be moved.
[10]For thou, O God, hast proved us:
thou hast tried us, as silver is tried.

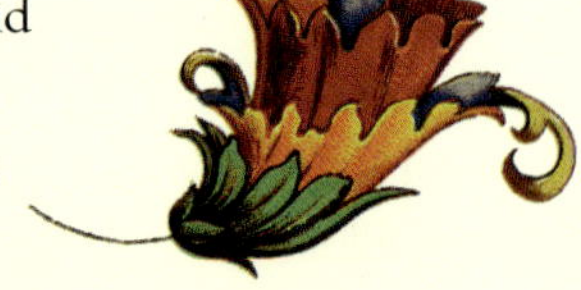

11 Thou broughtest us into the net; thou laidst affliction
upon our loins.
12 Thou hast caused men to ride over our heads; we went
through fire and through water: but thou broughtest us out
into a wealthy place.
13 I will go into thy house with burnt offerings: I will pay
thee my vows,
14 Which my lips have uttered, and my mouth hath spoken,
when I was in trouble.
15 I will offer unto thee burnt sacrifices of fatlings, with the
incense of rams; I will offer bullocks with goats. Selah.
16 Come and hear, all ye that fear God, and I will declare
what he hath done for my soul.
17 I cried unto him with my mouth, and he was extolled with
my tongue.
18 If I regard iniquity in my heart, the LORD will not hear me:
19 But verily God hath heard me; he hath attended to the
voice of my prayer.
20 Blessed be God, which hath not turned away my prayer,
nor his mercy from me.

PSALM 67

To the chief Musician on Neginoth,
A Psalm or Song.

God be merciful unto us, and bless us; and cause his
face to shine upon us; Selah.
2 That thy way may be known upon earth, thy saving health
among all nations.

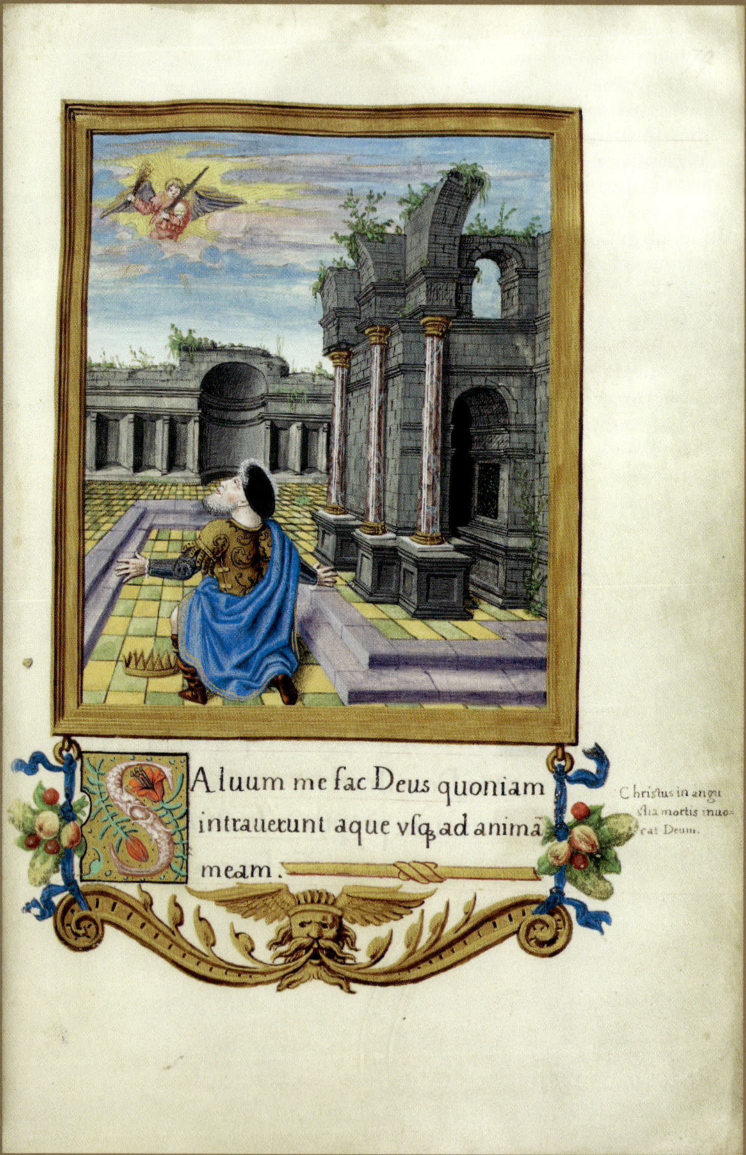

Psalter of Henry VIII, England, Psalm 68, 1530–1547

3Let the people praise thee, O God; let all the people praise
thee.
4O let the nations be glad and sing for joy: for thou shalt
judge the people righteously, and govern the nations upon
earth. Selah.
5Let the people praise thee, O God; let all the people praise
thee.
6Then shall the earth yield her increase; and God, even our
own God, shall bless us.
7God shall bless us; and all the ends of the earth shall fear him.

PSALM 68

To the chief Musician, A Psalm or Song of David.

Let God arise, let his enemies be scattered: let them
also that hate him flee before him.
2As smoke is driven away, so drive them away: as wax
melteth before the fire, so let the wicked perish at the
presence of God.
3But let the righteous be glad; let them rejoice before God:
yea, let them exceedingly rejoice.
4Sing unto God, sing praises to his name: extol him that rideth
upon the heavens by his name JAH, and rejoice before him.
5A father of the fatherless, and a judge of the widows, is
God in his holy habitation.
6God setteth the solitary in families: he bringeth out those
which are bound with chains: but the rebellious dwell in a
dry land.
7O God, when thou wentest forth before thy people, when

thou didst march through the wilderness; Selah:
8The earth shook, the heavens also dropped at the presence
of God: even Sinai itself was moved at the presence of God,
the God of Israel.
9Thou, O God, didst send a plentiful rain, whereby thou
didst confirm thine inheritance, when it was weary.
10Thy congregation hath dwelt therein: thou, O God, hast
prepared of thy goodness for the poor.
11The LORD gave the word: great was the company of
those that published it.
12Kings of armies did flee apace: and she that tarried at
home divided the spoil.
13Though ye have lien among the pots, yet shall ye be as the
wings of a dove covered with silver, and her feathers with
yellow gold.
14When the Almighty scattered kings in it, it was white as
snow in Salmon.
15The hill of God is as the hill of Bashan; an high hill as the
hill of Bashan.
16Why leap ye, ye high hills? this is the hill which God
desireth to dwell in; yea, the LORD will dwell in it for ever.
17The chariots of God are twenty thousand, even thousands of
angels: the LORD is among them, as in Sinai, in the holy place.
18Thou hast ascended on high, thou hast led captivity
captive: thou hast received gifts for men; yea, for the
rebellious also, that the LORD God might dwell among them.
19Blessed be the LORD, who daily loadeth us with benefits,
even the God of our salvation. Selah.
20He that is our God is the God of salvation; and unto God
the LORD belong the issues from death.
21But God shall wound the head of his enemies, and the
hairy scalp of such an one as goeth on still in his trespasses.

[22]The LORD said, I will bring again from Bashan, I will
bring my people again from the depths of the sea:
[23]That thy foot may be dipped in the blood of thine
enemies, and the tongue of thy dogs in the same.
[24]They have seen thy goings, O God; even the goings of my
God, my King, in the sanctuary.
[25]The singers went before, the players on instruments followed
after; among them were the damsels playing with timbrels.
[26]Bless ye God in the congregations, even the LORD, from
the fountain of Israel.
[27]There is little Benjamin with their ruler, the princes of
Judah and their council, the princes of Zebulun, and the
princes of Naphtali.
[28]Thy God hath commanded thy strength: strengthen, O
God, that which thou hast wrought for us.
[29]Because of thy temple at Jerusalem shall kings bring
presents unto thee.
[30]Rebuke the company of spearmen, the multitude of the
bulls, with the calves of the people, till every one submit
himself with pieces of silver: scatter thou the people that
delight in war.
[31]Princes shall come out of Egypt; Ethiopia shall soon
stretch out her hands unto God.
[32]Sing unto God, ye kingdoms of the earth; O sing praises
unto the LORD; Selah:

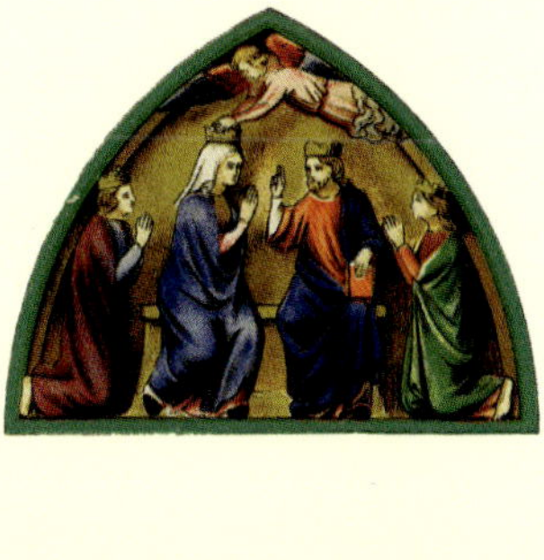

33 To him that rideth upon the heavens of heavens, which were
of old; lo, he doth send out his voice, and that a mighty voice.
34 Ascribe ye strength unto God: his excellency is over Israel,
and his strength is in the clouds.
35 O God, thou art terrible out of thy holy places: the God
of Israel is he that giveth strength and power unto his people.
Blessed be God.

PSALM 69

To chief Musician upon Shoshannim,
A Psalm of David.

Save me, O God; for the waters are come in unto my soul.
2 I sink in deep mire, where there is no standing: I
am come into deep waters, where the floods overflow me.
3 I am weary of my crying: my throat is dried: mine eyes fail
while I wait for my God.
4 They that hate me without a cause are more than the
hairs of mine head: they that would destroy me, being mine
enemies wrongfully, are mighty: then I restored that which I
took not away.
5 O God, thou knowest my foolishness; and my sins are not
hid from thee.
6 Let not them that wait on thee, O LORD God of hosts,
be ashamed for my sake: let not those that seek thee be
confounded for my sake, O God of Israel.
7 Because for thy sake I have borne reproach; shame hath
covered my face.
8 I am become a stranger unto my brethren, and an alien
unto my mother's children.

9 For the zeal of thine house hath eaten me up; and the
reproaches of them that reproached thee are fallen upon me.
10 When I wept, and chastened my soul with fasting, that
was to my reproach.
11 I made sackcloth also my garment; and I became a
proverb to them.
12 They that sit in the gate speak against me; and I was the
song of the drunkards.
13 But as for me, my prayer is unto thee, O LORD, in an
acceptable time: O God, in the multitude of thy mercy hear
me, in the truth of thy salvation.
14 Deliver me out of the mire, and let me not sink: let me be
delivered from them that hate me, and out of the deep waters.
15 Let not the waterflood overflow me, neither let the deep
swallow me up, and let not the pit shut her mouth upon me.
16 Hear me, O LORD; for thy lovingkindness is good: turn
unto me according to the multitude of thy tender mercies.
17 And hide not thy face from thy servant; for I am in
trouble: hear me speedily.
18 Draw nigh unto my soul, and redeem it: deliver me
because of mine enemies.
19 Thou hast known my reproach, and my shame, and my
dishonour: mine adversaries are all before thee.
20 Reproach hath broken my heart; and I am full of
heaviness: and I looked for some to take pity, but there was
none; and for comforters, but I found none.
21 They gave me also gall for my meat; and in my thirst they
gave me vinegar to drink.

22 Let their table become a snare before them: and that
which should have been for their welfare, let it become a trap.
23 Let their eyes be darkened, that they see not; and make
their loins continually to shake.
24 Pour out thine indignation upon them, and let thy
wrathful anger take hold of them.
25 Let their habitation be desolate; and let none dwell in
their tents.
26 For they persecute him whom thou hast smitten; and they
talk to the grief of those whom thou hast wounded.
27 Add iniquity unto their iniquity: and let them not come
into thy righteousness.
28 Let them be blotted out of the book of the living, and not
be written with the righteous.
29 But I am poor and sorrowful: let thy salvation, O God, set
me up on high.
30 I will praise the name of God with a song, and will
magnify him with thanksgiving.
31 This also shall please the LORD better than an ox or
bullock that hath horns and hoofs.
32 The humble shall see this, and be glad: and your heart
shall live that seek God.
33 For the LORD heareth the poor, and despiseth not his
prisoners.
34 Let the heaven and earth praise him, the seas, and every
thing that moveth therein.
35 For God will save Zion, and will build the
cities of Judah: that they may dwell there,
and have it in possession.
36 The seed also of his servants shall
inherit it: and they that love his name
shall dwell therein.

PSALM 70

To the chief Musician, A Psalm of David,
to bring to remembrance.

Make haste, O God, to deliver me; make haste to help me, O LORD.
2 Let them be ashamed and confounded that seek after my
soul: let them be turned backward, and put to confusion, that
desire my hurt.
3 Let them be turned back for a reward of their shame that
say, Aha, aha.
4 Let all those that seek thee rejoice and be glad in thee:
and let such as love thy salvation say continually, Let God be
magnified.
5 But I am poor and needy: make haste unto me, O God:
thou art my help and my deliverer; O LORD, make no
tarrying.

PSALM 71

In thee, O LORD, do I put my trust: let me never be put to confusion.
2 Deliver me in thy righteousness, and cause me to escape:
incline thine ear unto me, and save me.
3 Be thou my strong habitation, whereunto I may
continually resort: thou hast given commandment to save
me; for thou art my rock and my fortress.
4 Deliver me, O my God, out of the hand of the wicked, out
of the hand of the unrighteous and cruel man.

5For thou art my hope, O LORD God: thou art my trust
from my youth.
6By thee have I been holden up from the womb: thou art he
that took me out of my mother's bowels: my praise shall be
continually of thee.
7I am as a wonder unto many; but thou art my strong refuge.
8Let my mouth be filled with thy praise and with thy
honour all the day.
9Cast me not off in the time of old age; forsake me not
when my strength faileth.
10For mine enemies speak against me; and they that lay wait
for my soul take counsel together,
11Saying, God hath forsaken him: persecute and take him;
for there is none to deliver him.
12O God, be not far from me: O my God, make haste for
my help.
13Let them be confounded and consumed that are
adversaries to my soul; let them be covered with reproach
and dishonour that seek my hurt.
14But I will hope continually, and will yet praise thee more
and more.
15My mouth shall shew forth thy righteousness and thy
salvation all the day; for I know not the numbers thereof.
16I will go in the strength of the LORD God: I will make
mention of thy righteousness, even of thine only.
17O God, thou hast taught me from my youth: and hitherto
have I declared thy wondrous works.
18Now also when I am old and greyheaded, O God,
forsake me not; until I have shewed thy strength unto this
generation, and thy power to every one that is to come.
19Thy righteousness also, O God, is very high, who hast
done great things: O God, who is like unto thee!

20 Thou, which hast shewed me great and sore troubles,
shalt quicken me again, and shalt bring me up again from the
depths of the earth.
21 Thou shalt increase my greatness, and comfort me on
every side.
22 I will also praise thee with the psaltery, even thy truth, O
my God: unto thee will I sing with the harp, O thou Holy
One of Israel.
23 My lips shall greatly rejoice when I sing unto thee; and my
soul, which thou hast redeemed.
24 My tongue also shall talk of thy righteousness all the day
long: for they are confounded, for they are brought unto
shame, that seek my hurt.

PSALM 72

A Psalm for Solomon.

Give the king thy judgments, O God, and thy
righteousness unto the king's son.
2 He shall judge thy people with righteousness, and thy poor
with judgment.
3 The mountains shall bring peace to the people, and the
little hills, by righteousness.
4 He shall judge the poor of the people, he shall save the
children of the needy, and shall break in pieces the oppressor.
5 They shall fear thee as long as the sun and moon endure,
throughout all generations.

[6]He shall come down like rain upon the mown grass: as
showers that water the earth.
[7]In his days shall the righteous flourish; and abundance of
peace so long as the moon endureth.
[8]He shall have dominion also from sea to sea, and from the
river unto the ends of the earth.
[9]They that dwell in the wilderness shall bow before him;
and his enemies shall lick the dust.
[10]The kings of Tarshish and of the isles shall bring presents:
the kings of Sheba and Seba shall offer gifts.
[11]Yea, all kings shall fall down before him: all nations shall
serve him.
[12]For he shall deliver the needy when he crieth; the poor
also, and him that hath no helper.
[13]He shall spare the poor and needy, and shall save the souls
of the needy.
[14]He shall redeem their soul from deceit and violence: and
precious shall their blood be in his sight.
[15]And he shall live, and to him shall be given of the gold
of Sheba: prayer also shall be made for him continually; and
daily shall he be praised.
[16]There shall be an handful of corn in the earth upon the top
of the mountains; the fruit thereof shall shake like Lebanon:
and they of the city shall flourish like grass of the earth.
[17]His name shall endure for ever: his name shall be
continued as long as the sun: and men shall be blessed in him:
all nations shall call him blessed.
[18]Blessed be the LORD God, the God of Israel, who only
doeth wondrous things.
[19]And blessed be his glorious name for ever: and let the
whole earth be filled with his glory; Amen, and Amen.
[20]The prayers of David the son of Jesse are ended.

BOOK III

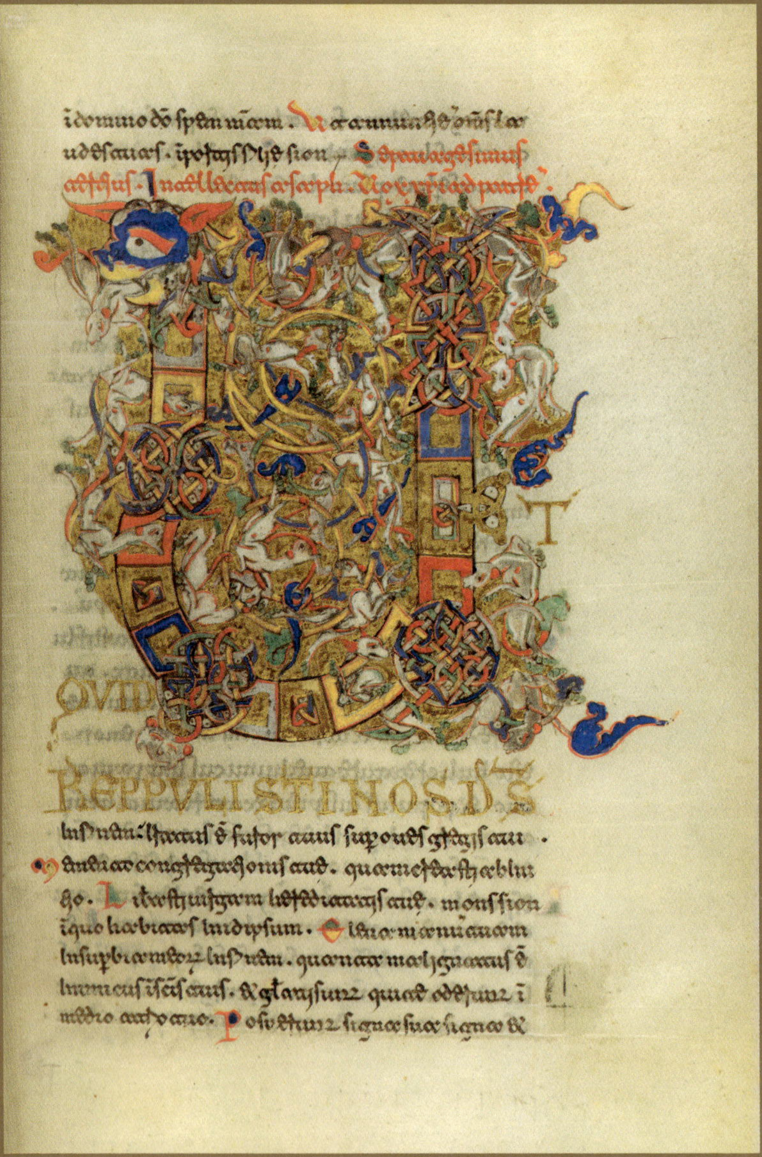

Monte Cassino Psalter, Southern Italy, Psalm 73, 12th century

PSALM 73

A Psalm of Asaph.

Truly God is good to Israel, even to such as are of a
clean heart.
2 But as for me, my feet were almost gone; my steps had well
nigh slipped.
3 For I was envious at the foolish, when I saw the prosperity
of the wicked.
4 For there are no bands in their death: but their strength is
firm.
5 They are not in trouble as other men; neither are they
plagued like other men.
6 Therefore pride compasseth them about as a chain;
violence covereth them as a garment.
7 Their eyes stand out with fatness: they have more than
heart could wish.
8 They are corrupt, and speak wickedly concerning
oppression: they speak loftily.
9 They set their mouth against the heavens, and their
tongue walketh through the earth.
10 Therefore his people return hither: and waters of a full
cup are wrung out to them.
11 And they say, How doth God know? and is there
knowledge in the most High?
12 Behold, these are the ungodly, who prosper in the world;
they increase in riches.
13 Verily I have cleansed my heart in vain, and washed my
hands in innocency.
14 For all the day long have I been plagued, and chastened
every morning.

15If I say, I will speak thus; behold, I should offend against
the generation of thy children.
16When I thought to know this, it was too painful for me;
17Until I went into the sanctuary of God; then understood
I their end.
18Surely thou didst set them in slippery places: thou castedst
them down into destruction.
19How are they brought into desolation, as in a moment!
they are utterly consumed with terrors.
20As a dream when one awaketh; so, O LORD, when thou
awakest, thou shalt despise their image.
21Thus my heart was grieved, and I was pricked in my reins.
22So foolish was I, and ignorant: I was as a beast before thee.
23Nevertheless I am continually with thee: thou hast holden
me by my right hand.
24Thou shalt guide me with thy counsel, and afterward
receive me to glory.
25Whom have I in heaven but thee? and there is none upon
earth that I desire beside thee.
26My flesh and my heart faileth: but God is the strength of
my heart, and my portion for ever.
27For, lo, they that are far from thee shall perish: thou hast
destroyed all them that go a whoring from thee.
28But it is good for me to draw near to God: I have put my
trust in the LORD God, that I may declare all thy works.

PSALM 74

Maschil of Asaph.

O God, why hast thou cast us off for ever? why doth
thine anger smoke against the sheep of thy pasture?
2 Remember thy congregation, which thou hast purchased
of old; the rod of thine inheritance, which thou hast
redeemed; this mount Zion, wherein thou hast dwelt.
3 Lift up thy feet unto the perpetual desolations; even all
that the enemy hath done wickedly in the sanctuary.
4 Thine enemies roar in the midst of thy congregations; they
set up their ensigns for signs.
5 A man was famous according as he had lifted up axes upon
the thick trees.
6 But now they break down the carved work thereof at once
with axes and hammers.
7 They have cast fire into thy sanctuary, they have defiled by
casting down the dwelling place of thy name to the ground.
8 They said in their hearts, Let us destroy them together:
they have burned up all the synagogues of God in the land.
9 We see not our signs: there is no more any prophet:

neither is there among us any that knoweth how long.
10 O God, how long shall the adversary reproach? shall the
enemy blaspheme thy name for ever?
11 Why withdrawest thou thy hand, even thy right hand?
pluck it out of thy bosom.
12 For God is my King of old, working salvation in the midst
of the earth.
13 Thou didst divide the sea by thy strength: thou brakest
the heads of the dragons in the waters.
14 Thou brakest the heads of leviathan in pieces, and gavest
him to be meat to the people inhabiting the wilderness.
15 Thou didst cleave the fountain and the flood: thou driedst
up mighty rivers.
16 The day is thine, the night also is thine: thou hast
prepared the light and the sun.
17 Thou hast set all the borders of the earth: thou hast made
summer and winter.
18 Remember this, that the enemy hath reproached, O LORD,
and that the foolish people have blasphemed thy name.
19 O deliver not the soul of thy turtledove unto the
multitude of the wicked: forget not the congregation of thy
poor for ever.
20 Have respect unto the covenant: for the dark places of the
earth are full of the habitations of cruelty.
21 O let not the oppressed return ashamed: let the poor and
needy praise thy name.
22 Arise, O God, plead thine own cause: remember how the
foolish man reproacheth thee daily.
23 Forget not the voice of thine enemies: the tumult of those
that rise up against thee increaseth continually.

PSALM 75

To the chief Musician, Altaschith,
A Psalm or Song of Asaph.

Unto thee, O God, do we give thanks, unto thee do we
give thanks: for that thy name is near thy wondrous
works declare.
2 When I shall receive the congregation I will judge
uprightly.
3 The earth and all the inhabitants thereof are dissolved: I
bear up the pillars of it. Selah.
4 I said unto the fools, Deal not foolishly: and to the wicked,
Lift not up the horn:
5 Lift not up your horn on high: speak not with a stiff neck.
6 For promotion cometh neither from the east, nor from the
west, nor from the south.
7 But God is the judge: he putteth down one, and setteth up
another.
8 For in the hand of the LORD there is a cup, and the wine
is red; it is full of mixture; and he poureth out of the same:
but the dregs thereof, all the wicked of the earth shall wring
them out, and drink them.
9 But I will declare for ever; I will sing praises to the
God of Jacob.
10 All the horns of the wicked also will I cut off; but
the horns of the righteous shall be exalted.

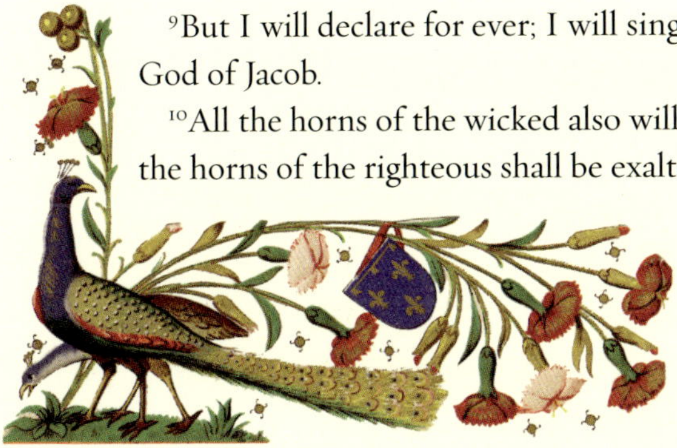

PSALM 76

To the chief Musician on Neginoth,
A Psalm or Song of Asaph.

In Judah is God known: his name is great in Israel.
2 In Salem also is his tabernacle, and his dwelling
place in Zion.
3 There brake he the arrows of the bow, the shield, and the
sword, and the battle. Selah.
4 Thou art more glorious and excellent than the mountains
of prey.
5 The stouthearted are spoiled, they have slept their sleep:
and none of the men of might have found their hands.
6 At thy rebuke, O God of Jacob, both the chariot and horse
are cast into a dead sleep.
7 Thou, even thou, art to be feared: and who may stand in
thy sight when once thou art angry?
8 Thou didst cause judgment to be heard from heaven; the
earth feared, and was still,
9 When God arose to judgment, to save all the meek of the
earth. Selah.
10 Surely the wrath of man shall praise thee: the remainder
of wrath shalt thou restrain.
11 Vow, and pay unto the LORD your God: let all that be
round about him bring presents unto
him that ought to be feared.
12 He shall cut off the spirit of
princes: he is terrible to the
kings of the earth.

PSALM 77

To the chief Musician, to Jeduthun,
A Psalm of Asaph.

I cried unto God with my voice, even unto God with
my voice; and he gave ear unto me.
2 In the day of my trouble I sought the LORD: my sore ran in
the night, and ceased not: my soul refused to be comforted.
3 I remembered God, and was troubled: I complained, and
my spirit was overwhelmed. Selah.
4 Thou holdest mine eyes waking: I am so troubled that I
cannot speak.
5 I have considered the days of old, the years of ancient
times.
6 I call to remembrance my song in the night: I commune
with mine own heart: and my spirit made diligent search.
7 Will the LORD cast off for ever? and will he be favourable
no more?
8 Is his mercy clean gone for ever? doth his promise fail for
evermore?
9 Hath God forgotten to be gracious? hath he in anger shut
up his tender mercies? Selah.
10 And I said, This is my infirmity: but I will remember the
years of the right hand of the most High.
11 I will remember the works of the LORD: surely I will
remember thy wonders of old.
12 I will meditate also of all thy work, and talk of thy doings.
13 Thy way, O God, is in the sanctuary: who is so great a God
as our God?
14 Thou art the God that doest wonders: thou hast declared
thy strength among the people.

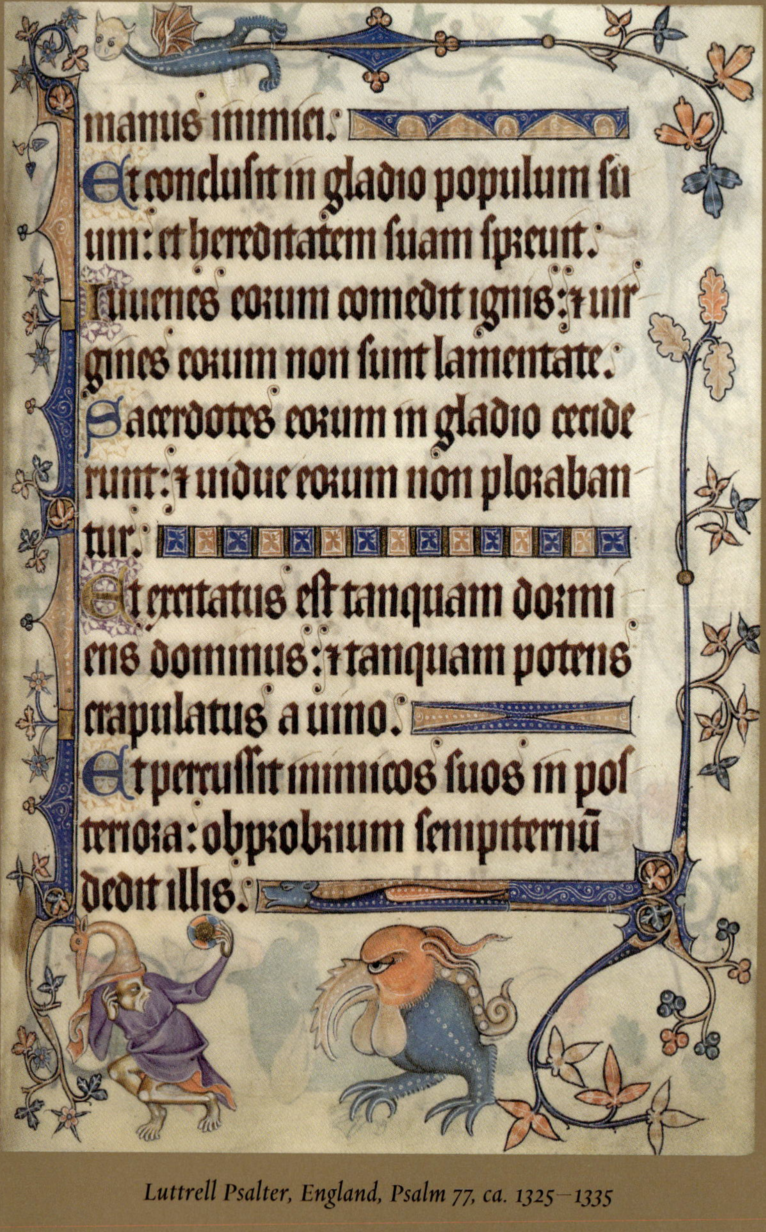

manus inimici.
Et conclusit in gladio populum su
um: et hereditatem suam spreuit.
Iuuenes eorum comedit ignis: ⁊ uir
gines eorum non sunt lamentate.
Sacerdotes eorum in gladio cecide
runt: ⁊ uidue eorum non ploraban
tur.
Et excitatus est tanquam dormi
ens dominus: ⁊ tanquam potens
crapulatus a uino.
Et percussit inimicos suos in pos
teriora: obprobrium sempiternū
dedit illis.

Luttrell Psalter, England, Psalm 77, ca. 1325–1335

15Thou hast with thine arm redeemed thy people, the sons
of Jacob and Joseph. Selah.
16The waters saw thee, O God, the waters saw thee; they
were afraid: the depths also were troubled.
17The clouds poured out water: the skies sent out a sound:
thine arrows also went abroad.
18The voice of thy thunder was in the heaven: the lightnings
lightened the world: the earth trembled and shook.
19Thy way is in the sea, and thy path in the great waters,
and thy footsteps are not known.
20Thou leddest thy people like a flock by the hand of Moses
and Aaron.

PSALM 78

Maschil of Asaph.

Give ear, O my people, to my law: incline your ears to
the words of my mouth.
2I will open my mouth in a parable: I will utter dark sayings
of old:
3Which we have heard and known, and our fathers have
told us.
4We will not hide them from their children, shewing to
the generation to come the praises of the LORD, and his
strength, and his wonderful works that he hath done.
5For he established a testimony in Jacob, and appointed
a law in Israel, which he commanded our fathers, that they
should make them known to their children:
6That the generation to come might know them, even the

children which should be born; who should arise and declare
them to their children:
7That they might set their hope in God, and not forget the
works of God, but keep his commandments:
8And might not be as their fathers, a stubborn and
rebellious generation; a generation that set not their heart
aright, and whose spirit was not stedfast with God.
9The children of Ephraim, being armed, and carrying bows,
turned back in the day of battle.
10They kept not the covenant of God, and refused to walk
in his law;
11And forgat his works, and his wonders that he had shewed
them.
12Marvellous things did he in the sight of their fathers, in
the land of Egypt, in the field of Zoan.
13He divided the sea, and caused them to pass through; and
he made the waters to stand as an heap.
14In the daytime also he led them with a cloud, and all the
night with a light of fire.
15He clave the rocks in the wilderness, and gave them drink
as out of the great depths.
16He brought streams also out of the rock, and caused
waters to run down like rivers.
17And they sinned yet more against him by provoking the
most High in the wilderness.
18And they tempted God in their heart by asking meat for
their lust.
19Yea, they spake against God; they said, Can God furnish a
table in the wilderness?

20 Behold, he smote the rock, that the waters gushed out,
and the streams overflowed; can he give bread also? can he
provide flesh for his people?
21 Therefore the LORD heard this, and was wroth: so a fire was
kindled against Jacob, and anger also came up against Israel;
22 Because they believed not in God, and trusted not in his
salvation:
23 Though he had commanded the clouds from above, and
opened the doors of heaven,
24 And had rained down manna upon them to eat, and had
given them of the corn of heaven.
25 Man did eat angels' food: he sent them meat to the full.
26 He caused an east wind to blow in the heaven: and by his
power he brought in the south wind.
27 He rained flesh also upon them as dust, and feathered
fowls like as the sand of the sea:
28 And he let it fall in the midst of their camp, round about
their habitations.
29 So they did eat, and were well filled: for he gave them
their own desire;
30 They were not estranged from their lust. But while their
meat was yet in their mouths,
31 The wrath of God came upon them, and slew the fattest
of them, and smote down the chosen men of Israel.
32 For all this they sinned still, and believed not for his
wondrous works.
33 Therefore their days did he consume in vanity,
and their years in trouble.
34 When he slew them, then they sought him:
and they returned and enquired early after God.
35 And they remembered that God was their
rock, and the high God their redeemer.

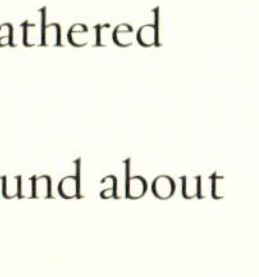

36 Nevertheless they did flatter him with their mouth, and
they lied unto him with their tongues.
37 For their heart was not right with him, neither were they
stedfast in his covenant.
38 But he, being full of compassion, forgave their iniquity,
and destroyed them not: yea, many a time turned he his
anger away, and did not stir up all his wrath.
39 For he remembered that they were but flesh; a wind that
passeth away, and cometh not again.
40 How oft did they provoke him in the wilderness, and
grieve him in the desert!
41 Yea, they turned back and tempted God, and limited the
Holy One of Israel.
42 They remembered not his hand, nor the day when he
delivered them from the enemy.
43 How he had wrought his signs in Egypt, and his wonders
in the field of Zoan:
44 And had turned their rivers into blood; and their floods,
that they could not drink.
45 He sent divers sorts of flies among them, which devoured
them; and frogs, which destroyed them.
46 He gave also their increase unto the caterpiller, and their
labour unto the locust.
47 He destroyed their vines with hail, and their sycomore
trees with frost.
48 He gave up their cattle also to the hail, and their flocks to
hot thunderbolts.

49 He cast upon them the fierceness of his anger, wrath,
and indignation, and trouble, by sending evil angels
among them.
50 He made a way to his anger; he spared not their soul from
death, but gave their life over to the pestilence;
51 And smote all the firstborn in Egypt; the chief of their
strength in the tabernacles of Ham:
52 But made his own people to go forth like sheep, and
guided them in the wilderness like a flock.
53 And he led them on safely, so that they feared not: but the
sea overwhelmed their enemies.
54 And he brought them to the border of his sanctuary, even
to this mountain, which his right hand had purchased.
55 He cast out the heathen also before them, and divided
them an inheritance by line, and made the tribes of Israel to
dwell in their tents.
56 Yet they tempted and provoked the most high God, and
kept not his testimonies:
57 But turned back, and dealt unfaithfully like their fathers:
they were turned aside like a deceitful bow.
58 For they provoked him to anger with their high places,
and moved him to jealousy with their graven images.
59 When God heard this, he was wroth, and greatly abhorred
Israel:
60 So that he forsook the tabernacle of Shiloh, the tent
which he placed among men;
61 And delivered his strength into captivity, and his glory
into the enemy's hand.
62 He gave his people over also unto the sword; and was
wroth with his inheritance.
63 The fire consumed their young men; and their maidens
were not given to marriage.

64 Their priests fell by the sword; and their widows made no
lamentation.
65 Then the LORD awaked as one out of sleep, and like a
mighty man that shouteth by reason of wine.
66 And he smote his enemies in the hinder parts: he put
them to a perpetual reproach.
67 Moreover he refused the tabernacle of Joseph, and chose
not the tribe of Ephraim:
68 But chose the tribe of Judah, the mount Zion which he loved.
69 And he built his sanctuary like high palaces, like the earth
which he hath established for ever.
70 He chose David also his servant, and took him from the
sheepfolds:
71 From following the ewes great with young he brought him
to feed Jacob his people, and Israel his inheritance.
72 So he fed them according to the integrity of his heart; and
guided them by the skilfulness of his hands.

PSALM 79

A Psalm of Asaph.

O God, the heathen are come into thine inheritance;
thy holy temple have they defiled; they have laid
Jerusalem on heaps.
2 The dead bodies of thy servants have they given to be meat
unto the fowls of the heaven, the flesh of thy saints unto the
beasts of the earth.
3 Their blood have they shed like water round about
Jerusalem; and there was none to bury them.

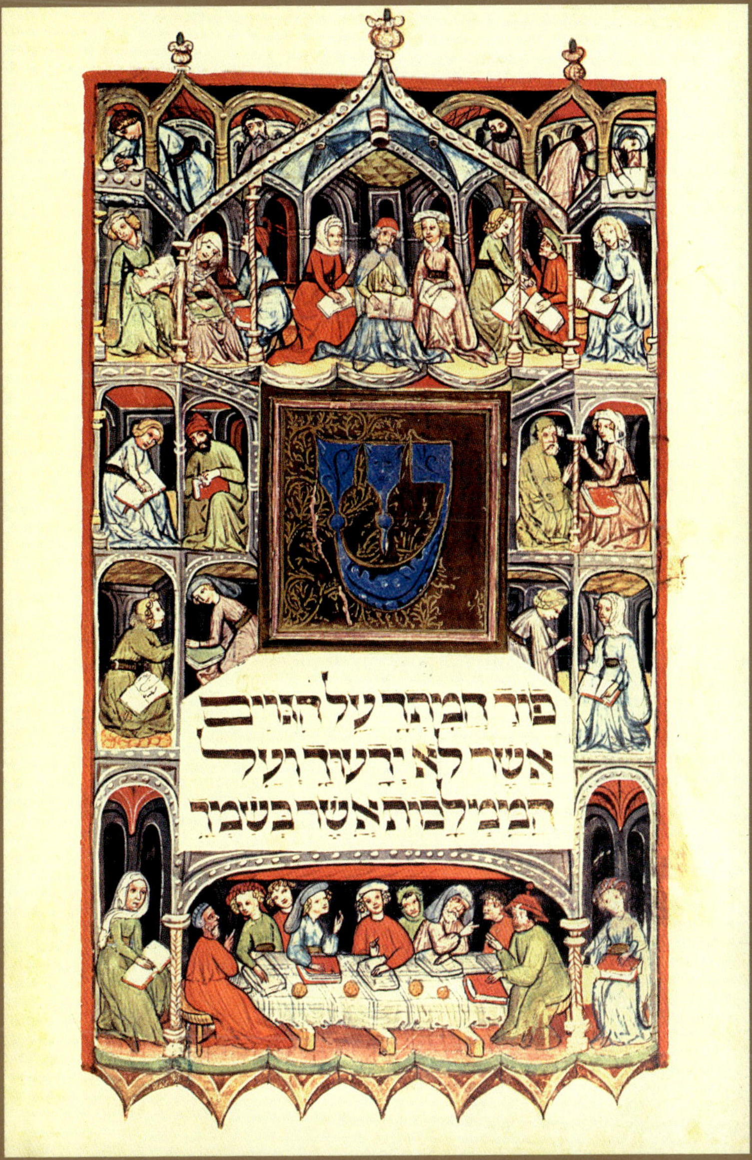

Darmstadt Haggadah, Psalm 79, Upper Rhine, 1420–1430

4 We are become a reproach to our neighbours, a scorn and
derision to them that are round about us.
5 How long, LORD? wilt thou be angry for ever? shall thy
jealousy burn like fire?
6 Pour out thy wrath upon the heathen that have not
known thee, and upon the kingdoms that have not called
upon thy name.

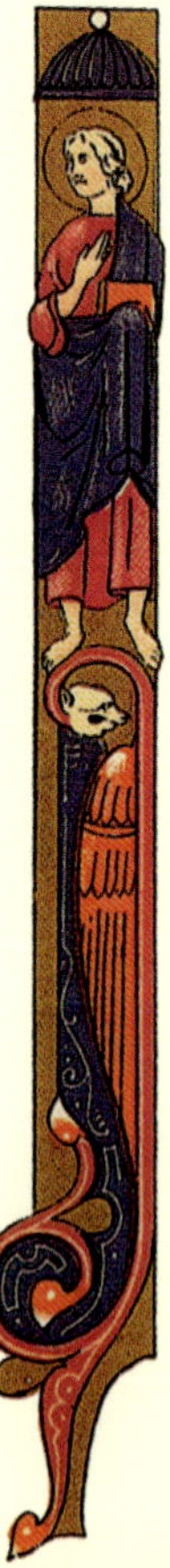

7 For they have devoured Jacob, and laid waste his
dwelling place.
8 O remember not against us former iniquities: let
thy tender mercies speedily prevent us: for we are
brought very low.
9 Help us, O God of our salvation, for the glory of
thy name: and deliver us, and purge away our sins,
for thy name's sake.
10 Wherefore should the heathen say, Where is
their God? let him be known among the heathen
in our sight by the revenging of the blood of thy
servants which is shed.
11 Let the sighing of the prisoner come before thee;
according to the greatness of thy power preserve
thou those that are appointed to die;
12 And render unto our neighbours sevenfold into
their bosom their reproach, wherewith they have
reproached thee, O LORD.
13 So we thy people and sheep of thy pasture will
give thee thanks for ever: we will shew forth thy
praise to all generations.

PSALM 80

To the chief Musician upon Shoshannim-Eduth,
A Psalm of Asaph.

Give ear, O Shepherd of Israel, thou that leadest Joseph
like a flock; thou that dwellest between the
cherubims, shine forth.
2Before Ephraim and Benjamin and Manasseh stir up thy
strength, and come and save us.
3Turn us again, O God, and cause thy face to shine; and we
shall be saved.
4O LORD God of hosts, how long wilt thou be angry
against the prayer of thy people?
5Thou feedest them with the bread of tears; and givest
them tears to drink in great measure.
6Thou makest us a strife unto our neighbours: and our
enemies laugh among themselves.
7Turn us again, O God of hosts, and cause thy face to shine;
and we shall be saved.
8Thou hast brought a vine out of Egypt: thou hast cast out
the heathen, and planted it.
9Thou preparedst room before it, and didst cause it to take
deep root, and it filled the land.
10The hills were covered with the shadow of it, and the
boughs thereof were like the goodly cedars.
11She sent out her boughs unto the sea, and her branches
unto the river.
12Why hast thou then broken down her hedges, so that all
they which pass by the way do pluck her?
13The boar out of the wood doth waste it, and the wild
beast of the field doth devour it.

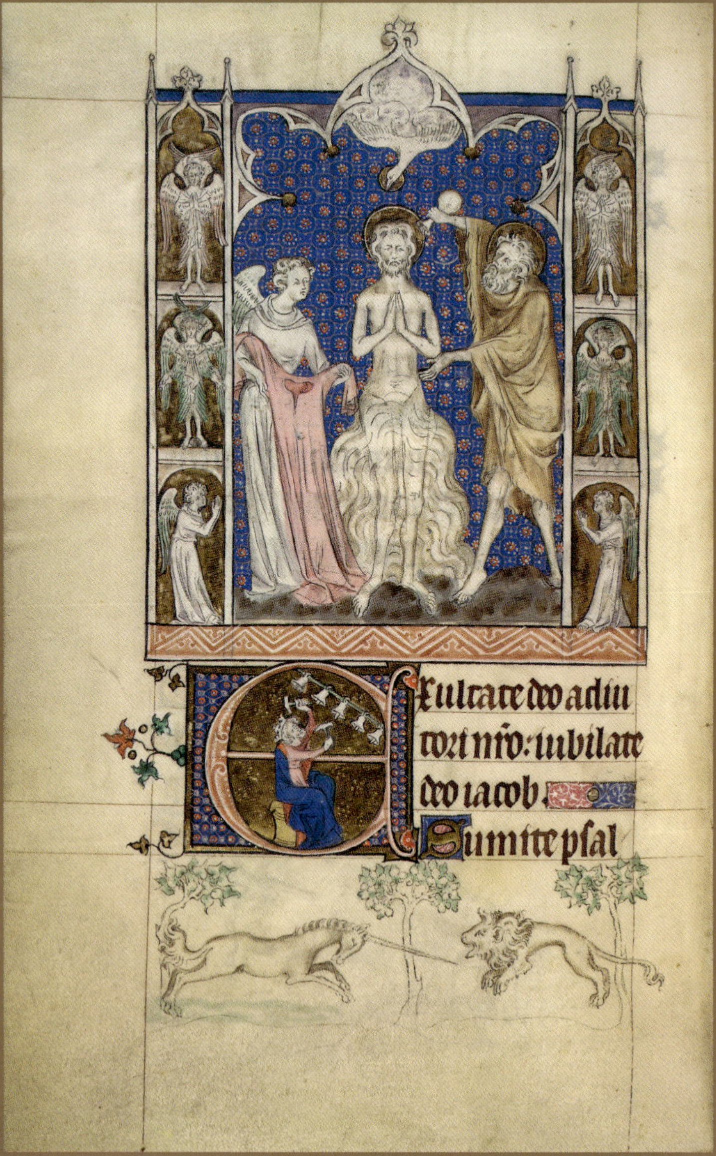

Queen Mary Psalter, England, Psalm 80, ca. 1310–1320

14Return, we beseech thee, O God of hosts: look down from
heaven, and behold, and visit this vine;
15And the vineyard which thy right hand hath planted, and
the branch that thou madest strong for thyself.
16It is burned with fire, it is cut down: they perish at the
rebuke of thy countenance.
17Let thy hand be upon the man of thy right hand, upon the
son of man whom thou madest strong for thyself.
18So will not we go back from thee: quicken us, and we will
call upon thy name.
19Turn us again, O LORD God of hosts, cause thy face to
shine; and we shall be saved.

PSALM 81

To the chief Musician upon Gittith,
A Psalm of Asaph.

Sing aloud unto God our strength: make a joyful noise
unto the God of Jacob.
2Take a psalm, and bring hither the timbrel, the pleasant
harp with the psaltery.
3Blow up the trumpet in the new moon, in the time
appointed, on our solemn feast day.
4For this was a statute for Israel, and a law of the God of Jacob.
5This he ordained in Joseph for a testimony, when he went
out through the land of Egypt: where I heard a language that
I understood not.
6I removed his shoulder from the burden: his hands were
delivered from the pots.

7 Thou calledst in trouble, and I delivered thee; I answered
thee in the secret place of thunder: I proved thee at the
waters of Meribah. Selah.
8 Hear, O my people, and I will testify unto thee: O Israel, if
thou wilt hearken unto me;
9 There shall no strange god be in thee; neither shalt thou
worship any strange god.
10 I am the LORD thy God, which brought thee out of the
land of Egypt: open thy mouth wide, and I will fill it.
11 But my people would not hearken to my voice; and Israel
would none of me.
12 So I gave them up unto their own hearts' lust: and they
walked in their own counsels.
13 Oh that my people had hearkened unto me, and Israel had
walked in my ways!
14 I should soon have subdued their enemies, and turned my
hand against their adversaries.
15 The haters of the LORD should have submitted
themselves unto him: but their time should have endured for
ever.
16 He should have fed them also with the finest of the wheat:
and with honey out of the rock should I have satisfied thee.

PSALM 82

A Psalm of Asaph.

God standeth in the congregation of the mighty; he
judgeth among the gods.
2 How long will ye judge unjustly, and accept the persons of
the wicked? Selah.
3 Defend the poor and fatherless: do justice to the afflicted
and needy.
4 Deliver the poor and needy: rid them out of the hand of
the wicked.
5 They know not, neither will they understand; they walk on
in darkness: all the foundations of the earth are out of course.
6 I have said, Ye are gods; and all of you are children of the
most High.
7 But ye shall die like men, and fall like one of the princes.
8 Arise, O God, judge the earth: for thou shalt inherit all
nations.

PSALM 83

A Song or Psalm of Asaph.

Keep not thou silence, O God: hold not thy peace, and
be not still, O God.
2 For, lo, thine enemies make a tumult: and they that hate
thee have lifted up the head.
3 They have taken crafty counsel against thy people, and
consulted against thy hidden ones.
4 They have said, Come, and let us cut them off from
being a nation; that the name of Israel may be no more in
remembrance.
5 For they have consulted together with one consent: they
are confederate against thee:
6 The tabernacles of Edom, and the Ishmaelites; of Moab,
and the Hagarenes;
7 Gebal, and Ammon, and Amalek; the Philistines with the
inhabitants of Tyre;
8 Assur also is joined with them: they have holpen the
children of Lot. Selah.
9 Do unto them as unto the Midianites; as to Sisera, as to
Jabin, at the brook of Kison:
10 Which perished at Endor: they became as dung for the earth.
11 Make their nobles like Oreb, and like Zeeb: yea, all their
princes as Zebah, and as Zalmunna:
12 Who said, Let us take to ourselves the houses of God in
possession.
13 O my God, make them like a wheel; as the stubble before
the wind.
14 As the fire burneth a wood, and as the flame setteth the
mountains on fire;

[15]So persecute them with thy tempest, and make them
afraid with thy storm.
[16]Fill their faces with shame; that they may seek thy name,
O LORD.
[17]Let them be confounded and troubled for ever; yea, let
them be put to shame, and perish:
[18]That men may know that thou, whose name alone is
JEHOVAH, art the most high over all the earth.

PSALM 84

To the chief Musician upon Gittith,
A Psalm for the sons of Korah.

How amiable are thy tabernacles, O LORD of hosts!
[2]My soul longeth, yea, even fainteth for the courts of
the LORD: my heart and my flesh crieth out for the living God.
[3]Yea, the sparrow hath found an house, and the swallow
a nest for herself, where she may lay her young, even thine
altars, O LORD of hosts, my King, and my God.
[4]Blessed are they that dwell in thy house: they will be still
praising thee. Selah.
[5]Blessed is the man whose strength is in thee; in whose
heart are the ways of them.
[6]Who passing through the valley of Baca make it a well; the
rain also filleth the pools.

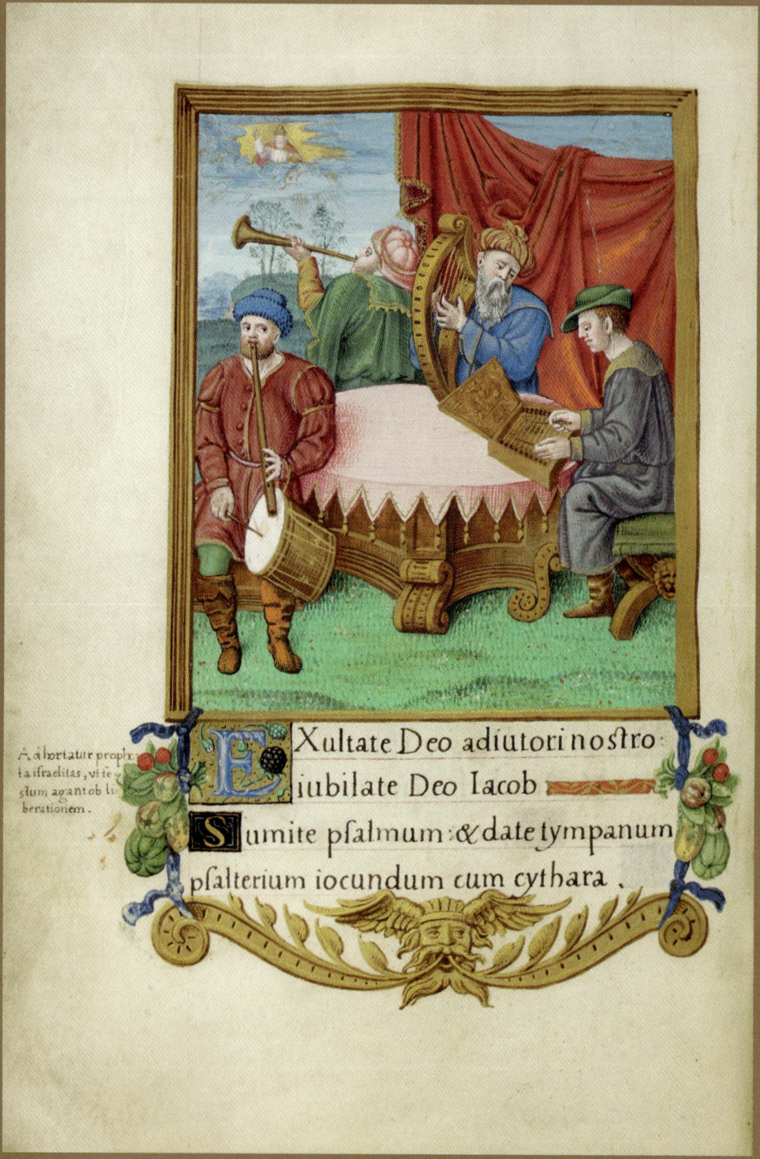

Psalter of Henry VIII, England, Psalm 84, 1530–1547

7 They go from strength to strength, every one of them in
Zion appeareth before God.
8 O LORD God of hosts, hear my prayer: give ear, O God
of Jacob. Selah.
9 Behold, O God our shield, and look upon the face of thine
anointed.
10 For a day in thy courts is better than a thousand. I had
rather be a doorkeeper in the house of my God, than to dwell
in the tents of wickedness.
11 For the LORD God is a sun and shield: the LORD will
give grace and glory: no good thing will he withhold from
them that walk uprightly.
12 O LORD of hosts, blessed is the man that trusteth
in thee.

PSALM 85

To the chief Musician,
A Psalm for the sons of Korah.

LORD, thou hast been favourable unto thy land:
thou hast brought back the captivity of Jacob.
2 Thou hast forgiven the iniquity of thy people, thou hast
covered all their sin. Selah.
3 Thou hast taken away all thy wrath: thou hast turned
thyself from the fierceness of thine anger.
4 Turn us, O God of our salvation, and cause thine anger
toward us to cease.
5 Wilt thou be angry with us for ever? wilt thou draw out
thine anger to all generations?

6Wilt thou not revive us again: that thy people may rejoice
in thee?
7Shew us thy mercy, O LORD, and grant us thy salvation.
8I will hear what God the LORD will speak: for he will
speak peace unto his people, and to his saints: but let them
not turn again to folly.
9Surely his salvation is nigh them that fear him; that glory
may dwell in our land.
10Mercy and truth are met together; righteousness and
peace have kissed each other.
11Truth shall spring out of the earth; and righteousness shall
look down from heaven.
12Yea, the LORD shall give that which is good; and our land
shall yield her increase.
13Righteousness shall go before him; and shall set us in the
way of his steps.

PSALM 86

A Prayer of David.

Bow down thine ear, O LORD, hear me: for I am
poor and needy.
2Preserve my soul; for I am holy: O thou my God, save thy
servant that trusteth in thee.
3Be merciful unto me, O LORD: for I cry unto thee daily.
4Rejoice the soul of thy servant: for unto thee, O LORD,
do I lift up my soul.
5For thou, LORD, art good, and ready to forgive; and
plenteous in mercy unto all them that call upon thee.

6Give ear, O LORD, unto my prayer; and attend to the
voice of my supplications.
7In the day of my trouble I will call upon thee: for thou wilt
answer me.
8Among the gods there is none like unto thee, O LORD;
neither are there any works like unto thy works.
9All nations whom thou hast made shall come and worship
before thee, O LORD; and shall glorify thy name.
10For thou art great, and doest wondrous things: thou art
God alone.
11Teach me thy way, O LORD; I will walk in thy truth:
unite my heart to fear thy name.
12I will praise thee, O LORD my God, with all my heart:
and I will glorify thy name for evermore.
13For great is thy mercy toward me: and thou hast delivered
my soul from the lowest hell.
14O God, the proud are risen against me, and the assemblies
of violent men have sought after my soul; and have not set
thee before them.
15But thou, O LORD, art a God full of compassion, and
gracious, longsuffering, and plenteous in mercy and truth.
16O turn unto me, and have mercy upon me; give thy
strength unto thy servant, and save the son of thine
handmaid.
17Shew me a token for good; that they which hate me may
see it, and be ashamed: because thou, LORD, hast holpen
me, and comforted me.

PSALM 87

A Psalm or Song for the sons of Korah.

His foundation is in the holy mountains.
2 The LORD loveth the gates of Zion more than all
the dwellings of Jacob.
3 Glorious things are spoken of thee, O city of God. Selah.
4 I will make mention of Rahab and Babylon to them that
know me: behold Philistia, and Tyre, with Ethiopia; this man
was born there.
5 And of Zion it shall be said, This and that man was born in
her: and the highest himself shall establish her.
6 The LORD shall count, when he writeth up the people,
that this man was born there. Selah.
7 As well the singers as the players on instruments shall be
there: all my springs are in thee.

PSALM 88

A Song or Psalm for the sons of Korah,
to the chief Musician upon Mahalath Leannoth,
Maschil of Heman the Ezrahite.

O LORD God of my salvation, I have cried day and
night before thee:
2 Let my prayer come before thee: incline thine ear unto
my cry;
3 For my soul is full of troubles: and my life draweth nigh
unto the grave.

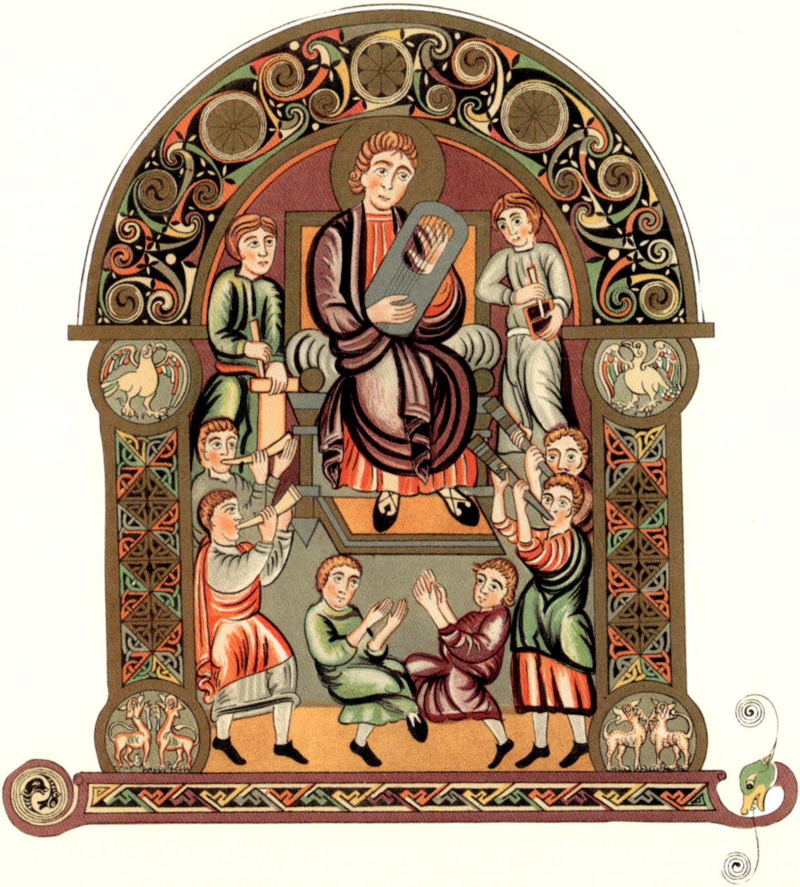

4I am counted with them that go down into the pit: I am as
a man that hath no strength:
5Free among the dead, like the slain that lie in the grave,
whom thou rememberest no more: and they are cut off from
thy hand.
6Thou hast laid me in the lowest pit, in darkness, in the deeps.
7Thy wrath lieth hard upon me, and thou hast afflicted me
with all thy waves. Selah.
8Thou hast put away mine acquaintance far from me; thou
hast made me an abomination unto them: I am shut up, and
I cannot come forth.
9Mine eye mourneth by reason of affliction: LORD, I have
called daily upon thee, I have stretched out my hands unto
thee.
10Wilt thou shew wonders to the dead? shall the dead arise
and praise thee? Selah.
11Shall thy lovingkindness be declared in the grave? or thy
faithfulness in destruction?
12Shall thy wonders be known in the dark? and thy
righteousness in the land of forgetfulness?
13But unto thee have I cried, O LORD; and in the morning
shall my prayer prevent thee.
14LORD, why castest thou off my soul? why hidest thou thy
face from me?
15I am afflicted and ready to die from my youth up: while I
suffer thy terrors I am distracted.
16Thy fierce wrath goeth over me; thy terrors have cut me off.
17They came round about me daily like water; they
compassed me about together.
18Lover and friend hast thou put far from me, and mine
acquaintance into darkness.

PSALM 89

Maschil of Ethan the Ezrahite.

I will sing of the mercies of the LORD for ever:
with my mouth will I make known thy faithfulness to
all generations.
2 For I have said, Mercy shall be built up for ever: thy
faithfulness shalt thou establish in the very heavens.
3 I have made a covenant with my chosen, I have sworn
unto David my servant,
4 Thy seed will I establish for ever, and build up thy throne
to all generations. Selah.
5 And the heavens shall praise thy wonders, O LORD: thy
faithfulness also in the congregation of the saints.
6 For who in the heaven can be compared unto the LORD?
who among the sons of the mighty can be likened unto the
LORD?
7 God is greatly to be feared in the assembly of the saints,
and to be had in reverence of all them that are about him.
8 O LORD God of hosts, who is a strong LORD like unto
thee? or to thy faithfulness round about thee?
9 Thou rulest the raging of the sea: when the waves thereof
arise, thou stillest them.
10 Thou hast broken Rahab in pieces, as one that is slain;
thou hast scattered thine enemies with thy strong arm.
11 The heavens are thine, the earth also is thine: as for the
world and the fulness thereof, thou hast founded them.

[12] The north and the south thou hast created them: Tabor
and Hermon shall rejoice in thy name.
[13] Thou hast a mighty arm: strong is thy hand, and high is
thy right hand.
[14] Justice and judgment are the habitation of thy throne:
mercy and truth shall go before thy face.
[15] Blessed is the people that know the joyful sound: they
shall walk, O LORD, in the light of thy countenance.
[16] In thy name shall they rejoice all the day: and in thy
righteousness shall they be exalted.
[17] For thou art the glory of their strength: and in thy favour
our horn shall be exalted.
[18] For the LORD is our defence; and the Holy One of Israel
is our king.
[19] Then thou spakest in vision to thy holy one, and saidst,
I have laid help upon one that is mighty; I have exalted one
chosen out of the people.
[20] I have found David my servant; with my holy oil have I
anointed him:
[21] With whom my hand shall be established: mine arm also
shall strengthen him.
[22] The enemy shall not exact upon him; nor the son of
wickedness afflict him.
[23] And I will beat down his foes before his face, and plague
them that hate him.
[24] But my faithfulness and my mercy shall be with him: and
in my name shall his horn be exalted.
[25] I will set his hand also in the sea, and his right hand in the
rivers.

26 He shall cry unto me, Thou art my father, my God, and
the rock of my salvation.
27 Also I will make him my firstborn, higher than the kings
of the earth.
28 My mercy will I keep for him for evermore, and my
covenant shall stand fast with him.
29 His seed also will I make to endure for ever, and his
throne as the days of heaven.
30 If his children forsake my law, and walk not in my
judgments;
31 If they break my statutes, and keep not my
commandments;
32 Then will I visit their transgression with the rod, and
their iniquity with stripes.
33 Nevertheless my lovingkindness will I not utterly take
from him, nor suffer my faithfulness to fail.
34 My covenant will I not break, nor alter the thing that is
gone out of my lips.
35 Once have I sworn by my holiness that I will not lie unto
David.
36 His seed shall endure for ever, and his throne as the sun
before me.
37 It shall be established for ever as the moon, and as a
faithful witness in heaven. Selah.

38 But thou hast cast off and abhorred, thou hast been wroth
with thine anointed.
39 Thou hast made void the covenant of thy servant: thou
hast profaned his crown by casting it to the ground.
40 Thou hast broken down all his hedges; thou hast brought
his strong holds to ruin.
41 All that pass by the way spoil him: he is a reproach to his
neighbours.
42 Thou hast set up the right hand of his adversaries; thou
hast made all his enemies to rejoice.
43 Thou hast also turned the edge of his sword, and hast not
made him to stand in the battle.
44 Thou hast made his glory to cease, and cast his throne
down to the ground.
45 The days of his youth hast thou shortened: thou hast
covered him with shame. Selah.
46 How long, LORD? wilt thou hide thyself for ever? shall
thy wrath burn like fire?
47 Remember how short my time is: wherefore hast thou
made all men in vain?
48 What man is he that liveth, and shall not see death? shall
he deliver his soul from the hand of the grave? Selah.
49 LORD, where are thy former lovingkindnesses, which
thou swarest unto David in thy truth?
50 Remember, LORD, the reproach of thy servants; how I
do bear in my bosom the reproach of all the mighty people;
51 Wherewith thine enemies have reproached, O LORD;
wherewith they have reproached the footsteps of thine
anointed.
52 Blessed be the LORD for evermore. Amen, and Amen.

BOOK IV

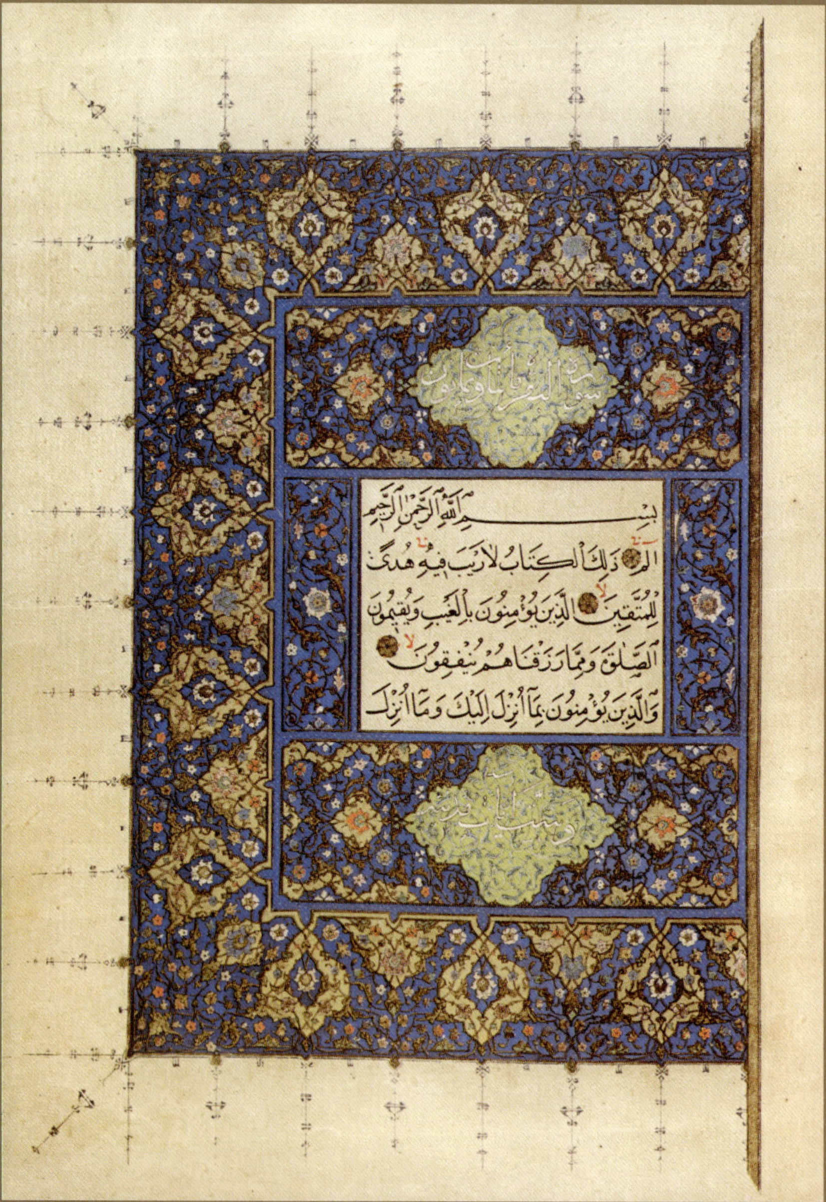
بِسْمِ اللهِ الرَّحْمٰنِ الرَّحِيمِ
الٓمٓ ذٰلِكَ الْكِتَابُ لَا رَيْبَ فِيهِ هُدًى
لِلْمُتَّقِينَ الَّذِينَ يُؤْمِنُونَ بِالْغَيْبِ وَيُقِيمُونَ
الصَّلٰوةَ وَمِمَّا رَزَقْنَاهُمْ يُنْفِقُونَ
وَالَّذِينَ يُؤْمِنُونَ بِمَا أُنْزِلَ إِلَيْكَ وَمَا أُنْزِلَ

PSALM 90

A Prayer of Moses the man of God.

LORD, thou hast been our dwelling place in all
generations.
2 Before the mountains were brought forth, or ever thou
hadst formed the earth and the world, even from everlasting
to everlasting, thou art God.
3 Thou turnest man to destruction; and sayest, Return, ye
children of men.
4 For a thousand years in thy sight are but as yesterday when
it is past, and as a watch in the night.
5 Thou carriest them away as with a flood; they are as a
sleep: in the morning they are like grass which groweth up.
6 In the morning it flourisheth, and groweth up; in the
evening it is cut down, and withereth.
7 For we are consumed by thine anger, and by thy wrath are
we troubled.
8 Thou hast set our iniquities before thee, our secret sins in
the light of thy countenance.
9 For all our days are passed away in thy wrath: we spend our
years as a tale that is told.
10 The days of our years are threescore years and ten; and if by
reason of strength they be fourscore years, yet is their strength
labour and sorrow; for it is soon cut off, and we fly away.
11 Who knoweth the power of thine anger? even according
to thy fear, so is thy wrath.
12 So teach us to number our days, that we
may apply our hearts unto wisdom.
13 Return, O LORD, how long? and let
it repent thee concerning thy servants.

14 O satisfy us early with thy mercy; that we may rejoice and
be glad all our days.
15 Make us glad according to the days wherein thou hast
afflicted us, and the years wherein we have seen evil.
16 Let thy work appear unto thy servants, and thy glory unto
their children.
17 And let the beauty of the LORD our God be upon us: and
establish thou the work of our hands upon us; yea, the work
of our hands establish thou it.

PSALM 91

He that dwelleth in the secret place of the most High
shall abide under the shadow of the Almighty.
2 I will say of the LORD, He is my refuge and my fortress:
my God; in him will I trust.
3 Surely he shall deliver thee from the snare of the fowler,
and from the noisome pestilence.
4 He shall cover thee with his feathers, and under his wings
shalt thou trust: his truth shall be thy shield and buckler.
5 Thou shalt not be afraid for the terror by night; nor for the
arrow that flieth by day;
6 Nor for the pestilence that walketh in darkness; nor for
the destruction that wasteth at noonday.
7 A thousand shall fall at thy side, and ten thousand at thy
right hand; but it shall not come nigh thee.
8 Only with thine eyes shalt thou behold and see the reward
of the wicked.
9 Because thou hast made the LORD, which is my refuge,
even the most High, thy habitation;

10 There shall no evil befall thee, neither shall any plague
come nigh thy dwelling.
11 For he shall give his angels charge over thee, to keep thee
in all thy ways.
12 They shall bear thee up in their hands, lest thou dash thy
foot against a stone.
13 Thou shalt tread upon the lion and adder: the young lion
and the dragon shalt thou trample under feet.
14 Because he hath set his love upon me, therefore will I
deliver him: I will set him on high, because he hath known
my name.
15 He shall call upon me, and I will answer him: I will be
with him in trouble; I will deliver him, and honour him.
16 With long life will I satisfy him, and shew him my
salvation.

PSALM 92

A Psalm or Song for the sabbath day.

It is a good thing to give thanks unto the LORD, and
to sing praises unto thy name, O most High:
2 To shew forth thy lovingkindness in the morning, and thy
faithfulness every night,
3 Upon an instrument of ten strings, and upon the psaltery;
upon the harp with a solemn sound.
4 For thou, LORD, hast made me glad through thy work: I
will triumph in the works of thy hands.
5 O LORD, how great are thy works! and thy thoughts are
very deep.

6 A brutish man knoweth not; neither doth a fool
understand this.
7 When the wicked spring as the grass, and when all the
workers of iniquity do flourish; it is that they shall be
destroyed for ever:
8 But thou, LORD, art most high for evermore.
9 For, lo, thine enemies, O LORD, for, lo, thine enemies
shall perish; all the workers of iniquity shall be scattered.
10 But my horn shalt thou exalt like the horn of an unicorn:
I shall be anointed with fresh oil.
11 Mine eye also shall see my desire on mine enemies, and
mine ears shall hear my desire of the wicked that rise up
against me.
12 The righteous shall flourish like the palm tree: he shall
grow like a cedar in Lebanon.
13 Those that be planted in the house of the LORD shall
flourish in the courts of our God.
14 They shall still bring forth fruit in old age; they shall be fat
and flourishing;
15 To shew that the LORD is upright: he is my rock, and
there is no unrighteousness in him.

PSALM 93

The LORD reigneth, he is clothed with majesty; the LORD is clothed with strength, wherewith he hath girded himself: the world also is stablished, that it cannot be moved.
2 Thy throne is established of old: thou art from everlasting.
3 The floods have lifted up, O LORD, the floods have lifted

up their voice; the floods lift up their waves.
4 The LORD on high is mightier than the noise of many
waters, yea, than the mighty waves of the sea.
5 Thy testimonies are very sure: holiness becometh thine
house, O LORD, for ever.

PSALM 94

O LORD God, to whom vengeance belongeth; O God,
to whom vengeance belongeth, shew thyself.
2 Lift up thyself, thou judge of the earth: render a reward to
the proud.
3 LORD, how long shall the wicked, how long shall the
wicked triumph?
4 How long shall they utter and speak hard things? and all
the workers of iniquity boast themselves?
5 They break in pieces thy people, O LORD, and afflict
thine heritage.
6 They slay the widow and the stranger, and murder the
fatherless.
7 Yet they say, The LORD shall not see, neither shall the
God of Jacob regard it.
8 Understand, ye brutish among the people: and ye fools,
when will ye be wise?
9 He that planted the ear, shall he not hear? he that formed
the eye, shall he not see?
10 He that chastiseth the heathen, shall not he correct? he
that teacheth man knowledge, shall not he know?
11 The LORD knoweth the thoughts of man, that they
are vanity.

12 Blessed is the man whom thou chastenest, O LORD, and teachest him out of thy law;

13 That thou mayest give him rest from the days of adversity, until the pit be digged for the wicked.

14 For the LORD will not cast off his people, neither will he forsake his inheritance.

15 But judgment shall return unto righteousness: and all the upright in heart shall follow it.

16 Who will rise up for me against the evildoers? or who will stand up for me against the workers of iniquity?

17 Unless the LORD had been my help, my soul had almost dwelt in silence.

18 When I said, My foot slippeth; thy mercy, O LORD, held me up.

19 In the multitude of my thoughts within me thy comforts delight my soul.

20 Shall the throne of iniquity have fellowship with thee, which frameth mischief by a law?

21 They gather themselves together against the soul of the righteous, and condemn the innocent blood.

22 But the LORD is my defence; and my God is the rock of my refuge.

23 And he shall bring upon them their own iniquity, and shall cut them off in their own wickedness; yea, the LORD our God shall cut them off.

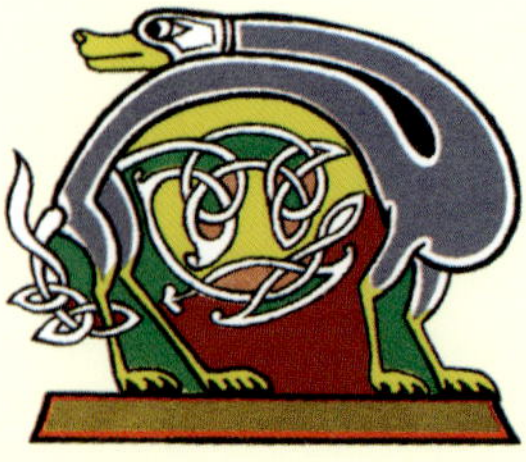

PSALM 95

O come, let us sing unto the LORD: let us make a
joyful noise to the rock of our salvation.
2 Let us come before his presence with thanksgiving, and
make a joyful noise unto him with psalms.
3 For the LORD is a great God, and a great King above
all gods.
4 In his hand are the deep places of the earth: the strength
of the hills is his also.
5 The sea is his, and he made it: and his hands formed the
dry land.
6 O come, let us worship and bow down: let us kneel before
the LORD our maker.
7 For he is our God; and we are the people of his pasture,
and the sheep of his hand. To day if ye will hear his voice,
8 Harden not your heart, as in the provocation, and as in the
day of temptation in the wilderness:
9 When your fathers tempted me, proved me, and saw my
work.
10 Forty years long was I grieved with this generation, and
said, It is a people that do err in their heart, and they have
not known my ways:
11 Unto whom I sware in my wrath that they should not
enter into my rest.

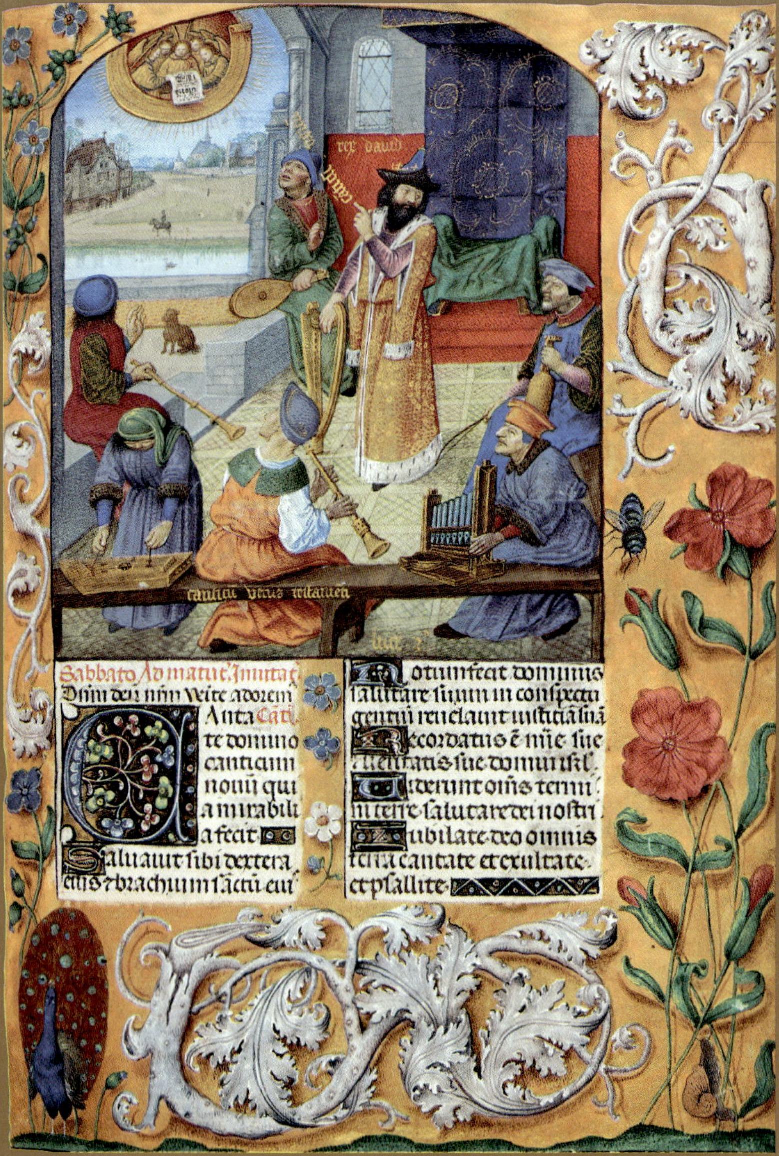

Master of the Dresden Prayer Book, South Netherlands, Psalm 95, ca. 1490–1497

PSALM 96

O sing unto the LORD a new song: sing unto the
LORD, all the earth.
2 Sing unto the LORD, bless his name; shew forth his
salvation from day to day.
3 Declare his glory among the heathen, his wonders among
all people.
4 For the LORD is great, and greatly to be praised: he is to
be feared above all gods.
5 For all the gods of the nations are idols: but the LORD
made the heavens.
6 Honour and majesty are before him: strength and beauty
are in his sanctuary.
7 Give unto the LORD, O ye kindreds of the people, give
unto the LORD glory and strength.
8 Give unto the LORD the glory due unto his name: bring
an offering, and come into his courts.
9 O worship the LORD in the beauty of holiness: fear
before him, all the earth.
10 Say among the heathen that the LORD reigneth: the
world also shall be established that it shall not be moved: he
shall judge the people righteously.
11 Let the heavens rejoice, and let the earth be glad; let the
sea roar, and the fulness thereof.
12 Let the field be joyful, and all that is therein: then shall all
the trees of the wood rejoice
13 Before the LORD: for he cometh, for he cometh to judge
the earth: he shall judge the world with righteousness, and
the people with his truth.

PSALM 97

The LORD reigneth; let the earth rejoice; let the
multitude of isles be glad thereof.
2 Clouds and darkness are round about him: righteousness
and judgment are the habitation of his throne.
3 A fire goeth before him, and burneth up his enemies round
about.
4 His lightnings enlightened the world: the earth saw, and
trembled.
5 The hills melted like wax at the presence of the LORD, at
the presence of the LORD of the whole earth.
6 The heavens declare his righteousness, and all the people
see his glory.
7 Confounded be all they that serve graven images, that
boast themselves of idols: worship him, all ye gods.
8 Zion heard, and was glad; and the daughters of Judah
rejoiced because of thy judgments, O LORD.
9 For thou, LORD, art high above all the earth: thou art
exalted far above all gods.
10 Ye that love the LORD, hate evil:
he preserveth the souls of his saints;
he delivereth them out of the hand
of the wicked.
11 Light is sown for the righteous,
and gladness for the upright in heart.
12 Rejoice in the LORD, ye righteous;
and give thanks at the remembrance
of his holiness.

PSALM 98

O sing unto the LORD a new song; for he hath done
marvellous things: his right hand, and his holy arm,
hath gotten him the victory.
2 The LORD hath made known his salvation: his righteousness
hath he openly shewed in the sight of the heathen.
3 He hath remembered his mercy and his truth toward
the house of Israel: all the ends of the earth have seen the
salvation of our God.
4 Make a joyful noise unto the LORD, all the earth: make a
loud noise, and rejoice, and sing praise.
5 Sing unto the LORD with the harp; with the harp, and the
voice of a psalm.
6 With trumpets and sound of cornet make a joyful noise
before the LORD, the King.
7 Let the sea roar, and the fulness thereof; the world, and
they that dwell therein.
8 Let the floods clap their hands: let the hills be joyful together
9 Before the LORD; for he cometh to judge the earth: with
righteousness shall he judge the world, and the people with
equity.

PSALM 99

The LORD reigneth; let the people tremble: he
sitteth between the cherubims; let the earth be moved.
2 The LORD is great in Zion; and he is high above all the
people.
3 Let them praise thy great and terrible name; for it is holy.

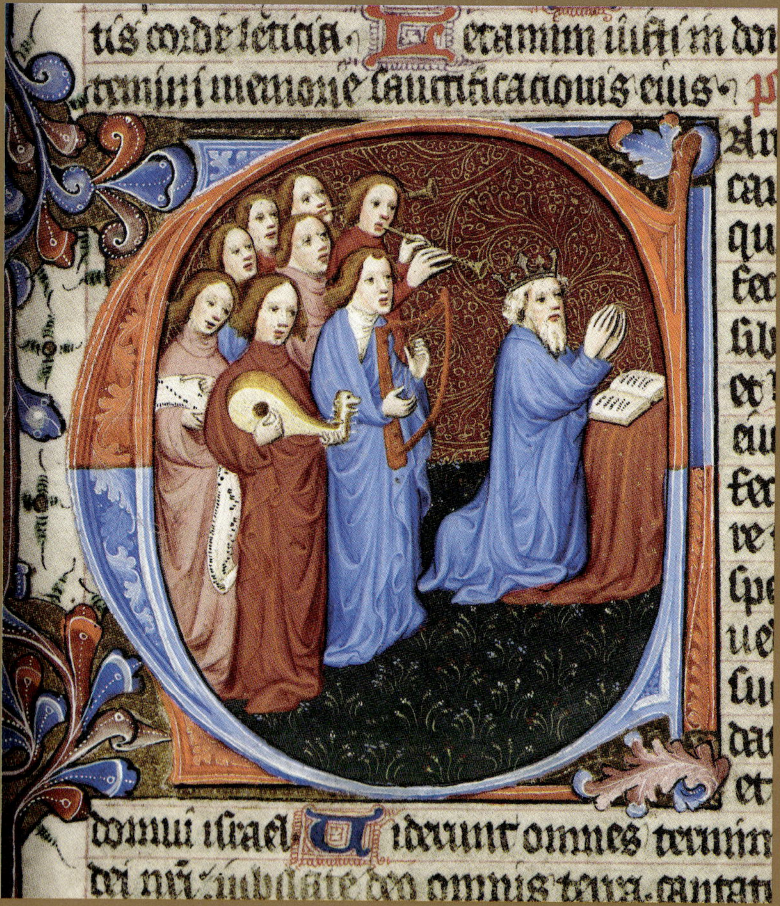

England, Psalm 95, 1405–1415

4The king's strength also loveth judgment;
thou dost establish equity, thou executest
judgment and righteousness in Jacob.
5Exalt ye the LORD our God, and worship
at his footstool; for he is holy.
6Moses and Aaron among his priests, and Samuel among
them that call upon his name; they called upon the LORD,
and he answered them.
7He spake unto them in the cloudy pillar: they kept his
testimonies, and the ordinance that he gave them.
8Thou answeredst them, O LORD our God: thou wast a
God that forgavest them, though thou tookest vengeance of
their inventions.
9Exalt the LORD our God, and worship at his holy hill; for
the LORD our God is holy.

PSALM 100

A Psalm of praise.

Make a joyful noise unto the LORD, all ye lands.
2Serve the LORD with gladness: come before his
presence with singing.
3Know ye that the LORD he is God: it is he that hath made
us, and not we ourselves; we are his people, and the sheep of
his pasture.
4Enter into his gates with thanksgiving, and into his courts
with praise: be thankful unto him, and bless his name.
5For the LORD is good; his mercy is everlasting; and his
truth endureth to all generations.

PSALM 101

A Psalm of David.

I will sing of mercy and judgment: unto thee, O
LORD, will I sing.
2 I will behave myself wisely in a perfect way. O when wilt
thou come unto me? I will walk within my house with a
perfect heart.
3 I will set no wicked thing before mine eyes: I hate the
work of them that turn aside; it shall not cleave to me.
4 A froward heart shall depart from me: I will not know a
wicked person.
5 Whoso privily slandereth his neighbour, him will I cut off:
him that hath an high look and a proud heart will not I suffer.
6 Mine eyes shall be upon the faithful of the land, that they
may dwell with me: he that walketh in a perfect way, he shall
serve me.
7 He that worketh deceit shall not dwell within my house:
he that telleth lies shall not tarry in my sight.
8 I will early destroy all the wicked of the land; that I may
cut off all wicked doers from the city of the LORD.

PSALM 102

A Prayer of the afflicted,
when he is overwhelmed, and poureth out
his complaint before the LORD.

Hear my prayer, O LORD, and let my cry come
unto thee.
2 Hide not thy face from me in the day when I am in
trouble; incline thine ear unto me: in the day when I call
answer me speedily.
3 For my days are consumed like smoke, and my bones are
burned as an hearth.
4 My heart is smitten, and withered like grass; so that I
forget to eat my bread.
5 By reason of the voice of my groaning my bones cleave to
my skin.
6 I am like a pelican of the wilderness: I am like an owl of
the desert.
7 I watch, and am as a sparrow alone upon the house top.
8 Mine enemies reproach me all the day; and they that are
mad against me are sworn against me.
9 For I have eaten ashes like bread, and mingled my drink
with weeping,
10 Because of thine indignation and thy wrath: for thou hast
lifted me up, and cast me down.
11 My days are like a shadow that declineth; and I am
withered like grass.
12 But thou, O LORD, shalt endure for ever; and thy
remembrance unto all generations.
13 Thou shalt arise, and have mercy upon Zion: for the time
to favour her, yea, the set time, is come.

14 For thy servants take pleasure in her stones, and favour
the dust thereof.
15 So the heathen shall fear the name of the LORD, and all
the kings of the earth thy glory.
16 When the LORD shall build up Zion, he shall appear in
his glory.
17 He will regard the prayer of the destitute, and not despise
their prayer.
18 This shall be written for the generation to come: and the
people which shall be created shall praise the LORD.
19 For he hath looked down from the height of his sanctuary;
from heaven did the LORD behold the earth;
20 To hear the groaning of the prisoner; to loose those that
are appointed to death;
21 To declare the name of the LORD in Zion, and his praise
in Jerusalem;
22 When the people are gathered together, and the
kingdoms, to serve the LORD.
23 He weakened my strength in the way; he shortened my days.
24 I said, O my God, take me not away in the midst of my
days: thy years are throughout all generations.
25 Of old hast thou laid the foundation of the earth: and the
heavens are the work of thy hands.
26 They shall perish, but thou shalt endure: yea, all of them
shall wax old like a garment; as a vesture shalt thou change
them, and they shall be changed:
27 But thou art the same, and thy years shall have no end.
28 The children of thy servants shall
continue, and their seed
shall be established
before thee.

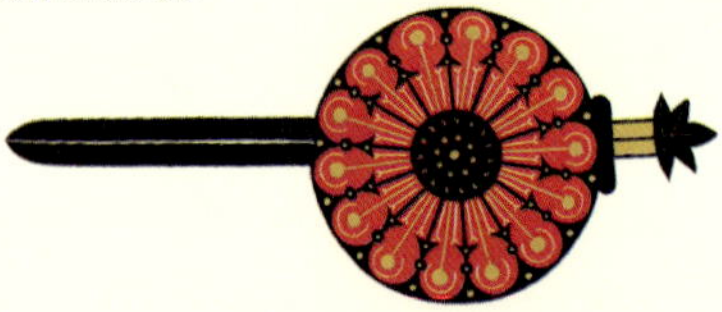

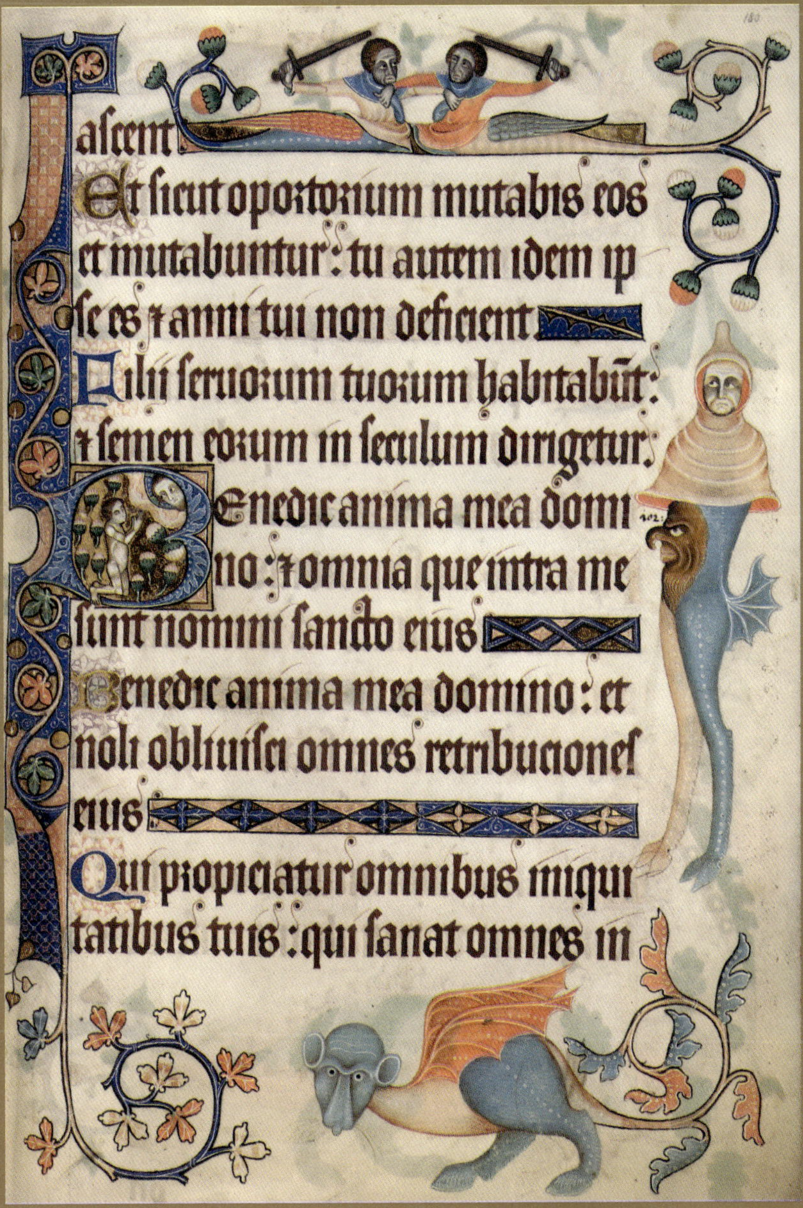
ascent
Et sicut opertorium mutabis eos
et mutabuntur: tu autem idem ip
se es et anni tui non deficient.
Filii seruorum tuorum habitabunt:
et semen eorum in seculum dirigetur.
Benedic anima mea domi
no: et omnia que intra me
sunt nomini sancto eius
Benedic anima mea domino: et
noli obliuisci omnes retribuciones
eius
Qui propiciatur omnibus iniqui
tatibus tuis: qui sanat omnes in

Luttrel Psalter, England, Psalm 102, ca. 1325–1335

PSALM 103

A Psalm of David.

Bless the LORD, O my soul: and all that is within me,
bless his holy name.
2 Bless the LORD, O my soul, and forget not all his benefits:
3 Who forgiveth all thine iniquities; who healeth all thy diseases;
4 Who redeemeth thy life from destruction; who crowneth
thee with lovingkindness and tender mercies;
5 Who satisfieth thy mouth with good things; so that thy
youth is renewed like the eagle's.
6 The LORD executeth righteousness and
judgment for all that are oppressed.
7 He made known his ways unto Moses, his
acts unto the children of Israel.
8 The LORD is merciful and gracious, slow
to anger, and plenteous in mercy.
9 He will not always chide: neither will he
keep his anger for ever.
10 He hath not dealt with us after our sins;
nor rewarded us according to our iniquities.
11 For as the heaven is high above the earth, so
great is his mercy toward them that fear him.
12 As far as the east is from the west, so far
hath he removed our transgressions from us.
13 Like as a father pitieth his children, so the
LORD pitieth them that fear him.
14 For he knoweth our frame; he remembereth
that we are dust.
15 As for man, his days are as grass: as a
flower of the field, so he flourisheth.

[16]For the wind passeth over it, and it is gone; and the place
thereof shall know it no more.
[17]But the mercy of the LORD is from everlasting to
everlasting upon them that fear him, and his righteousness
unto children's children;
[18]To such as keep his covenant, and to those that remember
his commandments to do them.
[19]The LORD hath prepared his throne in the heavens; and
his kingdom ruleth over all.
[20]Bless the LORD, ye his angels, that excel in strength, that
do his commandments, hearkening unto the voice of
his word.
[21]Bless ye the LORD, all ye his hosts; ye ministers of his,
that do his pleasure.
[22]Bless the LORD, all his works in all places of his
dominion: bless the LORD, O my soul.

PSALM 104

Bless the LORD, O my soul. O LORD my God,
thou art very great; thou art clothed with honour
and majesty.
[2]Who coverest thyself with light as with a garment: who
stretchest out the heavens like a curtain:
[3]Who layeth the beams of his chambers in the waters: who
maketh the clouds his chariot: who walketh upon the wings
of the wind:
[4]Who maketh his angels spirits; his ministers a flaming fire:
[5]Who laid the foundations of the earth, that it should not
be removed for ever.

6 Thou coveredst it with the deep as with a garment: the
waters stood above the mountains.
7 At thy rebuke they fled; at the voice of thy thunder they
hasted away.
8 They go up by the mountains; they go down by the valleys
unto the place which thou hast founded for them.
9 Thou hast set a bound that they may not pass over; that
they turn not again to cover the earth.
10 He sendeth the springs into the valleys, which run among
the hills.
11 They give drink to every beast of the field: the wild asses
quench their thirst.
12 By them shall the fowls of the heaven have their
habitation, which sing among the branches.
13 He watereth the hills from his chambers: the earth is
satisfied with the fruit of thy works.
14 He causeth the grass to grow for the cattle, and herb for the
service of man: that he may bring forth food out of the earth;
15 And wine that maketh glad the heart of man, and oil to make
his face to shine, and bread which strengtheneth man's heart.
16 The trees of the LORD are full of sap; the cedars of
Lebanon, which he hath planted;
17 Where the birds make their nests: as for the stork, the fir
trees are her house.
18 The high hills are a refuge for the wild goats; and the
rocks for the conies.
19 He appointed the moon for seasons: the sun knoweth his
going down.
20 Thou makest darkness, and it is night: wherein all the
beasts of the forest do creep forth.
21 The young lions roar after their prey, and seek their meat
from God.

22 The sun ariseth, they gather themselves together, and lay
them down in their dens.
23 Man goeth forth unto his work and to his labour until the
evening.
24 O LORD, how manifold are thy works! in wisdom hast
thou made them all: the earth is full of thy riches.
25 So is this great and wide sea, wherein are things creeping
innumerable, both small and great beasts.
26 There go the ships: there is that leviathan, whom thou
hast made to play therein.
27 These wait all upon thee; that thou mayest give them
their meat in due season.
28 That thou givest them they gather: thou openest thine
hand, they are filled with good.
29 Thou hidest thy face, they are troubled: thou takest away
their breath, they die, and return to their dust.
30 Thou sendest forth thy spirit, they are created: and thou
renewest the face of the earth.
31 The glory of the LORD shall endure for ever: the LORD
shall rejoice in his works.
32 He looketh on the earth, and it trembleth: he toucheth
the hills, and they smoke.
33 I will sing unto the LORD as long as I live: I will sing
praise to my God while I have my being.
34 My meditation of him shall be sweet: I will be glad in the
LORD.
35 Let the sinners be consumed out of
the earth, and let the wicked be no
more. Bless thou the LORD,
O my soul. Praise ye the LORD.

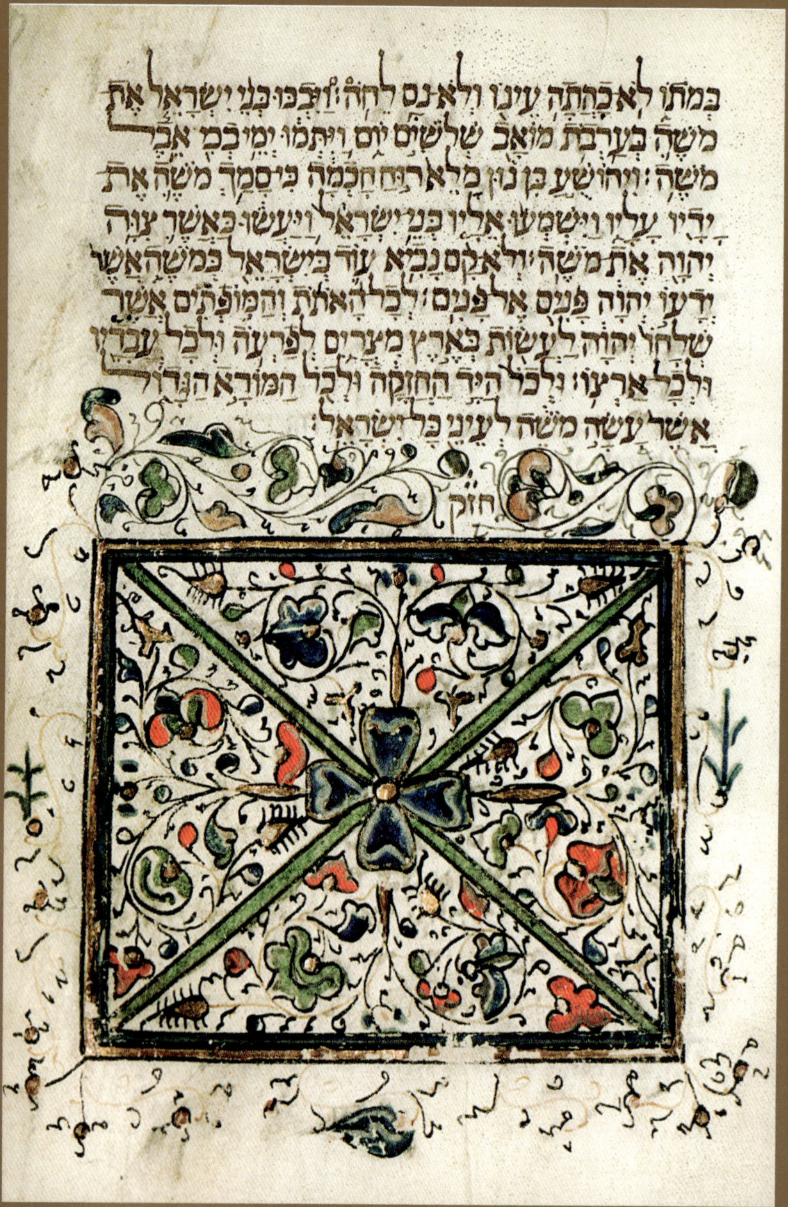
במתו לא כהתה עינו ולא נס לחה׃ ויבכו בני ישראל את
משה בערבת מואב שלשים יום ויתמו ימי בכי אבל
משה׃ ויהושע בן נון מלא רוח חכמה כי סמך משה את
ידיו עליו וישמעו אליו בני ישראל ויעשו כאשר צוה
יהוה את משה׃ ולא קם נביא עוד בישראל כמשה אשר
ידעו יהוה פנים אל פנים׃ לכל האתת והמופתים אשר
שלחו יהוה לעשות בארץ מצרים לפרעה ולכל עבדיו
ולכל ארצו׃ ולכל היד החזקה ולכל המורא הגדול
אשר עשה משה לעיני כל ישראל׃

חזק

PSALM 105

O give thanks unto the LORD; call upon his name:
make known his deeds among the people.
2 Sing unto him, sing psalms unto him: talk ye of all his
wondrous works.
3 Glory ye in his holy name: let the heart of them rejoice
that seek the LORD.
4 Seek the LORD, and his strength: seek his face evermore.
5 Remember his marvellous works that he hath done; his
wonders, and the judgments of his mouth;
6 O ye seed of Abraham his servant, ye children of Jacob his
chosen.
7 He is the LORD our God: his judgments are in all the earth.
8 He hath remembered his covenant for ever, the word
which he commanded to a thousand generations.
9 Which covenant he made with Abraham, and his oath
unto Isaac;
10 And confirmed the same unto Jacob for a law, and to
Israel for an everlasting covenant:
11 Saying, Unto thee will I give the land of Canaan, the lot of
your inheritance:
12 When they were but a few men in number; yea, very few,
and strangers in it.
13 When they went from one nation to another, from one
kingdom to another people;
14 He suffered no man to do them wrong: yea, he reproved
kings for their sakes;
15 Saying, Touch not mine anointed, and do my prophets no
harm.
16 Moreover he called for a famine upon the land: he brake
the whole staff of bread.

17 He sent a man before them, even Joseph, who was sold for
a servant:
18 Whose feet they hurt with fetters: he was laid in iron:
19 Until the time that his word came: the word of the
LORD tried him.
20 The king sent and loosed him; even the ruler of the
people, and let him go free.
21 He made him lord of his house, and ruler of all his
substance:
22 To bind his princes at his pleasure; and teach his senators
wisdom.
23 Israel also came into Egypt; and Jacob sojourned in the
land of Ham.
24 And he increased his people greatly; and made them
stronger than their enemies.
25 He turned their heart to hate his people, to deal subtilly
with his servants.
26 He sent Moses his servant; and Aaron whom he had chosen.
27 They shewed his signs among them, and wonders in the
land of Ham.
28 He sent darkness, and made it dark; and they rebelled not
against his word.
29 He turned their waters into blood, and slew their fish.
30 Their land brought forth frogs in abundance, in the
chambers of their kings.
31 He spake, and there came divers sorts of flies, and lice in
all their coasts.
32 He gave them hail for rain, and flaming fire in their land.
33 He smote their vines also and their fig trees; and brake the
trees of their coasts.
34 He spake, and the locusts came, and caterpillers, and that
without number,

35 And did eat up all the herbs in their land, and devoured
the fruit of their ground.
36 He smote also all the firstborn in their land, the chief of
all their strength.
37 He brought them forth also with silver and gold: and
there was not one feeble person among their tribes.
38 Egypt was glad when they departed: for the fear of them
fell upon them.
39 He spread a cloud for a covering; and fire to give light in
the night.
40 The people asked, and he brought quails, and satisfied
them with the bread of heaven.
41 He opened the rock, and the waters gushed out; they ran
in the dry places like a river.
42 For he remembered his holy promise, and Abraham his
servant.
43 And he brought forth his people with joy, and his chosen
with gladness:
44 And gave them the lands of the heathen: and they
inherited the labour of the people;
45 That they might observe his statutes, and keep his laws.
Praise ye the LORD.

PSALM 106

Praise ye the LORD. O give thanks unto the LORD;
for he is good: for his mercy endureth for ever.
2 Who can utter the mighty acts of the LORD? who can
shew forth all his praise?
3 Blessed are they that keep judgment, and he that doeth
righteousness at all times.
4 Remember me, O LORD, with the favour that thou
bearest unto thy people: O visit me with thy salvation;
5 That I may see the good of thy chosen, that I may rejoice in the
gladness of thy nation, that I may glory with thine inheritance.
6 We have sinned with our fathers, we have committed
iniquity, we have done wickedly.
7 Our fathers understood not thy wonders in Egypt; they
remembered not the multitude of thy mercies; but provoked
him at the sea, even at the Red sea.
8 Nevertheless he saved them for his name's sake, that he
might make his mighty power to be known.
9 He rebuked the Red sea also, and it was dried up: so he led
them through the depths, as through the wilderness.
10 And he saved them from the hand of him that hated
them, and redeemed them from the hand of the enemy.
11 And the waters covered their enemies: there was not one
of them left.
12 Then believed they his words; they sang his praise.
13 They soon forgat his works; they waited not for his counsel:
14 But lusted exceedingly in the wilderness, and tempted
God in the desert.
15 And he gave them their request; but sent leanness into their soul.
16 They envied Moses also in the camp, and Aaron the saint
of the LORD.

17 The earth opened and swallowed up Dathan, and covered
the company of Abiram.
18 And a fire was kindled in their company; the flame burned
up the wicked.
19 They made a calf in Horeb, and worshipped the molten image.
20 Thus they changed their glory into the similitude of an ox
that eateth grass.
21 They forgat God their saviour, which had done great
things in Egypt;
22 Wondrous works in the land of Ham, and terrible things
by the Red sea.
23 Therefore he said that he would destroy them, had not
Moses his chosen stood before him in the breach, to turn
away his wrath, lest he should destroy them.
24 Yea, they despised the pleasant land, they believed not
his word:
25 But murmured in their tents, and hearkened not unto the
voice of the LORD.
26 Therefore he lifted up his hand against them, to
overthrow them in the wilderness:
27 To overthrow their seed also among the nations, and to
scatter them in the lands.
28 They joined themselves also unto Baal-peor, and ate the
sacrifices of the dead.
29 Thus they provoked him to anger with their inventions:
and the plague brake in upon them.
30 Then stood up Phinehas, and executed judgment: and so
the plague was stayed.
31 And that was counted unto him for righteousness unto all
generations for evermore.
32 They angered him also at the waters of strife, so that it
went ill with Moses for their sakes:

33 Because they provoked his spirit, so that he spake
unadvisedly with his lips.
34 They did not destroy the nations, concerning whom the
LORD commanded them:
35 But were mingled among the heathen, and learned their
works.
36 And they served their idols: which were a snare unto them.
37 Yea, they sacrificed their sons and their daughters unto devils,
38 And shed innocent blood, even the blood of their sons
and of their daughters, whom they sacrificed unto the idols
of Canaan: and the land was polluted with blood.
39 Thus were they defiled with their own works, and went a
whoring with their own inventions.
40 Therefore was the wrath of the LORD kindled against
his people, insomuch that he abhorred his own inheritance.
41 And he gave them into the hand of the heathen; and they
that hated them ruled over them.
42 Their enemies also oppressed them, and they were
brought into subjection under their hand.
43 Many times did he deliver them; but they provoked him
with their counsel, and were brought low for their iniquity.
44 Nevertheless he regarded their affliction, when he heard
their cry:
45 And he remembered for them his covenant, and repented
according to the multitude of his mercies.
46 He made them also to be pitied of all those that carried
them captives.
47 Save us, O LORD our God, and gather us from among
the heathen, to give thanks unto thy holy name, and to
triumph in thy praise.
48 Blessed be the LORD God of Israel from everlasting to
everlasting: and let all the people say, Amen. Praise ye the LORD.

BOOK V

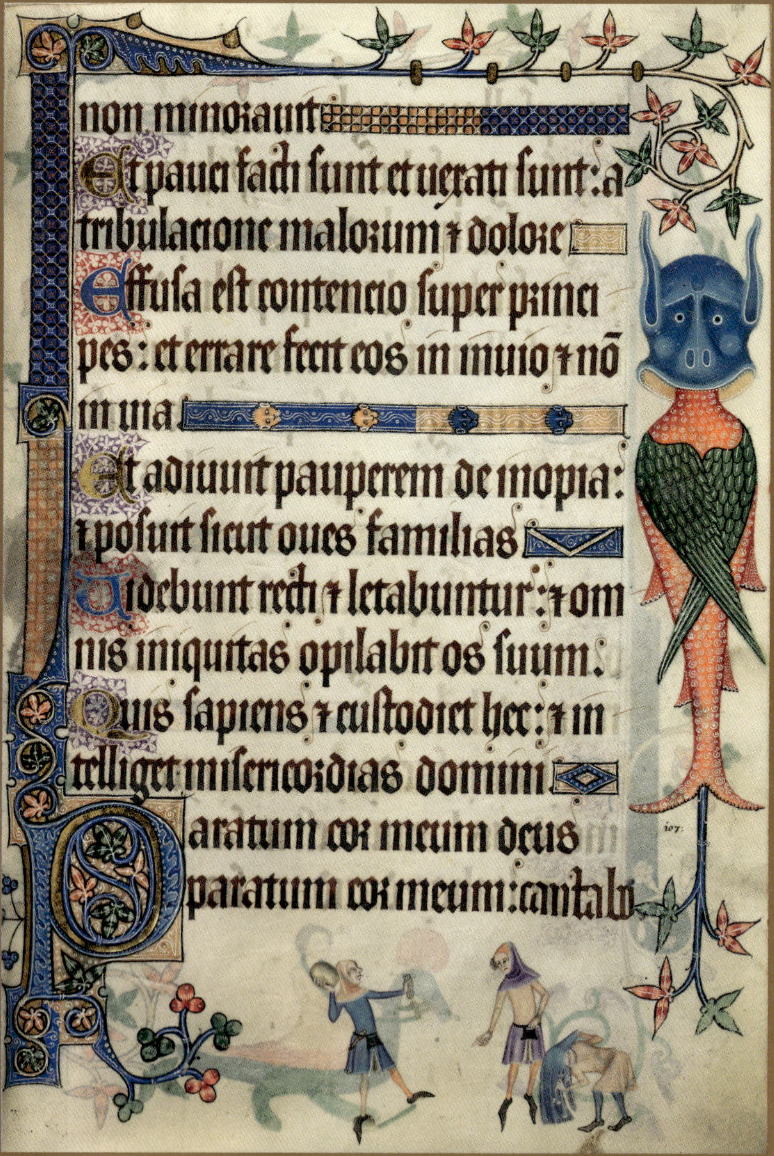
non minorauit
Et pauci facti sunt et uexati sunt: a
tribulacione malorum ⁊ dolore
Effusa est contencio super princi
pes: et errare fecit eos in inuio ⁊ nō
in uia
Et adiuuit pauperem de inopia:
⁊ posuit sicut oues familias
Videbunt recti ⁊ letabuntur: ⁊ om
nis iniquitas oppilabit os suum.
Quis sapiens ⁊ custodiet hec: ⁊ in
telliget misericordias domini
Paratum cor meum deus
paratum cor meum: cantabo

Luttrell Psalter, England, Psalm 107, ca. 1325–1335

PSALM 107

O give thanks unto the LORD, for he is good: for his
mercy endureth for ever.
2 Let the redeemed of the LORD say so, whom he hath
redeemed from the hand of the enemy;
3 And gathered them out of the lands, from the east, and
from the west, from the north, and from the south.
4 They wandered in the wilderness in a solitary way; they
found no city to dwell in.
5 Hungry and thirsty, their soul fainted in them.
6 Then they cried unto the LORD in their trouble, and he
delivered them out of their distresses.
7 And he led them forth by the right way, that they might go
to a city of habitation.
8 Oh that men would praise the LORD for his goodness,
and for his wonderful works to the children of men!
9 For he satisfieth the longing soul, and filleth the hungry
soul with goodness.
10 Such as sit in darkness and in the shadow of death, being
bound in affliction and iron;
11 Because they rebelled against the words of God, and
contemned the counsel of the most High:
12 Therefore he brought down their heart with labour; they
fell down, and there was none to help.
13 Then they cried unto the LORD in their trouble, and he
saved them out of their distresses.
14 He brought them out of darkness and the shadow of
death, and brake their bands in sunder.
15 Oh that men would praise the LORD for his goodness,
and for his wonderful works to the children of men!

16 For he hath broken the gates of brass, and cut the bars of
iron in sunder.
17 Fools because of their transgression, and because of their
iniquities, are afflicted.
18 Their soul abhorreth all manner of meat; and they draw
near unto the gates of death.
19 Then they cry unto the LORD in their trouble, and he
saveth them out of their distresses.
20 He sent his word, and healed them, and delivered them
from their destructions.
21 Oh that men would praise the LORD for his goodness,
and for his wonderful works to the children of men!
22 And let them sacrifice the sacrifices of thanksgiving, and
declare his works with rejoicing.
23 They that go down to the sea in ships, that do business in
great waters;
24 These see the works of the LORD, and his wonders in
the deep.
25 For he commandeth, and raiseth the stormy wind, which
lifteth up the waves thereof.
26 They mount up to the heaven, they go down again to the
depths: their soul is melted because of trouble.
27 They reel to and fro, and stagger like a drunken man, and
are at their wit's end.
28 Then they cry unto the LORD in their trouble, and he
bringeth them out of their distresses.
29 He maketh the storm a calm, so that the waves thereof
are still.
30 Then are they glad because they be quiet; so he bringeth
them unto their desired haven.
31 Oh that men would praise the LORD for his goodness,
and for his wonderful works to the children of men!

32 Let them exalt him also in the congregation of the people,
and praise him in the assembly of the elders.
33 He turneth rivers into a wilderness, and the watersprings
into dry ground;
34 A fruitful land into barrenness, for the wickedness of
them that dwell therein.
35 He turneth the wilderness into a standing water, and dry
ground into watersprings.
36 And there he maketh the hungry to dwell, that they may
prepare a city for habitation;
37 And sow the fields, and plant vineyards, which may yield
fruits of increase.
38 He blesseth them also, so that they are multiplied greatly;
and suffereth not their cattle to decrease.
39 Again, they are minished and brought low through
oppression, affliction, and sorrow.
40 He poureth contempt upon princes, and causeth them to
wander in the wilderness, where there is no way.
41 Yet setteth he the poor on high from affliction, and
maketh him families like a flock.
42 The righteous shall see it, and rejoice: and all iniquity
shall stop her mouth.
43 Whoso is wise, and will observe these things, even they
shall understand the lovingkindness of the LORD.

PSALM 108

A Song or Psalm of David.

O God, my heart is fixed; I will sing and give praise,
even with my glory.
2 Awake, psaltery and harp: I myself will awake early.
3 I will praise thee, O LORD, among the people: and I will
sing praises unto thee among the nations.
4 For thy mercy is great above the heavens: and thy truth
reacheth unto the clouds.
5 Be thou exalted, O God, above the heavens: and thy glory
above all the earth;
6 That thy beloved may be delivered: save with thy right
hand, and answer me.
7 God hath spoken in his holiness; I will rejoice, I will divide
Shechem, and mete out the valley of Succoth.
8 Gilead is mine; Manasseh is mine; Ephraim also is the
strength of mine head; Judah is my lawgiver;
9 Moab is my washpot; over Edom will I cast out my shoe;
over Philistia will I triumph.
10 Who will bring me into the strong city? who will lead me
into Edom?
11 Wilt not thou, O God, who hast cast us off? and wilt not
thou, O God, go forth with our hosts?
12 Give us help from trouble: for vain is the help of man.
13 Through God we shall do valiantly: for he it is that shall
tread down our enemies.

PSALM 109

To the chief Musician, A Psalm of David.

Hold not thy peace, O God of my praise;
2 For the mouth of the wicked and the mouth of the
deceitful are opened against me: they have spoken against me
with a lying tongue.
3 They compassed me about also with words of hatred; and
fought against me without a cause.
4 For my love they are my adversaries: but I give myself unto
prayer.
5 And they have rewarded me evil for good, and hatred for
my love.
6 Set thou a wicked man over him: and let Satan stand at his
right hand.
7 When he shall be judged, let him be condemned: and let
his prayer become sin.
8 Let his days be few; and let another take his office.
9 Let his children be fatherless, and his wife a widow.
10 Let his children be continually vagabonds, and beg: let
them seek their bread also out of their desolate places.
11 Let the extortioner catch all that he hath; and let the
strangers spoil his labour.
12 Let there be none to extend mercy unto him: neither let
there be any to favour his fatherless children.
13 Let his posterity be cut off; and in the generation
following let their name be blotted out.
14 Let the iniquity of his fathers be remembered with the
LORD; and let not the sin of his mother be blotted out.
15 Let them be before the LORD continually, that he may
cut off the memory of them from the earth.

16 Because that he remembered not to shew mercy, but
persecuted the poor and needy man, that he might even slay
the broken in heart.
17 As he loved cursing, so let it come unto him: as he
delighted not in blessing, so let it be far from him.
18 As he clothed himself with cursing like as with his garment, so
let it come into his bowels like water, and like oil into his bones.
19 Let it be unto him as the garment which covereth him,
and for a girdle wherewith he is girded continually.
20 Let this be the reward of mine adversaries from the
LORD, and of them that speak evil against my soul.
21 But do thou for me, O God the LORD, for thy name's
sake: because thy mercy is good, deliver thou me.
22 For I am poor and needy, and my heart is wounded within me.
23 I am gone like the shadow when it declineth: I am tossed
up and down as the locust.
24 My knees are weak through fasting; and my flesh faileth of
fatness.
25 I became also a reproach unto them: when they looked
upon me they shaked their heads.
26 Help me, O LORD my God: O save me according to thy
mercy:
27 That they may know that this is thy hand; that thou,
LORD, hast done it.
28 Let them curse, but bless thou: when they arise, let them
be ashamed; but let thy servant rejoice.
29 Let mine adversaries be clothed with shame, and let them
cover themselves with their own confusion, as with a mantle.
30 I will greatly praise the LORD with my mouth; yea, I will
praise him among the multitude.
31 For he shall stand at the right hand of the poor, to save
him from those that condemn his soul.

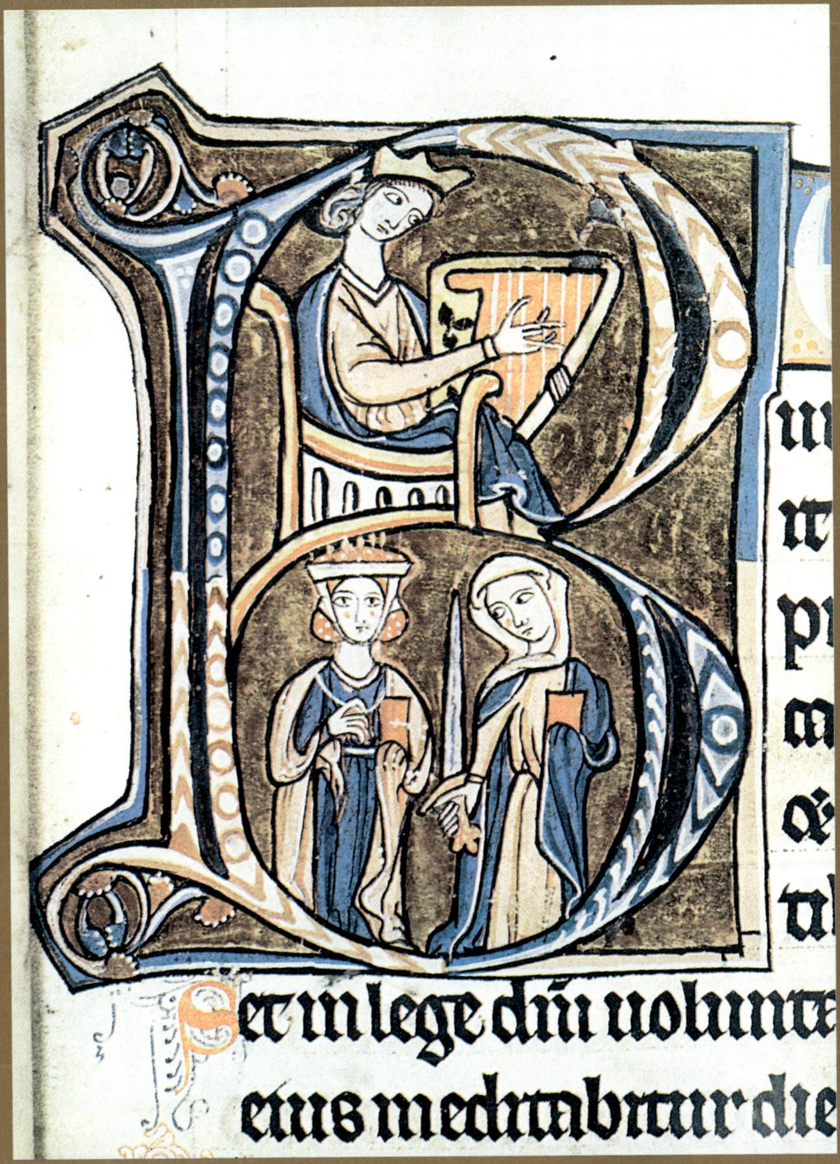

Miniature Gothic Psalter, Psalm 13, 13th century

PSALM 110

The LORD said unto my LORD, Sit thou at my right hand, until I make thine enemies thy footstool.
2 The LORD shall send the rod of thy strength out of Zion: rule thou in the midst of thine enemies.
3 Thy people shall be willing in the day of thy power, in the beauties of holiness from the womb of the morning: thou hast the dew of thy youth.
4 The LORD hath sworn, and will not repent, Thou art a priest for ever after the order of Melchizedek.
5 The LORD at thy right hand shall strike through kings in the day of his wrath.
6 He shall judge among the heathen, he shall fill the places with the dead bodies; he shall wound the heads over many countries.
7 He shall drink of the brook in the way: therefore shall he lift up the head.

PSALM 111

Praise ye the LORD. I will praise the LORD with my whole heart, in the assembly of the upright, and in the congregation.
2 The works of the LORD are great, sought out of all them that have pleasure therein.
3 His work is honourable and glorious: and his righteousness endureth for ever.
4 He hath made his wonderful works to be remembered: the LORD is gracious and full of compassion.

5 He hath given meat unto them that fear him: he will ever
be mindful of his covenant.
6 He hath shewed his people the power of his works, that he
may give them the heritage of the heathen.
7 The works of his hands are verity and judgment; all his
commandments are sure.
8 They stand fast for ever and ever, and are done in truth
and uprightness.
9 He sent redemption unto his people: he hath commanded
his covenant for ever: holy and reverend is his name.
10 The fear of the LORD is the beginning of wisdom: a good
understanding have all they that do his commandments: his
praise endureth for ever.

PSALM 112

Praise ye the LORD. Blessed is the man
that feareth the LORD, that delighteth
greatly in his commandments.
2 His seed shall be mighty upon earth: the
generation of the upright shall be blessed.
3 Wealth and riches shall be in his house:
and his righteousness endureth for ever.
4 Unto the upright there ariseth light in
the darkness: he is gracious, and full of
compassion, and righteous.
5 A good man sheweth favour, and lendeth:
he will guide his affairs with discretion.
6 Surely he shall not be moved for ever: the
righteous shall be in everlasting remembrance.

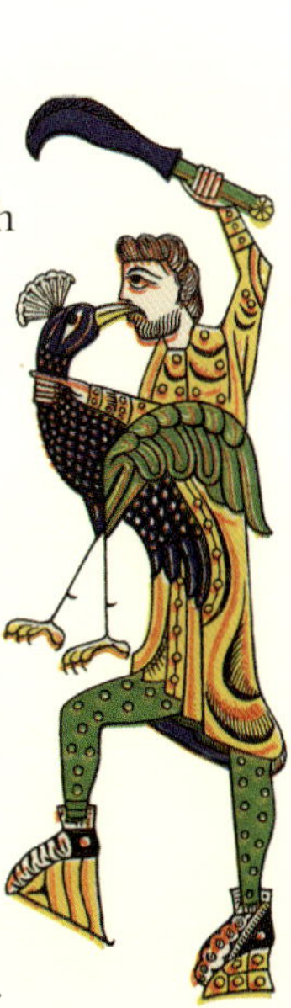

7 He shall not be afraid of evil tidings: his heart
is fixed, trusting in the LORD.
8 His heart is established, he shall not be afraid,
until he see his desire upon his enemies.
9 He hath dispersed, he hath given to the poor; his
righteousness endureth for ever; his horn shall be exalted
with honour.
10 The wicked shall see it, and be grieved; he shall gnash with
his teeth, and melt away: the desire of the wicked shall perish.

PSALM 113

Praise ye the LORD. Praise, O ye servants of the
LORD, praise the name of the LORD.
2 Blessed be the name of the LORD from this time forth
and for evermore.
3 From the rising of the sun unto the going down of the
same the LORD'S name is to be praised.
4 The LORD is high above all nations, and his glory above
the heavens.
5 Who is like unto the LORD our God, who dwelleth on high,
6 Who humbleth himself to behold the things that are in
heaven, and in the earth!
7 He raiseth up the poor out of the dust, and lifteth the
needy out of the dunghill;
8 That he may set him with princes, even with the princes of
his people.
9 He maketh the barren woman to keep house, and to be a
joyful mother of children. Praise ye the LORD.

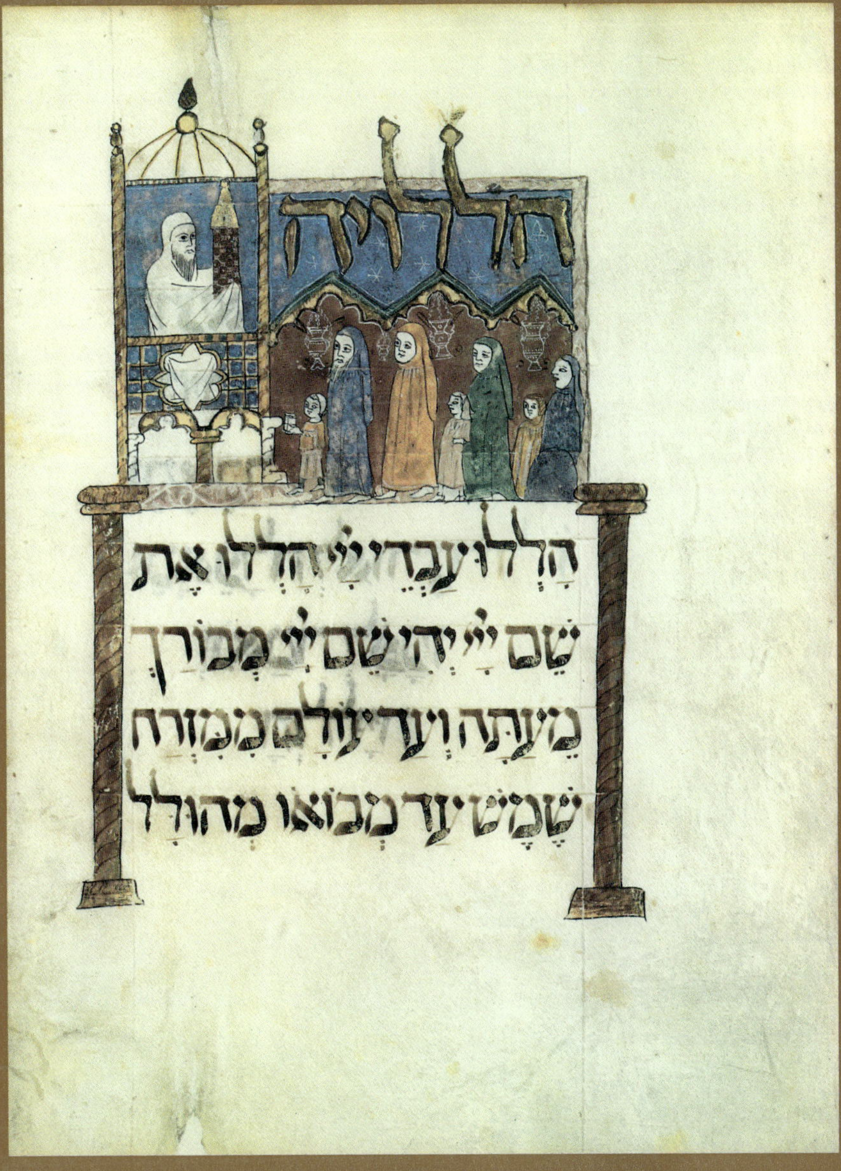

Barcelona Haggadah, Catalonia, Psalm 13, 14th century

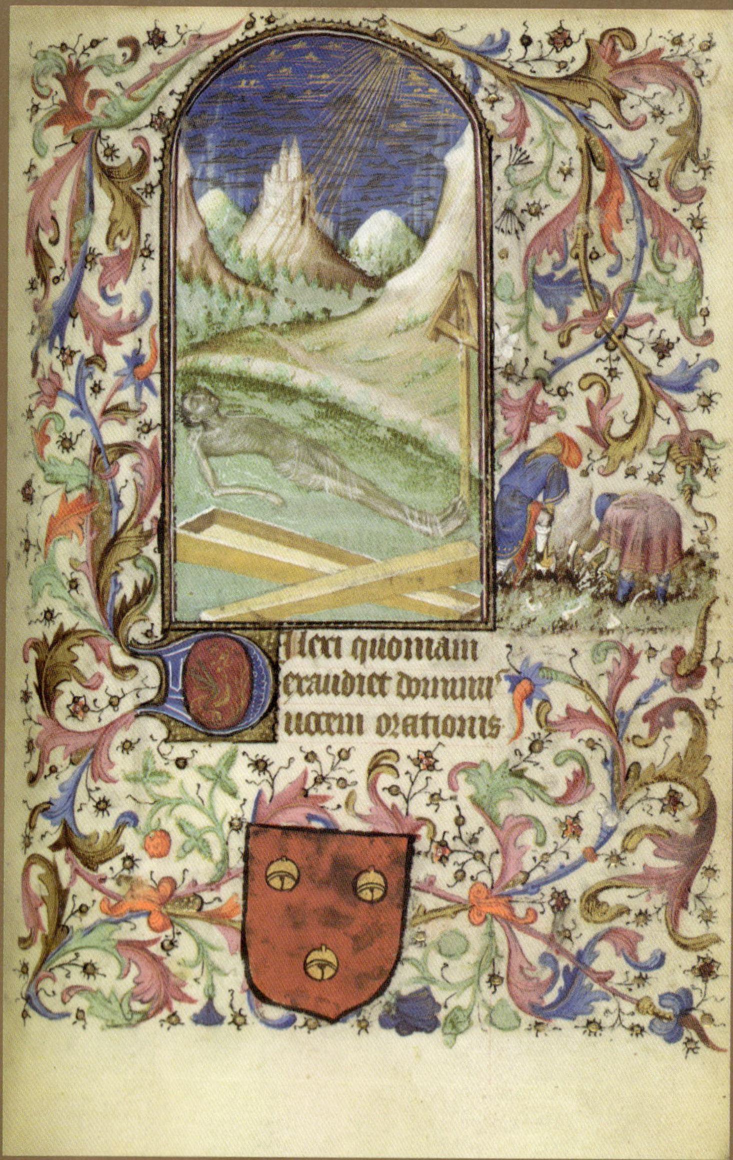

Book of Hours, France, Psalm 114, 1410

PSALM 114

When Israel went out of Egypt, the house of Jacob
from a people of strange language;
2Judah was his sanctuary, and Israel his dominion.
3The sea saw it, and fled: Jordan was driven back.
4The mountains skipped like rams, and the little hills
like lambs.
5What ailed thee, O thou sea, that thou fleddest? thou
Jordan, that thou wast driven back?
6Ye mountains, that ye skipped like rams; and ye little hills,
like lambs?
7Tremble, thou earth, at the presence of the
LORD, at the presence of the God of Jacob;
8Which turned the rock into a standing
water, the flint into a fountain of waters.

PSALM 115

Not unto us, O LORD, not unto us, but unto thy name
give glory, for thy mercy, and for thy truth's sake.
2Wherefore should the heathen say, Where is now their God?
3But our God is in the heavens: he hath done whatsoever he
hath pleased.
4Their idols are silver and gold, the work of men's hands.
5They have mouths, but they speak not: eyes have they, but
they see not:
6They have ears, but they hear not: noses have they, but
they smell not:
7They have hands, but they handle not: feet have they, but

they walk not: neither speak they through their throat.
8 They that make them are like unto them; so is every one
that trusteth in them.
9 O Israel, trust thou in the LORD: he is their help and
their shield.
10 O house of Aaron, trust in the LORD: he is their help
and their shield.
11 Ye that fear the LORD, trust in the LORD: he is their
help and their shield.
12 The LORD hath been mindful of us: he will bless us; he
will bless the house of Israel; he will bless the house of Aaron.
13 He will bless them that fear the LORD, both small and great.
14 The LORD shall increase you more and more, you and
your children.
15 Ye are blessed of the LORD which made heaven and earth.
16 The heaven, even the heavens, are the LORD'S: but the
earth hath he given to the children of men.
17 The dead praise not the LORD, neither any that go down
into silence.
18 But we will bless the LORD from this time forth and for
evermore. Praise the LORD.

PSALM 116

I love the LORD, because he hath heard my voice and
my supplications.
2 Because he hath inclined his ear unto me, therefore will I
call upon him as long as I live.
3 The sorrows of death compassed me, and the pains of hell
gat hold upon me: I found trouble and sorrow.

4 Then called I upon the name of the LORD; O LORD, I
beseech thee, deliver my soul.
5 Gracious is the LORD, and righteous; yea, our God is
merciful.
6 The LORD preserveth the simple: I was brought low, and
he helped me.
7 Return unto thy rest, O my soul; for the LORD hath dealt
bountifully with thee.
8 For thou hast delivered my soul from death, mine eyes
from tears, and my feet from falling.
9 I will walk before the LORD in the land of the living.
10 I believed, therefore have I spoken: I was greatly afflicted:
11 I said in my haste, All men are liars.
12 What shall I render unto the LORD for all his benefits
toward me?
13 I will take the cup of salvation, and call upon the name of
the LORD.
14 I will pay my vows unto the LORD now in the presence
of all his people.
15 Precious in the sight of the LORD is the death of his saints.
16 O LORD, truly I am thy servant; I am thy servant, and
the son of thine handmaid: thou hast loosed my bonds.
17 I will offer to thee the sacrifice of thanksgiving, and will
call upon the name of the LORD.
18 I will pay my vows unto the LORD
now in the presence of all his people,
19 In the courts of the LORD'S house,
in the midst of thee, O Jerusalem.
Praise ye the LORD.

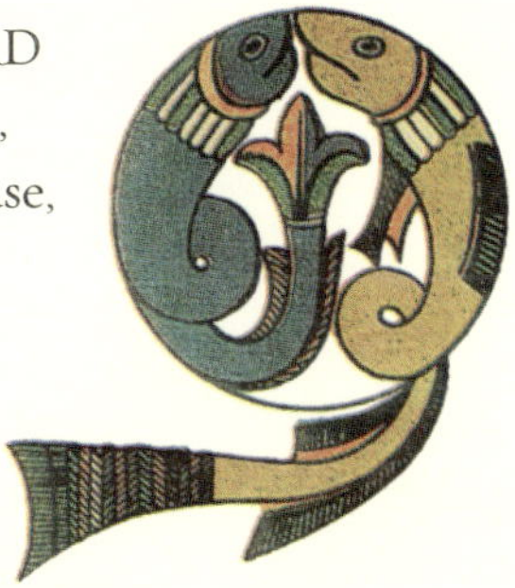

PSALM 117

O praise the LORD, all ye nations: praise him, all ye people.
2 For his merciful kindness is great toward us: and the
truth of the LORD endureth for ever. Praise ye the LORD.

PSALM 118

O give thanks unto the LORD; for he is good: because
his mercy endureth for ever.
2 Let Israel now say, that his mercy endureth for ever.
3 Let the house of Aaron now say, that his mercy endureth
for ever.
4 Let them now that fear the LORD say, that his mercy
endureth for ever.
5 I called upon the LORD in distress: the LORD answered
me, and set me in a large place.
6 The LORD is on my side; I will not fear: what can man do
unto me?
7 The LORD taketh my part with them that help me:
therefore shall I see my desire upon them that hate me.
8 It is better to trust in the LORD than to put confidence in
man.
9 It is better to trust in the LORD than to put confidence in
princes.
10 All nations compassed me about: but in the name of the
LORD will I destroy them.
11 They compassed me about; yea, they compassed me about:
but in the name of the LORD I will destroy them.
12 They compassed me about like bees; they are quenched as

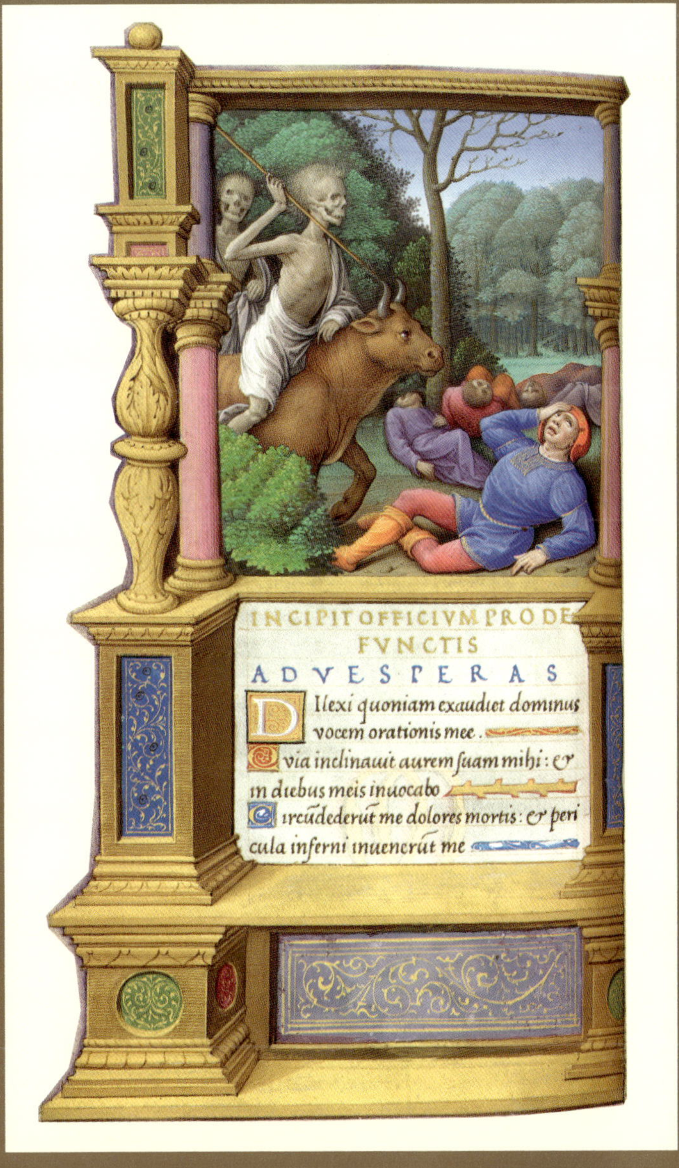

Book of Hours, France, Psalm 114, 16th century

the fire of thorns: for in the name of the LORD
I will destroy them.
13 Thou hast thrust sore at me that I might fall:
but the LORD helped me.
14 The LORD is my strength and song, and is
become my salvation.
15 The voice of rejoicing and salvation is in the
tabernacles of the righteous: the right hand of the
LORD doeth valiantly.
16 The right hand of the LORD is exalted: the
right hand of the LORD doeth valiantly.
17 I shall not die, but live, and declare the works of
the LORD.
18 The LORD hath chastened me sore: but
he hath not given me over unto death.
19 Open to me the gates of righteousness:
I will go into them, and I will praise the LORD:
20 This gate of the LORD, into which the righteous shall
enter.
21 I will praise thee: for thou hast heard me, and art become
my salvation.
22 The stone which the builders refused is become the head
stone of the corner.
23 This is the LORD'S doing; it is marvellous in our eyes.
24 This is the day which the LORD hath made; we will
rejoice and be glad in it.
25 Save now, I beseech thee, O LORD: O LORD, I beseech
thee, send now prosperity.
26 Blessed be he that cometh in the name of the LORD: we
have blessed you out of the house of the LORD.
27 God is the LORD, which hath shewed us light: bind the
sacrifice with cords, even unto the horns of the altar.

[28]Thou art my God, and I will praise thee: thou art my
God, I will exalt thee.
[29]O give thanks unto the LORD; for he is good: for his
mercy endureth for ever.

PSALM 119

ALEPH.

[1]Blessed are the undefiled in the way, who walk in the law of
the LORD.
[2]Blessed are they that keep his testimonies, and that seek
him with the whole heart.
[3]They also do no iniquity: they walk in his ways.
[4]Thou hast commanded us to keep thy precepts diligently.
[5]O that my ways were directed to keep thy statutes!
[6]Then shall I not be ashamed, when I have respect unto all
thy commandments.
[7]I will praise thee with uprightness of heart, when I shall
have learned thy righteous judgments.
[8]I will keep thy statutes: O forsake me not utterly.

BETH.

[9]Wherewithal shall a young man cleanse his way? by taking
heed thereto according to thy word.
[10]With my whole heart have I sought thee: O let me not
wander from thy commandments.
[11]Thy word have I hid in mine heart, that I might not sin
against thee.
[12]Blessed art thou, O LORD: teach me thy statutes.
[13]With my lips have I declared all the judgments of thy mouth.

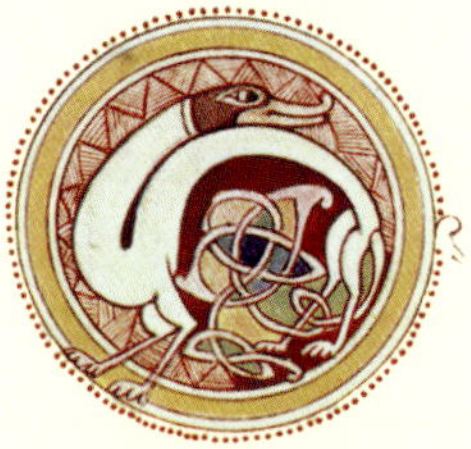

14 I have rejoiced in the way of thy
testimonies, as much as in all riches.
15 I will meditate in thy precepts,
and have respect unto thy ways.
16 I will delight myself in thy statutes:
I will not forget thy word.

GIMEL.

17 Deal bountifully with thy servant, that I may live, and
keep thy word.
18 Open thou mine eyes, that I may behold wondrous things
out of thy law.
19 I am a stranger in the earth: hide not thy commandments
from me.
20 My soul breaketh for the longing that it hath unto thy
judgments at all times.
21 Thou hast rebuked the proud that are cursed, which do
err from thy commandments.
22 Remove from me reproach and contempt; for I have kept
thy testimonies.
23 Princes also did sit and speak against me: but thy servant
did meditate in thy statutes.
24 Thy testimonies also are my delight and my counsellors.

DALETH.

25 My soul cleaveth unto the dust: quicken thou me
according to thy word.
26 I have declared my ways, and thou heardest me: teach me
thy statutes.
27 Make me to understand the way of thy precepts: so shall I
talk of thy wondrous works.
28 My soul melteth for heaviness: strengthen thou me

according unto thy word.
29 Remove from me the way of lying: and grant me thy law
graciously.
30 I have chosen the way of truth: thy judgments have I laid
before me.
31 I have stuck unto thy testimonies: O LORD, put me not
to shame.
32 I will run the way of thy commandments, when thou shalt
enlarge my heart.

HE.

33 Teach me, O LORD, the way of thy statutes; and I shall
keep it unto the end.
34 Give me understanding, and I shall keep thy law; yea, I
shall observe it with my whole heart.
35 Make me to go in the path of thy commandments; for
therein do I delight.
36 Incline my heart unto thy testimonies, and not to
covetousness.
37 Turn away mine eyes from beholding vanity; and quicken
thou me in thy way.
38 Stablish thy word unto thy servant, who is devoted to thy fear.
39 Turn away my reproach which I fear: for thy judgments
are good.
40 Behold, I have longed after thy precepts: quicken me in
thy righteousness.

VAU.

41 Let thy mercies come also unto
me, O LORD, even thy salvation,
according to thy word.
42 So shall I have wherewith to

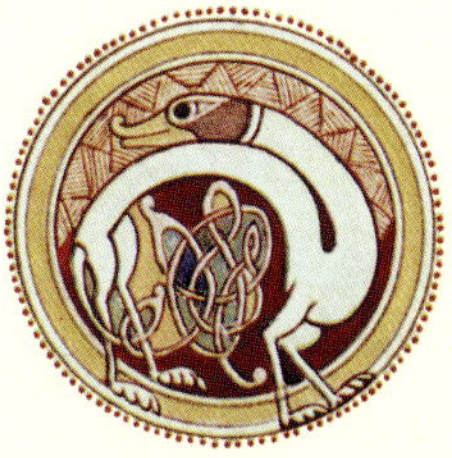

answer him that reproacheth me: for I trust in thy word.
43 And take not the word of truth utterly out of my mouth;
for I have hoped in thy judgments.
44 So shall I keep thy law continually for ever and ever.
45 And I will walk at liberty: for I seek thy precepts.
46 I will speak of thy testimonies also before kings, and will
not be ashamed.
47 And I will delight myself in thy commandments, which I
have loved.
48 My hands also will I lift up unto thy commandments,
which I have loved; and I will meditate in thy statutes.

ZAIN.

49 Remember the word unto thy servant, upon which thou
hast caused me to hope.
50 This is my comfort in my affliction: for thy word hath
quickened me.
51 The proud have had me greatly in derision: yet have I not
declined from thy law.
52 I remembered thy judgments of old, O LORD; and have
comforted myself.
53 Horror hath taken hold upon me because of the wicked
that forsake thy law.
54 Thy statutes have been my songs in the house of my
pilgrimage.
55 I have remembered thy name, O LORD, in the night, and
have kept thy law.
56 This I had, because I kept thy precepts.

CHETH.

57 Thou art my portion, O LORD: I have said that I would
keep thy words.

58 I intreated thy favour with my whole heart: be merciful
unto me according to thy word.
59 I thought on my ways, and turned my feet unto thy
testimonies.
60 I made haste, and delayed not to keep thy
commandments.
61 The bands of the wicked have robbed me: but I have not
forgotten thy law.
62 At midnight I will rise to give thanks unto thee because of
thy righteous judgments.
63 I am a companion of all them that fear thee, and of them
that keep thy precepts.
64 The earth, O LORD, is full of thy mercy: teach me thy
statutes.

TETH.

65 Thou hast dealt well with thy servant, O LORD,
according unto thy word.
66 Teach me good judgment and knowledge: for I have
believed thy commandments.
67 Before I was afflicted I went astray: but now have I kept
thy word.
68 Thou art good, and doest good; teach me thy statutes.
69 The proud have forged a lie against me: but I will keep
thy precepts with my whole heart.
70 Their heart is as fat as grease; but I
delight in thy law.
71 It is good for me that I have been
afflicted; that I might learn thy statutes.
72 The law of thy mouth is better unto
me than thousands of gold and silver.

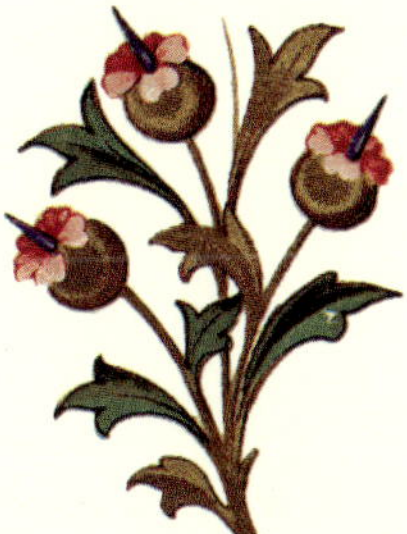

JOD.

73 Thy hands have made me and fashioned me: give me
understanding, that I may learn thy commandments.
74 They that fear thee will be glad when they see me; because
I have hoped in thy word.
75 I know, O LORD, that thy judgments are right, and that
thou in faithfulness hast afflicted me.
76 Let, I pray thee, thy merciful kindness be for my comfort,
according to thy word unto thy servant.
77 Let thy tender mercies come unto me, that I may live: for
thy law is my delight.
78 Let the proud be ashamed; for they dealt perversely with
me without a cause: but I will meditate in thy precepts.
79 Let those that fear thee turn unto me, and those that have
known thy testimonies.
80 Let my heart be sound in thy statutes; that I be not ashamed.

CAPH.

81 My soul fainteth for thy salvation: but I hope in thy word.
82 Mine eyes fail for thy word, saying, When wilt thou
comfort me?
83 For I am become like a bottle in the smoke; yet do I not
forget thy statutes.
84 How many are the days of thy servant? when wilt thou
execute judgment on them that persecute me?
85 The proud have digged pits for me, which are not after thy law.
86 All thy commandments are faithful: they
persecute me wrongfully; help thou me.
87 They had almost consumed me upon
earth; but I forsook not thy precepts.
88 Quicken me after thy lovingkindness;
so shall I keep the testimony of thy mouth.

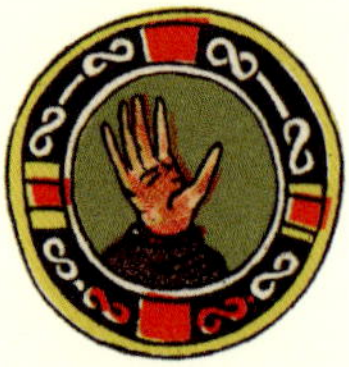

LAMED.

89 For ever, O LORD, thy word is settled in heaven.
90 Thy faithfulness is unto all generations: thou hast
established the earth, and it abideth.
91 They continue this day according to thine ordinances: for
all are thy servants.
92 Unless thy law had been my delights, I should then have
perished in mine affliction.
93 I will never forget thy precepts: for with them thou hast
quickened me.
94 I am thine, save me; for I have sought thy precepts.
95 The wicked have waited for me to destroy me: but I will
consider thy testimonies.
96 I have seen an end of all perfection: but thy
commandment is exceeding broad.

MEM.

97 O how love I thy law! it is my meditation all the day.
98 Thou through thy commandments hast made me wiser
than mine enemies: for they are ever with me.
99 I have more understanding than all my teachers: for thy
testimonies are my meditation.
100 I understand more than the ancients, because I keep thy
precepts.
101 I have refrained my feet from every evil way, that I might
keep thy word.
102 I have not departed from thy judgments: for thou hast
taught me.
103 How sweet are thy words unto my taste! yea, sweeter
than honey to my mouth!
104 Through thy precepts I get understanding: therefore I
hate every false way.

NUN.

105 Thy word is a lamp unto my feet, and a light unto my path.
106 I have sworn, and I will perform it, that I will keep thy
righteous judgments.
107 I am afflicted very much: quicken me, O LORD,
according unto thy word.
108 Accept, I beseech thee, the freewill offerings of my
mouth, O LORD, and teach me thy judgments.
109 My soul is continually in my hand: yet do I not forget thy law.
110 The wicked have laid a snare for me: yet I erred not from
thy precepts.
111 Thy testimonies have I taken as an heritage for ever: for
they are the rejoicing of my heart.
112 I have inclined mine heart to perform thy statutes alway,
even unto the end.

SAMECH.

113 I hate vain thoughts: but thy law do I love.
114 Thou art my hiding place and my shield: I hope in thy word.
115 Depart from me, ye evildoers: for I will keep the
commandments of my God.
116 Uphold me according unto thy word, that I may live: and
let me not be ashamed of my hope.
117 Hold thou me up, and I shall be safe: and I will have
respect unto thy statutes continually.
118 Thou hast trodden down all them that err from thy
statutes: for their deceit is falsehood.
119 Thou puttest away all the wicked of the earth like dross:
therefore I love thy testimonies.
120 My flesh trembleth for fear of thee; and I am afraid of
thy judgments.

AIN.

[121]I have done judgment and justice:
leave me not to mine oppressors.
[122]Be surety for thy servant for good: let not
the proud oppress me.
[123]Mine eyes fail for thy salvation, and for the word of thy
righteousness.
[124]Deal with thy servant according unto thy mercy, and
teach me thy statutes.
[125]I am thy servant; give me understanding, that I may
know thy testimonies.
[126]It is time for thee, LORD, to work: for they have made
void thy law.
[127]Therefore I love thy commandments above gold; yea,
above fine gold.
[128]Therefore I esteem all thy precepts concerning all things
to be right; and I hate every false way.

PE.

[129]Thy testimonies are wonderful: therefore doth my soul
keep them.
[130]The entrance of thy words giveth light; it giveth
understanding unto the simple.
[131]I opened my mouth, and panted: for I longed for thy
commandments.
[132]Look thou upon me, and be merciful unto me, as thou
usest to do unto those that love thy name.
[133]Order my steps in thy word: and let not any iniquity have
dominion over me.
[134]Deliver me from the oppression of man: so will I keep
thy precepts.
[135]Make thy face to shine upon thy servant; and teach me

thy statutes.

136 Rivers of waters run down mine
eyes, because they keep not thy law.

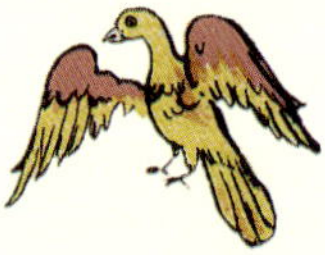

TZADDE.

137 Righteous art thou, O LORD, and upright are thy judgments.
138 Thy testimonies that thou hast commanded are righteous
and very faithful.
139 My zeal hath consumed me, because mine enemies have
forgotten thy words.
140 Thy word is very pure: therefore thy servant loveth it.
141 I am small and despised: yet do not I forget thy precepts.
142 Thy righteousness is an everlasting righteousness, and thy
law is the truth.
143 Trouble and anguish have taken hold on me: yet thy
commandments are my delights.
144 The righteousness of thy testimonies is everlasting: give
me understanding, and I shall live.

KOPH.

145 I cried with my whole heart; hear me, O LORD: I will
keep thy statutes.
146 I cried unto thee; save me, and I shall keep thy
testimonies.
147 I prevented the dawning of the morning, and cried: I
hoped in thy word.
148 Mine eyes prevent the night watches, that I might
meditate in thy word.
149 Hear my voice according unto thy lovingkindness: O
LORD, quicken me according to thy judgment.
150 They draw nigh that follow after mischief: they are far
from thy law.

151 Thou art near, O LORD; and all thy commandments are
truth.
152 Concerning thy testimonies, I have known of old that
thou hast founded them for ever.

RESH.

153 Consider mine affliction, and deliver me: for I do not
forget thy law.
154 Plead my cause, and deliver me: quicken me according to
thy word.
155 Salvation is far from the wicked: for they seek not thy
statutes.
156 Great are thy tender mercies, O LORD: quicken me
according to thy judgments.
157 Many are my persecutors and mine enemies; yet do I not
decline from thy testimonies.
158 I beheld the transgressors, and was grieved; because they
kept not thy word.
159 Consider how I love thy precepts: quicken me, O LORD,
according to thy lovingkindness.
160 Thy word is true from the beginning: and every one of
thy righteous judgments endureth for ever.

SCHIN.

161 Princes have persecuted me without a cause: but my heart
standeth in awe of thy word.
162 I rejoice at thy word, as one that findeth great spoil.
163 I hate and abhor lying: but thy law do I love.
164 Seven times a day do I praise thee because of thy
righteous judgments.
165 Great peace have they which love thy law: and nothing
shall offend them.

166 LORD, I have hoped for thy salvation, and done thy
commandments.
167 My soul hath kept thy testimonies; and I love them
exceedingly.
168 I have kept thy precepts and thy testimonies: for all my
ways are before thee.

TAU.

169 Let my cry come near before thee, O LORD: give me
understanding according to thy word.
170 Let my supplication come before thee: deliver me
according to thy word.
171 My lips shall utter praise, when thou hast taught me thy
statutes.
172 My tongue shall speak of thy word: for all thy
commandments are righteousness.
173 Let thine hand help me; for I have chosen thy precepts.
174 I have longed for thy salvation, O LORD; and thy law is
my delight.
175 Let my soul live, and it shall praise thee; and let thy
judgments help me.
176 I have gone astray like a lost sheep; seek thy servant; for I
do not forget thy commandments.

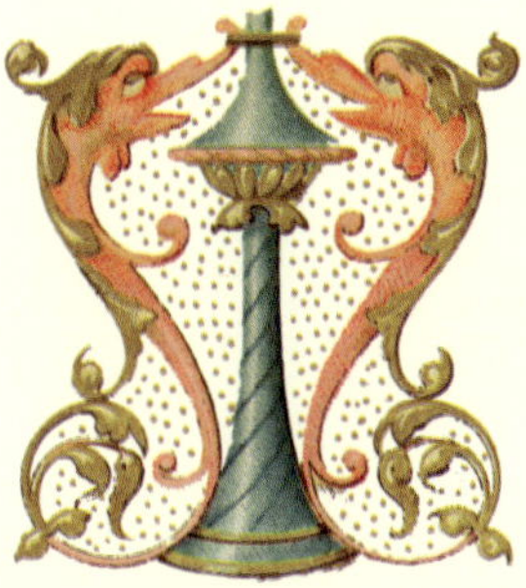

PSALM 120

A Song of degrees.

In my distress I cried unto the LORD, and he heard me.
2 Deliver my soul, O LORD, from lying lips, and from
a deceitful tongue.
3 What shall be given unto thee? or what shall be done unto
thee, thou false tongue?
4 Sharp arrows of the mighty, with coals of juniper.
5 Woe is me, that I sojourn in Mesech, that I dwell in the
tents of Kedar!
6 My soul hath long dwelt with him that hateth peace.
7 I am for peace: but when I speak, they are for war.

PSALM 121

A Song of degrees.

I will lift up mine eyes unto the hills, from whence
cometh my help.
2 My help cometh from the LORD, which made heaven and
earth.
3 He will not suffer thy foot to be moved: he that keepeth
thee will not slumber.
4 Behold, he that keepeth Israel shall neither slumber nor sleep.
5 The LORD is thy keeper: the LORD is thy shade upon
thy right hand.
6 The sun shall not smite thee by day, nor the moon by night.

7The LORD shall preserve thee from all evil: he shall
preserve thy soul.
8The LORD shall preserve thy going out and thy coming in
from this time forth, and even for evermore.

PSALM 122

A Song of degrees of David.

I was glad when they said unto me, Let us go into the
house of the LORD.
2Our feet shall stand within thy gates, O Jerusalem.
3Jerusalem is builded as a city that is compact together:
4Whither the tribes go up, the tribes of the LORD, unto the
testimony of Israel, to give thanks unto the name of the LORD.
5For there are set thrones of judgment, the thrones of the
house of David.
6Pray for the peace of Jerusalem: they shall prosper that
love thee.
7Peace be within thy walls, and prosperity within thy palaces.
8For my brethren and companions' sakes, I will now say,
Peace be within thee.
9Because of the house of the LORD our God I will seek
thy good.

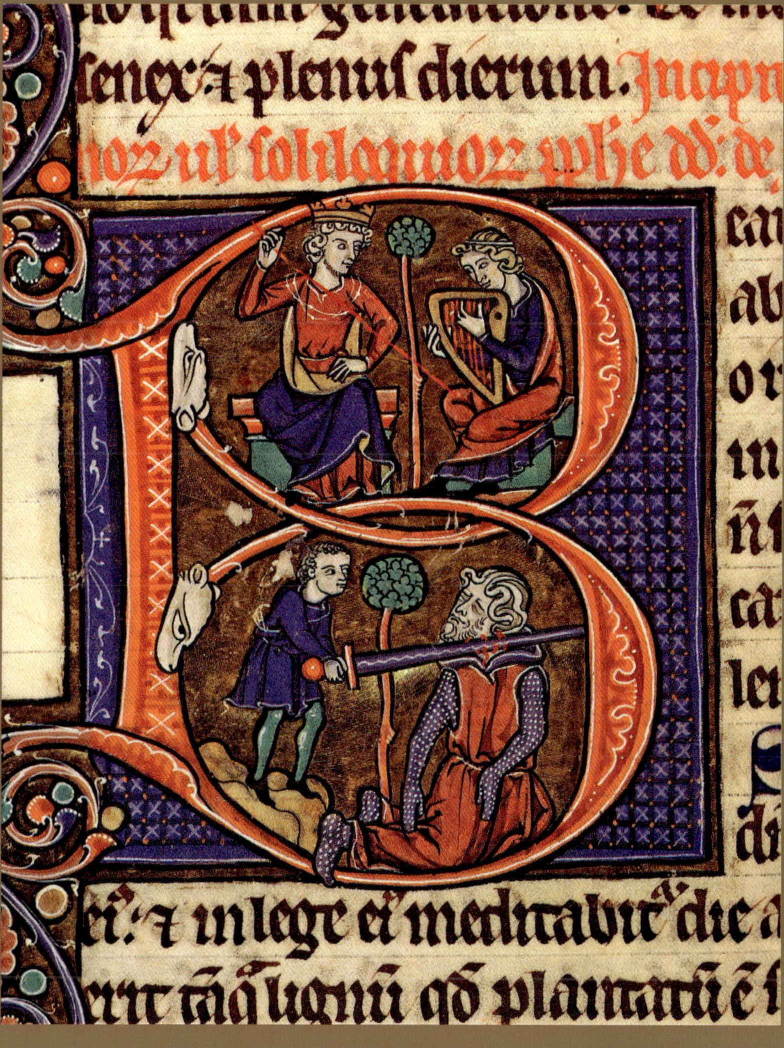

Abbey of Mont St. Eloi, France, Psalm 133, 13th century

PSALM 123

A Song of degrees.

Unto thee lift I up mine eyes, O thou that dwellest in
the heavens.
2 Behold, as the eyes of servants look unto the hand of their
masters, and as the eyes of a maiden unto the hand of her
mistress; so our eyes wait upon the LORD our God, until
that he have mercy upon us.
3 Have mercy upon us, O LORD, have mercy upon us: for
we are exceedingly filled with contempt.
4 Our soul is exceedingly filled with the scorning of those
that are at ease, and with the contempt of the proud.

PSALM 124

A Song of degrees of David.

If it had not been the LORD who was on our side,
now may Israel say;
2 If it had not been the LORD who was on our side, when
men rose up against us:
3 Then they had swallowed us up quick, when their wrath
was kindled against us:
4 Then the waters had overwhelmed us, the stream had gone
over our soul:
5 Then the proud waters had gone over our soul.
6 Blessed be the LORD, who hath not given us as a prey to
their teeth.

7Our soul is escaped as a bird out of the snare of the
fowlers: the snare is broken, and we are escaped.
8Our help is in the name of the LORD, who made heaven
and earth.

PSALM 125

A Song of degrees.

They that trust in the LORD shall be as mount Zion,
which cannot be removed, but abideth for ever.
2As the mountains are round about Jerusalem, so the LORD
is round about his people from henceforth even for ever.
3For the rod of the wicked shall not rest upon the lot of the
righteous; lest the righteous put forth their hands unto iniquity.
4Do good, O LORD, unto those that be good, and to them
that are upright in their hearts.
5As for such as turn aside unto their crooked ways, the
LORD shall lead them forth with the workers of iniquity:
but peace shall be upon Israel.

PSALM 126

A Song of degrees.

When the LORD turned again the captivity of Zion,
we were like them that dream.
2Then was our mouth filled with laughter, and our tongue

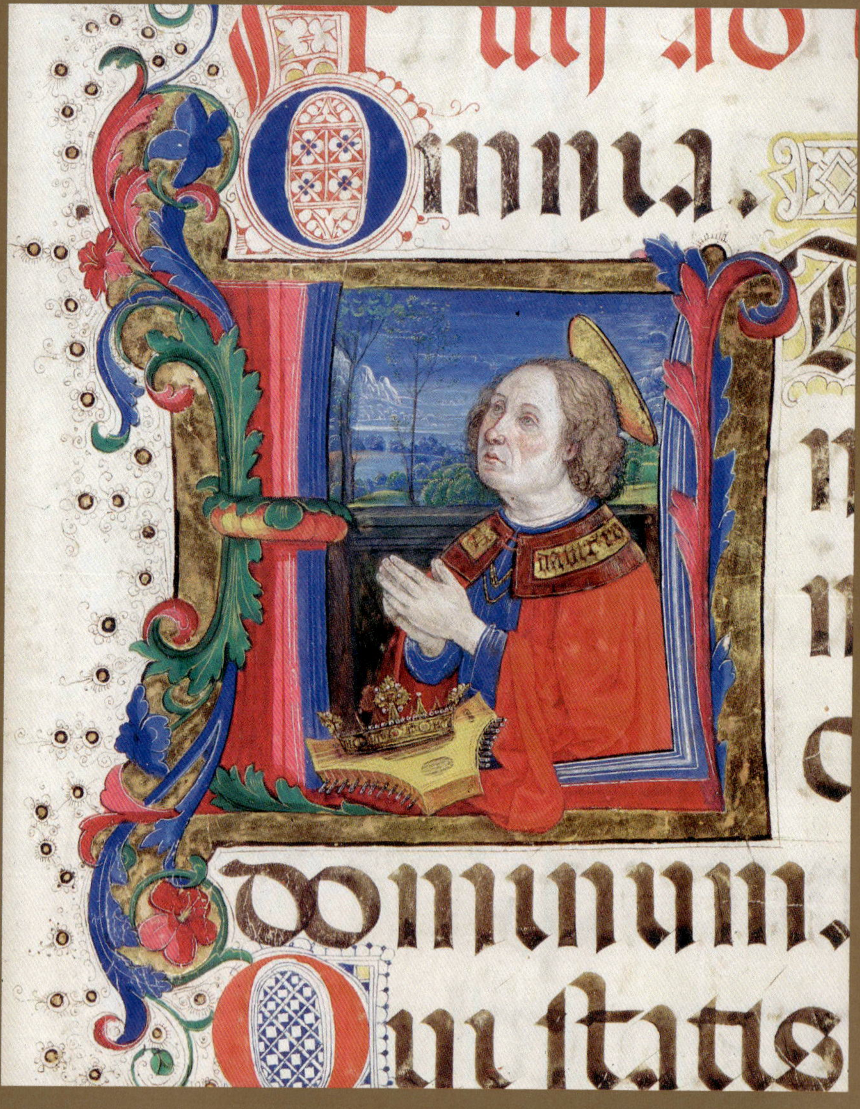

Monte di Giovanni, King David praying, detail of a Book of Psalms, ca. 1490

with singing: then said they among the heathen, The LORD
hath done great things for them.
3 The LORD hath done great things for us; whereof we are glad.
4 Turn again our captivity, O LORD, as the streams in the south.
5 They that sow in tears shall reap in joy.
6 He that goeth forth and weepeth, bearing precious seed,
shall doubtless come again with rejoicing, bringing his
sheaves with him.

PSALM 127

A Song of degrees for Solomon.

Except the LORD build the house, they labour
in vain that build it: except the LORD keep the
city, the watchman waketh but in vain.
2 It is vain for you to rise up early, to sit up late, to eat the
bread of sorrows: for so he giveth his beloved sleep.
3 Lo, children are an heritage of the LORD: and the fruit of
the womb is his reward.
4 As arrows are in the hand of a mighty man; so are children
of the youth.
5 Happy is the man that hath his quiver full of them: they
shall not be ashamed, but they shall speak with the enemies
in the gate.

PSALM 128

A Song of degrees.

Blessed is every one that feareth the LORD; that
walketh in his ways.
2 For thou shalt eat the labour of thine hands: happy shalt
thou be, and it shall be well with thee.
3 Thy wife shall be as a fruitful vine by the sides of thine
house: thy children like olive plants round about thy table.
4 Behold, that thus shall the man be blessed that feareth the
LORD.
5 The LORD shall bless thee out of Zion: and thou shalt see
the good of Jerusalem all the days of thy life.
6 Yea, thou shalt see thy children's children, and peace upon
Israel.

PSALM 129

A Song of degrees.

Many a time have they afflicted me from my youth,
may Israel now say:
2 Many a time have they afflicted me from my youth: yet
they have not prevailed against me.
3 The plowers plowed upon my back: they made long their
furrows.
4 The LORD is righteous: he hath cut asunder the cords of
the wicked.
5 Let them all be confounded and turned back that hate Zion.

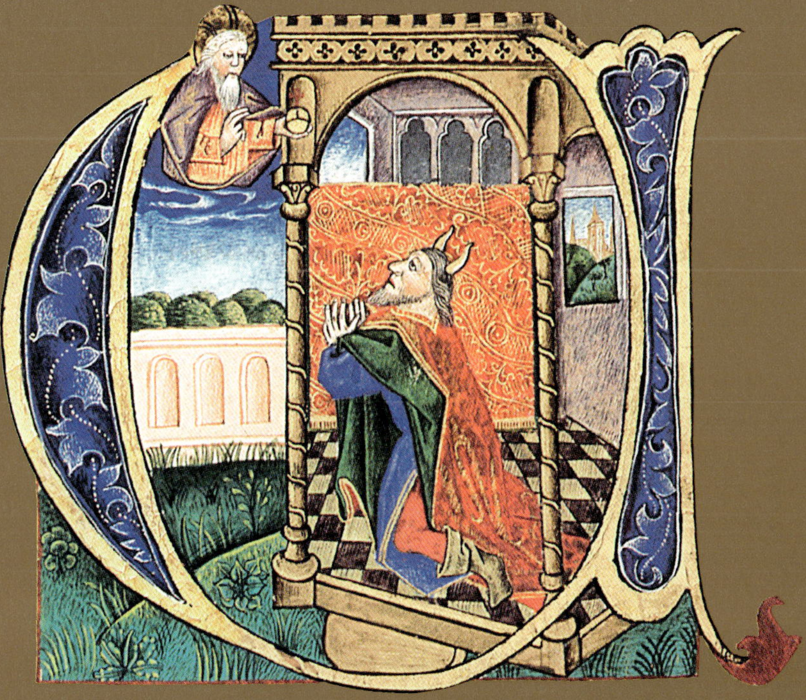

6 Let them be as the grass upon the housetops, which
withereth afore it groweth up:
7 Wherewith the mower filleth not his hand; nor he that
bindeth sheaves his bosom.
8 Neither do they which go by say, The blessing of the
LORD be upon you: we bless you in the name of the LORD.

PSALM 130

A Song of degrees.

Out of the depths have I cried unto thee, O LORD.
2 LORD, hear my voice: let thine ears be attentive to
the voice of my supplications.
3 If thou, LORD, shouldest mark iniquities, O LORD, who
shall stand?
4 But there is forgiveness with thee, that thou mayest be
feared.
5 I wait for the LORD, my soul doth wait, and in his word
do I hope.
6 My soul waiteth for the LORD more than they that watch
for the morning: I say, more than they that watch for the
morning.
7 Let Israel hope in the LORD: for with the LORD there is
mercy, and with him is plenteous redemption.
8 And he shall redeem Israel from all his iniquities.

PSALM 131

A Song of degrees of David.

LORD, my heart is not haughty, nor mine eyes lofty:
neither do I exercise myself in great matters, or in
things too high for me.
2 Surely I have behaved and quieted myself, as a child that is
weaned of his mother: my soul is even as a weaned child.
3 Let Israel hope in the LORD from henceforth and for ever.

PSALM 132

A Song of degrees.

LORD, remember David, and all his afflictions:
2 How he sware unto the LORD, and vowed unto
the mighty God of Jacob;
3 Surely I will not come into the tabernacle of my house, nor
go up into my bed;
4 I will not give sleep to mine eyes, or slumber to mine eyelids,
5 Until I find out a place for the LORD, an habitation for
the mighty God of Jacob.
6 Lo, we heard of it at Ephratah: we found it in the fields of
the wood.
7 We will go into his tabernacles: we will worship
at his footstool.
8 Arise, O LORD, into thy rest; thou, and
the ark of thy strength.
9 Let thy priests be clothed with
righteousness; and let thy saints shout for joy.

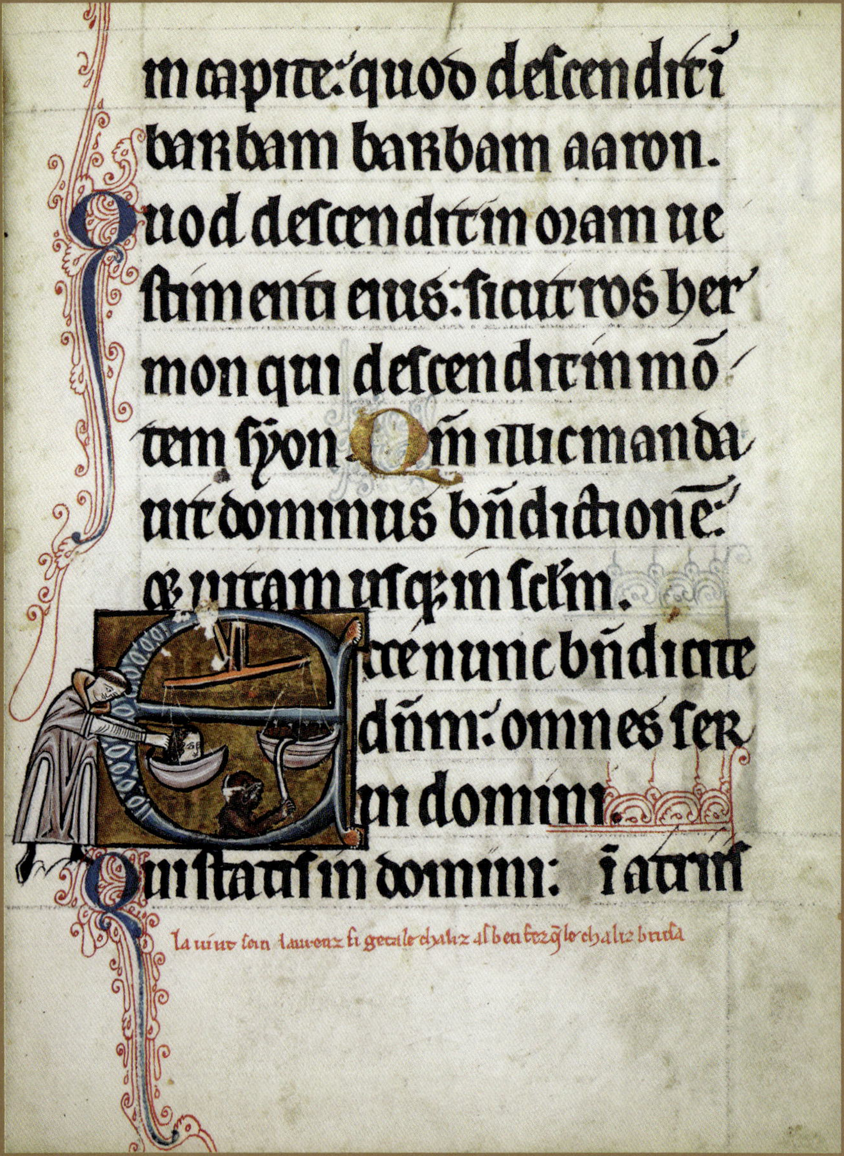

De Brailes Hours, England, Psalm 132, ca. 1240

10For thy servant David's sake turn not away the face of
thine anointed.
11The LORD hath sworn in truth unto David; he will not turn
from it; Of the fruit of thy body will I set upon thy throne.
12If thy children will keep my covenant and my testimony
that I shall teach them, their children shall also sit upon thy
throne for evermore.
13For the LORD hath chosen Zion; he hath desired it for
his habitation.
14This is my rest for ever: here will I dwell; for I have desired it.
15I will abundantly bless her provision: I will satisfy her
poor with bread.
16I will also clothe her priests with salvation: and her saints
shall shout aloud for joy.
17There will I make the horn of David to bud: I have
ordained a lamp for mine anointed.
18His enemies will I clothe with shame: but upon himself
shall his crown flourish.

PSALM 133

A Song of degrees of David.

Behold, how good and how pleasant it is for brethren
to dwell together in unity!
2It is like the precious ointment upon the head, that ran
down upon the beard, even Aaron's beard: that went down to
the skirts of his garments;
3As the dew of Hermon, and as the dew that descended
upon the mountains of Zion: for there the LORD
commanded the blessing, even life for evermore.

PSALM 134

A Song of degrees.

Behold, bless ye the LORD, all ye servants of the
LORD, which by night stand in the house of the
LORD.
2 Lift up your hands in the sanctuary, and bless the LORD.
3 The LORD that made heaven and earth bless thee out of
Zion.

PSALM 135

Praise ye the LORD. Praise ye the name of the LORD;
praise him, O ye servants of the LORD.
2 Ye that stand in the house of the LORD, in the courts of
the house of our God,
3 Praise the LORD; for the LORD is good: sing praises unto
his name; for it is pleasant.
4 For the LORD hath chosen Jacob unto himself, and Israel
for his peculiar treasure.
5 For I know that the LORD is great, and that our LORD is
above all gods.
6 Whatsoever the LORD pleased, that did he in heaven, and
in earth, in the seas, and all deep places.
7 He causeth the vapours to ascend from the ends of the
earth; he maketh lightnings for the rain; he bringeth the wind
out of his treasuries.
8 Who smote the firstborn of Egypt, both of man and beast.
9 Who sent tokens and wonders into the midst of thee, O

Egypt, upon Pharaoh, and upon all his servants.
10 Who smote great nations, and slew mighty kings;
11 Sihon king of the Amorites, and Og king of Bashan, and
all the kingdoms of Canaan:
12 And gave their land for an heritage, an heritage unto
Israel his people.
13 Thy name, O LORD, endureth for ever; and thy
memorial, O LORD, throughout all generations.
14 For the LORD will judge his people, and he will repent
himself concerning his servants.
15 The idols of the heathen are silver and gold, the work of
men's hands.
16 They have mouths, but they speak not; eyes have they, but
they see not;
17 They have ears, but they hear not; neither is there any
breath in their mouths.
18 They that make them are like unto them: so is every one
that trusteth in them.
19 Bless the LORD, O house of Israel: bless the LORD, O
house of Aaron:
20 Bless the LORD, O house of Levi: ye that fear the
LORD, bless the LORD.
21 Blessed be the LORD out of Zion, which dwelleth at
Jerusalem. Praise ye the LORD.

PSALM 136

O give thanks unto the LORD; for he is good: for his
mercy endureth for ever.
2 O give thanks unto the God of gods: for his mercy
endureth for ever.
3 O give thanks to the LORD of lords: for his mercy
endureth for ever.
4 To him who alone doeth great wonders: for his mercy
endureth for ever.
5 To him that by wisdom made the heavens: for his mercy
endureth for ever.
6 To him that stretched out the earth above the waters: for
his mercy endureth for ever.
7 To him that made great lights: for his mercy endureth for ever:
8 The sun to rule by day: for his mercy endureth for ever:
9 The moon and stars to rule by night: for his mercy
endureth for ever.
10 To him that smote Egypt in their firstborn: for his mercy
endureth for ever:
11 And brought out Israel from among them: for his mercy
endureth for ever:
12 With a strong hand, and with a stretched out arm: for his
mercy endureth for ever.
13 To him which divided the Red sea into parts: for his mercy
endureth for ever:
14 And made Israel to pass through the midst
of it: for his mercy endureth for ever:
15 But overthrew Pharaoh and his host in the
Red sea: for his mercy endureth for ever.
16 To him which led his people through the
wilderness: for his mercy endureth for ever.

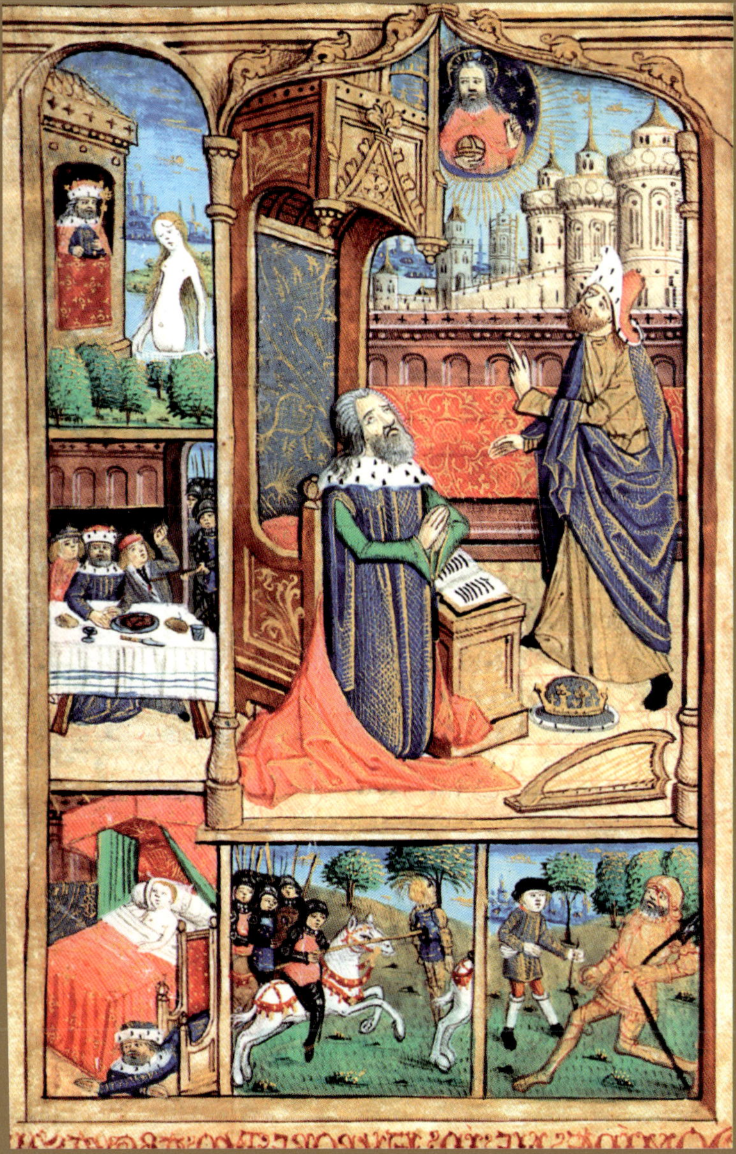

Playfair Book of Hours, France, late 15th century

17To him which smote great kings: for his mercy endureth
for ever:
18And slew famous kings: for his mercy endureth for ever:
19Sihon king of the Amorites: for his mercy endureth for ever:
20And Og the king of Bashan: for his mercy endureth for ever:
21And gave their land for an heritage: for his mercy
endureth for ever:
22Even an heritage unto Israel his servant: for his mercy
endureth for ever.
23Who remembered us in our low estate: for his mercy
endureth for ever:
24And hath redeemed us from our enemies: for his mercy
endureth for ever.
25Who giveth food to all flesh: for his mercy endureth for ever.
26O give thanks unto the God of heaven: for his mercy
endureth for ever.

PSALM 137

By the rivers of Babylon, there we sat down, yea, we
wept, when we remembered Zion.
2We hanged our harps upon the willows in the midst thereof.
3For there they that carried us away captive required of us
a song; and they that wasted us required of us mirth, saying,
Sing us one of the songs of Zion.
4How shall we sing the LORD'S song in a strange land?
5If I forget thee, O Jerusalem, let my right hand forget her
cunning.
6If I do not remember thee, let my tongue cleave to the roof
of my mouth; if I prefer not Jerusalem above my chief joy.

7Remember, O LORD, the children of Edom in the day of
Jerusalem; who said, Rase it, rase it, even to the foundation
thereof.
8O daughter of Babylon, who art to be destroyed; happy
shall he be, that rewardeth thee as thou hast served us.
9Happy shall he be, that taketh and dasheth thy little ones
against the stones.

PSALM 138

A Psalm of David.

I will praise thee with my whole heart: before the gods
will I sing praise unto thee.
2I will worship toward thy holy temple, and praise thy
name for thy lovingkindness and for thy truth: for thou hast
magnified thy word above all thy name.
3In the day when I cried thou answeredst me, and
strengthenedst me with strength in my soul.
4All the kings of the earth shall praise thee, O LORD,
when they hear the words of thy mouth.
5Yea, they shall sing in the ways of the LORD: for great is
the glory of the LORD.
6Though the LORD be high, yet hath he respect unto the
lowly: but the proud he knoweth afar off.
7Though I walk in the midst of trouble, thou wilt revive
me: thou shalt stretch forth thine hand against the wrath of
mine enemies, and thy right hand shall save me.
8The LORD will perfect that which concerneth me: thy
mercy, O LORD, endureth for ever: forsake not the works of
thine own hands.

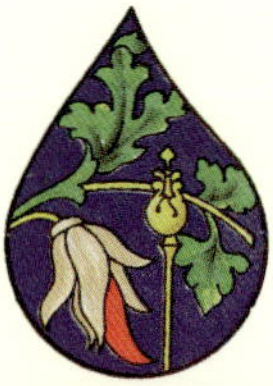

PSALM 139

To the chief Musician, A Psalm of David.

O LORD, thou hast searched me, and known me.
2 Thou knowest my downsitting and mine uprising,
thou understandest my thought afar off.
3 Thou compassest my path and my lying down, and art
acquainted with all my ways.
4 For there is not a word in my tongue, but, lo, O LORD,
thou knowest it altogether.
5 Thou hast beset me behind and before, and laid thine
hand upon me.
6 Such knowledge is too wonderful for me; it is high, I
cannot attain unto it.
7 Whither shall I go from thy spirit? or whither shall I flee
from thy presence?
8 If I ascend up into heaven, thou art there: if I make my
bed in hell, behold, thou art there.
9 If I take the wings of the morning, and dwell in the
uttermost parts of the sea;
10 Even there shall thy hand lead me, and thy right hand
shall hold me.
11 If I say, Surely the darkness shall cover me; even the night
shall be light about me.
12 Yea, the darkness hideth not from thee; but the night shineth

as the day: the darkness and the light are both alike to thee.
13 For thou hast possessed my reins: thou hast covered me in
my mother's womb.
14 I will praise thee; for I am fearfully and wonderfully
made: marvellous are thy works; and that my soul knoweth
right well.
15 My substance was not hid from thee, when I was made in
secret, and curiously wrought in the lowest parts of the earth.
16 Thine eyes did see my substance, yet being unperfect; and in
thy book all my members were written, which in continuance
were fashioned, when as yet there was none of them.
17 How precious also are thy thoughts unto me, O God! how
great is the sum of them!
18 If I should count them, they are more in number than the
sand: when I awake, I am still with thee.
19 Surely thou wilt slay the wicked, O God: depart from me
therefore, ye bloody men.
20 For they speak against thee wickedly, and thine enemies
take thy name in vain.
21 Do not I hate them, O LORD, that hate thee? and am not
I grieved with those that rise up against thee?
22 I hate them with perfect hatred: I count them mine enemies.
23 Search me, O God, and know my heart: try me, and know
my thoughts:
24 And see if there be any wicked way in me, and lead me in
the way everlasting.

PSALM 140

To the chief Musician, A Psalm of David.

Deliver me, O LORD, from the evil man: preserve me from the violent man;
2 Which imagine mischiefs in their heart; continually are they gathered together for war.
3 They have sharpened their tongues like a serpent; adders' poison is under their lips. Selah.
4 Keep me, O LORD, from the hands of the wicked; preserve me from the violent man; who have purposed to overthrow my goings.
5 The proud have hid a snare for me, and cords; they have spread a net by the wayside; they have set gins for me. Selah.
6 I said unto the LORD, Thou art my God: hear the voice of my supplications, O LORD.
7 O God the LORD, the strength of my salvation, thou hast covered my head in the day of battle.
8 Grant not, O LORD, the desires of the wicked: further not his wicked device; lest they exalt themselves. Selah.
9 As for the head of those that compass me about, let the mischief of their own lips cover them.
10 Let burning coals fall upon them: let them be cast into the fire; into deep pits, that they rise not up again.
11 Let not an evil speaker be established in the earth: evil shall hunt the violent man to overthrow him.
12 I know that the LORD will maintain the cause of the afflicted, and the right of the poor.
13 Surely the righteous shall give thanks unto thy name: the upright shall dwell in thy presence.

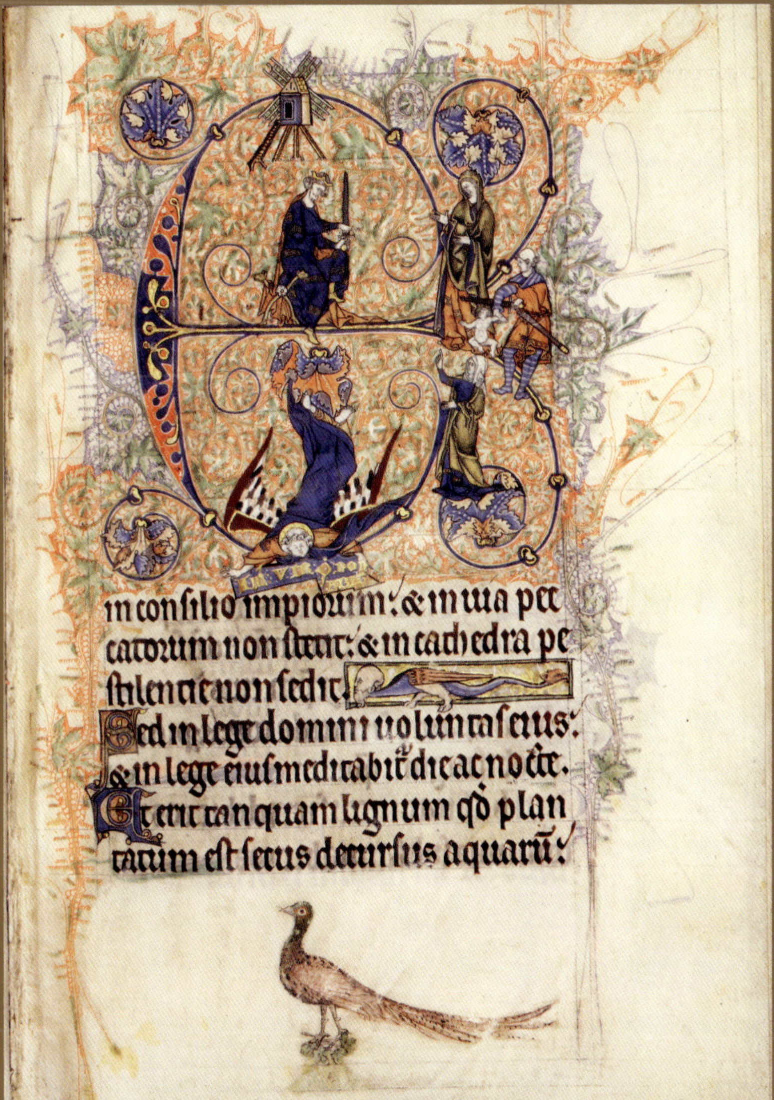

Windmill Psalter, England, ca. 1270–1280

PSALM 141

A Psalm of David.

LORD, I cry unto thee: make haste unto me; give ear
unto my voice, when I cry unto thee.
2 Let my prayer be set forth before thee as incense; and the
lifting up of my hands as the evening sacrifice.
3 Set a watch, O LORD, before my mouth; keep the door of
my lips.
4 Incline not my heart to any evil thing, to practise wicked
works with men that work iniquity: and let me not eat of
their dainties.
5 Let the righteous smite me; it shall be a kindness: and let him
reprove me; it shall be an excellent oil, which shall not break my
head: for yet my prayer also shall be in their calamities.
6 When their judges are overthrown in stony places, they
shall hear my words; for they are sweet.
7 Our bones are scattered at the grave's mouth, as when one
cutteth and cleaveth wood upon the earth.
8 But mine eyes are unto thee, O God the LORD: in thee is
my trust; leave not my soul destitute.
9 Keep me from the snares which they have laid for me, and
the gins of the workers of iniquity.
10 Let the wicked fall into their own nets, whilst that I
withal escape.

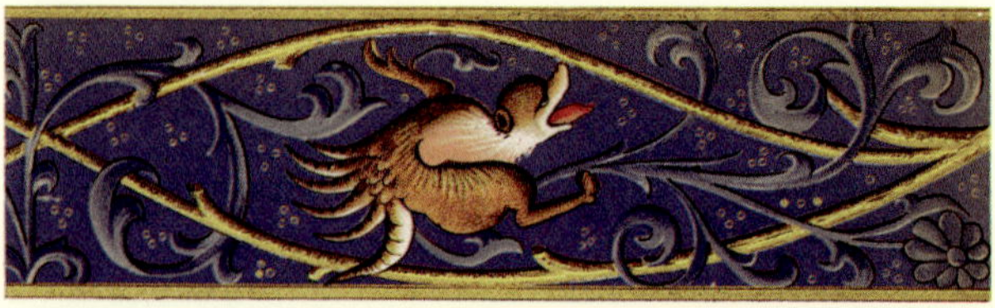

PSALM 142

Maschil of David;
A Prayer when he was in the cave.

I cried unto the LORD with my voice; with my voice unto the LORD did I make my supplication.
2 I poured out my complaint before him; I shewed before
him my trouble.
3 When my spirit was overwhelmed within me, then thou
knewest my path. In the way wherein I walked have they
privily laid a snare for me.
4 I looked on my right hand, and beheld, but there was no
man that would know me: refuge failed me; no man cared for
my soul.
5 I cried unto thee, O LORD: I said, Thou art my refuge
and my portion in the land of the living.
6 Attend unto my cry; for I am brought very low: deliver me
from my persecutors; for they are stronger than I.
7 Bring my soul out of prison, that I may praise thy name:
the righteous shall compass me about; for thou shalt deal
bountifully with me.

PSALM 143

A Psalm of David.

Hear my prayer, O LORD, give ear to my supplications: in thy faithfulness answer me, and in thy righteousness.

2 And enter not into judgment with thy servant: for in thy
sight shall no man living be justified.
3 For the enemy hath persecuted my soul; he hath smitten
my life down to the ground; he hath made me to dwell in
darkness, as those that have been long dead.
4 Therefore is my spirit overwhelmed within me; my heart
within me is desolate.
5 I remember the days of old; I meditate on all thy works; I
muse on the work of thy hands.
6 I stretch forth my hands unto thee: my soul thirsteth after
thee, as a thirsty land. Selah.
7 Hear me speedily, O LORD: my spirit faileth: hide not thy face
from me, lest I be like unto them that go down into the pit.
8 Cause me to hear thy lovingkindness in the morning;
for in thee do I trust: cause me to know the way wherein I
should walk; for I lift up my soul unto thee.
9 Deliver me, O LORD, from mine enemies: I flee unto
thee to hide me.
10 Teach me to do thy will; for thou art my God: thy spirit is
good; lead me into the land of uprightness.
11 Quicken me, O LORD, for thy name's sake: for thy
righteousness' sake bring my soul out of trouble.
12 And of thy mercy cut off mine enemies, and destroy all
them that afflict my soul: for I am thy servant.

PSALM 144

A Psalm of David.

Blessed be the LORD my strength, which teacheth
my hands to war, and my fingers to fight:
2 My goodness, and my fortress; my high tower, and my
deliverer; my shield, and he in whom I trust; who subdueth
my people under me.
3 LORD, what is man, that thou takest knowledge of him! or
the son of man, that thou makest account of him!
4 Man is like to vanity: his days are as a shadow that passeth
away.
5 Bow thy heavens, O LORD, and come down: touch the
mountains, and they shall smoke.
6 Cast forth lightning, and scatter them: shoot out thine
arrows, and destroy them.
7 Send thine hand from above; rid me, and deliver me out of
great waters, from the hand of strange children;
8 Whose mouth speaketh vanity, and their right hand is a
right hand of falsehood.
9 I will sing a new song unto thee, O God: upon a psaltery
and an instrument of ten strings will I sing praises unto thee.
10 It is he that giveth salvation unto kings: who delivereth
David his servant from the hurtful sword.
11 Rid me, and deliver me from the hand of strange children,
whose mouth speaketh vanity, and their right hand is a right
hand of falsehood:
12 That our sons may be as plants grown up in their youth;
that our daughters may be as corner stones, polished after the
similitude of a palace:
13 That our garners may be full, affording all manner of

store: that our sheep may bring forth thousands
and ten thousands in our streets:
14 That our oxen may be strong to labour; that
there be no breaking in, nor going out; that there
be no complaining in our streets.
15 Happy is that people, that is in such a case: yea, happy is
that people, whose God is the LORD.

PSALM 145

David's Psalm of praise.

I will extol thee, my God, O king; and I will bless thy
name for ever and ever.
2 Every day will I bless thee; and I will praise thy name for
ever and ever.
3 Great is the LORD, and greatly to be praised; and his
greatness is unsearchable.
4 One generation shall praise thy works to another, and shall
declare thy mighty acts.
5 I will speak of the glorious honour of thy majesty, and of
thy wondrous works.
6 And men shall speak of the might of thy terrible acts: and
I will declare thy greatness.
7 They shall abundantly utter the memory of thy great
goodness, and shall sing of thy righteousness.
8 The LORD is gracious, and full of compassion; slow to
anger, and of great mercy.
9 The LORD is good to all: and his tender mercies are over
all his works.

[10]All thy works shall praise thee, O LORD; and thy saints
shall bless thee.
[11]They shall speak of the glory of thy kingdom, and talk of
thy power;
[12]To make known to the sons of men his mighty acts, and
the glorious majesty of his kingdom.
[13]Thy kingdom is an everlasting kingdom, and thy
dominion endureth throughout all generations.
[14]The LORD upholdeth all that fall, and raiseth up all
those that be bowed down.
[15]The eyes of all wait upon thee; and thou givest them their
meat in due season.
[16]Thou openest thine hand, and satisfiest the desire of
every living thing.
[17]The LORD is righteous in all his ways, and holy in all his
works.
[18]The LORD is nigh unto all them that call upon him, to all
that call upon him in truth.
[19]He will fulfil the desire of them that fear him: he also will
hear their cry, and will save them.
[20]The LORD preserveth all them that love him: but all the
wicked will he destroy.
[21]My mouth shall speak the praise of the LORD: and let all
flesh bless his holy name for ever and ever.

PSALM 146

Praise ye the LORD. Praise the LORD, O my soul.
[2]While I live will I praise the LORD: I will sing
praises unto my God while I have any being.

3Put not your trust in princes, nor in the son of man, in
whom there is no help.
4His breath goeth forth, he returneth to his earth; in that
very day his thoughts perish.
5Happy is he that hath the God of Jacob for his help, whose
hope is in the LORD his God:
6Which made heaven, and earth, the sea, and all that
therein is: which keepeth truth for ever:
7Which executeth judgment for the oppressed: which
giveth food to the hungry. The LORD looseth the prisoners:
8The LORD openeth the eyes of the blind: the LORD
raiseth them that are bowed down: the LORD loveth the
righteous:
9The LORD preserveth the strangers; he relieveth the
fatherless and widow: but the way of the wicked he turneth
upside down.
10The LORD shall reign for ever, even thy God, O Zion,
unto all generations. Praise ye the LORD.

PSALM 147

Praise ye the LORD: for it is good to sing praises unto
our God; for it is pleasant; and praise is comely.
2The LORD doth build up Jerusalem: he gathereth
together the outcasts of Israel.
3He healeth the broken in heart, and bindeth up their wounds.
4He telleth the number of the stars; he calleth them all by
their names.
5Great is our LORD, and of great power: his understanding
is infinite.

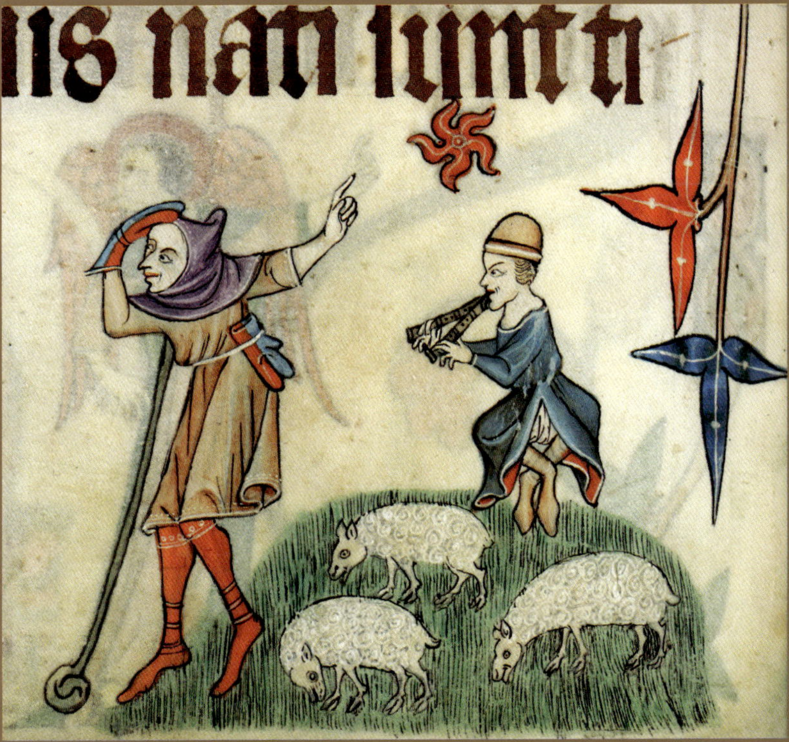

Luttrell Psalter, detail: Two Shepherds, England, ca. 1325–1335

6 The LORD lifteth up the meek: he casteth the wicked
down to the ground.
7 Sing unto the LORD with thanksgiving; sing praise upon
the harp unto our God:
8 Who covereth the heaven with clouds, who prepareth rain
for the earth, who maketh grass to grow upon the mountains.
9 He giveth to the beast his food, and to the young ravens
which cry.
10 He delighteth not in the strength of the horse: he taketh
not pleasure in the legs of a man.
11 The LORD taketh pleasure in them that fear him, in
those that hope in his mercy.
12 Praise the LORD, O Jerusalem; praise thy God, O Zion.
13 For he hath strengthened the bars of thy gates; he hath
blessed thy children within thee.
14 He maketh peace in thy borders, and filleth thee with the
finest of the wheat.
15 He sendeth forth his commandment upon
earth: his word runneth very swiftly.
16 He giveth snow like wool: he scattereth the
hoar frost like ashes.
17 He casteth forth his ice like morsels: who
can stand before his cold?
18 He sendeth out his word, and melteth them:
he causeth his wind to blow, and the waters flow.
19 He sheweth his word unto Jacob, his statutes
and his judgments unto Israel.
20 He hath not dealt so with any nation: and as
for his judgments, they have not known them.
Praise ye the LORD.

PSALM 148

Praise ye the LORD. Praise ye the LORD from the
heavens: praise him in the heights.
2 Praise ye him, all his angels: praise ye him, all his hosts.
3 Praise ye him, sun and moon: praise him, all ye stars of light.
4 Praise him, ye heavens of heavens, and ye waters that be
above the heavens.
5 Let them praise the name of the LORD: for he
commanded, and they were created.
6 He hath also stablished them for ever and ever: he hath
made a decree which shall not pass.
7 Praise the LORD from the earth, ye dragons, and all deeps:
8 Fire, and hail; snow, and vapours; stormy wind fulfilling
his word:
9 Mountains, and all hills; fruitful trees, and all cedars:
10 Beasts, and all cattle; creeping things, and flying fowl:
11 Kings of the earth, and all people; princes, and all judges
of the earth:
12 Both young men, and maidens; old men, and children:
13 Let them praise the name of the LORD: for his name
alone is excellent; his glory is above the earth and heaven.
14 He also exalteth the horn of his people, the praise of all his
saints; even of the children of Israel, a people near unto him.
Praise ye the LORD.

PSALM 149

Praise ye the LORD. Sing unto the LORD a new song,
and his praise in the congregation of saints.
2 Let Israel rejoice in him that made him: let the children of

Zion be joyful in their King.
3Let them praise his name in the dance: let them sing
praises unto him with the timbrel and harp.
4For the LORD taketh pleasure in his people: he will
beautify the meek with salvation.
5Let the saints be joyful in glory: let them sing aloud upon
their beds.
6Let the high praises of God be in their mouth, and a two-
edged sword in their hand;
7To execute vengeance upon the heathen, and punishments
upon the people;
8To bind their kings with chains, and their nobles with
fetters of iron;
9To execute upon them the judgment written: this honour
have all his saints. Praise ye the LORD.

PSALM 150

Praise ye the LORD. Praise God in his sanctuary: praise
him in the firmament of his power.
2Praise him for his mighty acts: praise him according
to his excellent greatness.
3Praise him with the sound of the trumpet: praise
him with the psaltery and harp.
4Praise him with the timbrel and dance: praise
him with stringed instruments and organs.
5Praise him upon the loud cymbals: praise him
upon the high sounding cymbals.
6Let every thing that hath breath praise the
LORD. Praise ye the LORD.

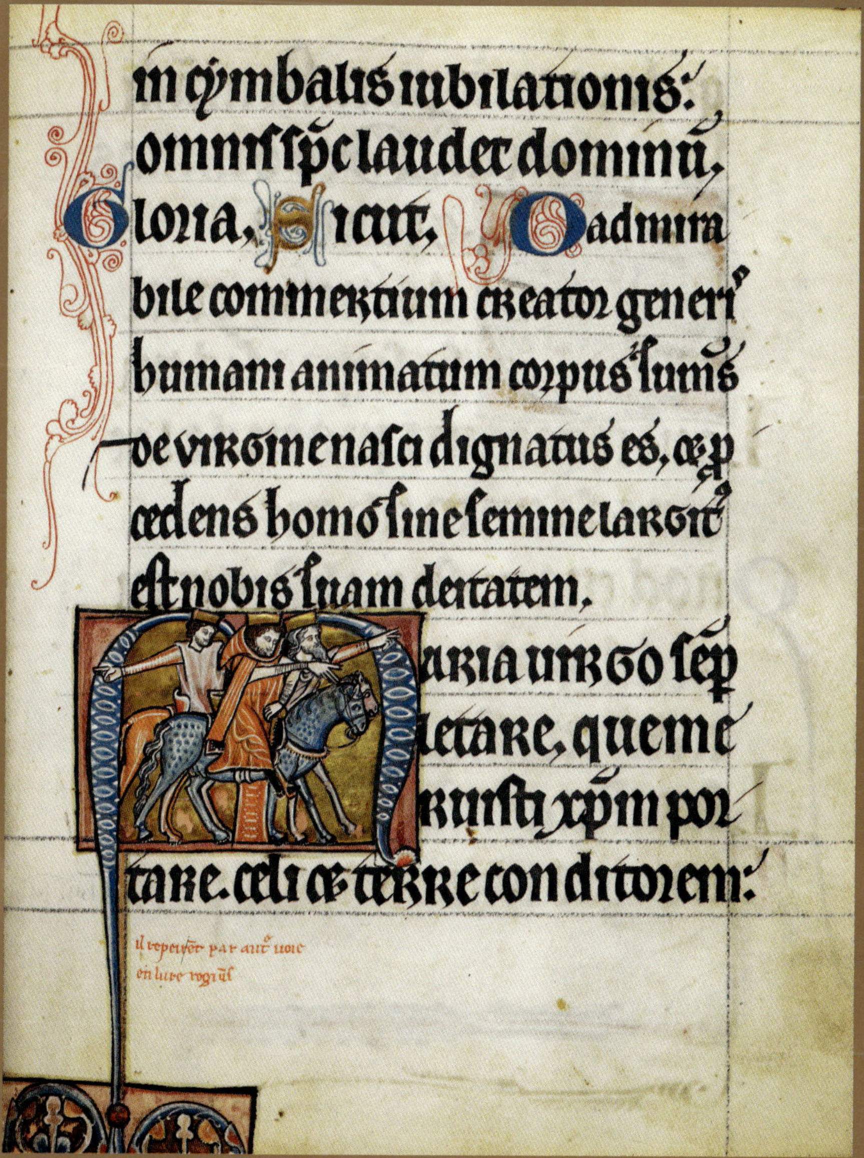

De Brailes Hours, England, Psalm 150, ca. 1240

INDEX OF ARTWORK